GATEWAY to SOCIAL STUDIES
VOCABULARY AND CONCEPTS

Bárbara C. Cruz

Stephen J. Thornton

Australia • Brazil • Japan • Korea • Singapore • Spain • United Kingdom • United States

Gateway to Social Studies

Bárbara C. Cruz, Stephen J. Thornton

Publisher: Sherrise Roehr

Executive Editor: Carmela Fazzino-Farah

Managing Editor: Kellie Cardone

Development Editor: Jill Korey O'Sullivan

Director, U.S. Marketing: Jim McDonough

Director of Professional Development and
Technology Marketing: Stacy Hilliard

Director of Content and Media Production:
Michael Burggren

Content Project Manager: Andrea Bobotas

Senior Print Buyer: Mary Beth Hennebury

Production Service/Compositor: Integra

Cover Designer: Integra

Portions of the glossary Copyright © HarperCollins

Credits appear on pages 291 which constitutes a
continuation of the copyright page.

Gateway to Social Studies Teacher's Edition
includes details on scientifically based research in
Gateway to Social Studies.

For product information and technology assistance, contact us at
Cengage Learning Customer & Sales Support, 1-800-354-9706

For permission to use material from this text or product,
submit all requests online at **www.cengage.com/permissions**
Further permissions questions can be emailed to
permissionrequest@cengage.com

Library of Congress Control Number: 2010941139

Student Edition (Hardcover)

ISBN-13: 978-1-4240-1811-6

Student Edition (Softcover)

ISBN-13: 978-1-1112-2222-2

Cengage Learning is a leading provider of customized learning solutions with
office locations around the globe, including Singapore, the United Kingdom,
Australia, Mexico, Brazil, and Japan. Locate your local office at:
international.cengage.com/region

Cengage Learning products are represented in Canada by Nelson Education, Ltd.

Visit Heinle online at **elt.heinle.com**

Visit our corporate website at **cengage.com**

Printed in the United States of America
1 2 3 4 5 6 7 8 9 10   15 14 13 12

Reviewers

We gratefully acknowledge the contribution of the following educators who reviewed materials at various stages of development. Their input and insight provided us with valuable perspective and ensure the integrity of the program.

Reviewers

Helene Becker
Norwalk Public Schools
Norwalk, CT

Ann Blessinger
Houston ISD
Houston, TX

Tammy Deleray
Bret Harte Elementary School
Modesto City Schools
Modesto, CA

Hilda Diaz
Dunn Middle School
Trenton, NJ

Michele Gatlin
Overton High School
Nashville, TN

Denise Grant
Stamford Public Schools
Stamford, CT

Kularb Griffiths
Fresno Unified School District/
Sequoia Middle School
Caruthers, CA

Sara Hamerla
Fuller Middle School
Framingham, MA

Laurie Hartwick
Health and Human Service
High School
Lawrence, MA

Patricia Hubble
John H. Pitman High School
Turlock, CA

Susan Iratene
SJUSD/Rio Americano
El Camino and Del Campo
High Schools
Sacramento, CA

Rosemary Jebari
Framingham Public Schools
Framingham, MA

Tina Johnson
Fresno Unified School District
Clovis, CA

Patricia Leftridge
E.V. Cain Middle School
Auburn, CA

Amanda Mahoney
Natick Public Schools
Natick, MA

Matt Makowetski
Maple High School/Lompoc
Unified School District
Lompoc, CA

Saideh Malekfzali
Visions in Education
Carmichael, CA

Lauren Lemons Odell
Fresno Unified School District/
Hoover High School
Fresno, CA

Heidi Perez
Lawrence Public Schools
Lawrence, MA

Sashi Rayasam
Durham Public Schools
Durham, NC

Katie Saldarriaga
Gwinnett County Public Schools
North Gwinnett High School
Suwanee, GA

Katherine Stocking
Cobb County School District
Campbell High School
Smyrna, GA

Troy Tenhet
PBVUSD/Bill Williams
Elementary School
Bakersfield, CA

Jennifer Villalobos
Los Banos High School
Los Banos, CA

Contents

Gateway to Social Studies Scope and Sequence

Lesson title	Social Studies Vocabulary	Academic Vocabulary	Word Study	Concepts	Critical Thinking	Social Studies Skill	National Social Studies Standards
Physical Geography	geography, ocean, lake, stream, river, cliff, waterfall, valley, canyon, mountain, forest, desert, grassland	Only 29 **percent** of Earth is made up of land.	Word Origins: geography	Water on Earth · Landforms on Earth · Interactions between Water and Land	Making Inferences · Analyzing Information	Comparing Photographs	People, Places, and Environments · Global Connections
Human and Cultural Geography	human, religion, culture, language, economics, government, city, built environment, monument	People **exchange** money for the things they want or need.	Prefixes: *inter-*	Culture, Language, and Religion · Government and Economics · The Built Environment	Relating to Your Own Experiences · Relating to Your Own Experiences	Reading a Pie Chart	People, Places, and Environments · Culture · Power, Authority, and Governance · Production, Distribution, and Consumption
North America	North America, Atlantic Ocean, Pacific Ocean, Arctic Ocean, isthmus, strait, settlement, indigenous people	Seeds **develop** into plants that have roots and leaves.	Parts of Speech: settle, settler, settlement	Physical Geography · Human and Cultural Geography · North America Today	Making Inferences · Making Inferences	Reading a Physical Map	People, Places, and Environments · Culture · Time, Continuity, and Change
South America	South America, Andes Mountains, Amazon River, Spanish, Portuguese, rainforest, volcano	There are many **diverse** cultures in South America.	Superlative Adjectives: Comparing three or more things	Physical Geography · Human and Cultural Geography · South America Today	Making Inferences · Recognizing Cause and Effect	Reading a Population Pyramid	People, Places, and Environments · Culture · Time, Continuity, and Change
Europe	Europe, Eurasia, Alps, European Union, currency, euro, peninsula, landlocked	**Literacy** is developed through instruction in reading and writing.	Word Origins: peninsula	Physical Geography · Human and Cultural Geography · Europe Today	Making Inferences · Making Inferences	Reading a Line Graph	People, Places, and Environments · Culture · Time, Continuity, and Change · Production, Distribution, and

Geography

Lesson title	Social Studies Vocabulary	Academic Vocabulary	Word Study	Concepts	Critical Thinking	Social Studies Skill	National Social Studies Standards
North Africa and the Middle East	North Africa, Middle East, Arab, oasis, desert, Nile River, Dead Sea, Suez Canal, camel	The friends had a **conflict** that they worked to resolve.	Commonly Confused Words: desert, dessert	Physical Geography; Human and Cultural Geography; North Africa and the Middle East Today	Making Inferences; Recognizing Cause and Effect	Reading a Climate Map	People, Places, and Environments; Culture; Time, Continuity, and Change
Sub-Saharan Africa	Sub-Saharan Africa, Sahel, drought, savanna, vegetation, refugee	Lions **consume** an average of 5,500 pounds of meat a year.	Compound Words: grasslands	Physical Geography; Human and Cultural Geography; Sub-Saharan Africa Today	Making Inferences; Relating to Your Own Experiences	Reading a Population Density Map	People, Places, and Environments; Culture; Time, Continuity, and Change
South Asia	Himalaya Mountains, South Asia, Taj Mahal, monsoon, Ganges, Hindu, Hindu temple, Muslim, mosque	Deaf people often use sign language to **communicate** with others.	Suffixes: -ous / -ious	Physical Geography; Human and Cultural Geography; South Asia Today	Comparing and Contrasting; Hypothesizing	Reading a Natural Vegetation Map	People, Places, and Environments; Culture; Time, Continuity, and Change
East Asia	emperor, East Asia, walled city, herder, nomads, Chinese characters, Great Wall, steppe	Mongolia is surrounded by land. Japan, in **contrast**, is surrounded by water.	Suffixes: -er	Physical Geography; Human and Cultural Geography; East Asia Today	Hypothesizing; Comparing and Contrasting	Reading a Physical Map	People, Places, and Environments; Culture; Time, Continuity, and Change
Southeast Asia and Australia	Southeast Asia, Australia, rice paddy, water buffalo, kangaroo, Aborigine, Outback	Marisela felt **isolated** when her friends left the island.	Compound Words: rice paddy water buffalo	Physical Geography; Human and Cultural Geography; Southeast Asia and Australia Today	Comparing and Contrasting; Analyzing Information	Making Observations	People, Places, and Environments; Culture; Time, Continuity, and Change

Geography

World History

Lesson title	Social Studies Vocabulary	Academic Vocabulary	Word Study	Concepts	Critical Thinking	Social Studies Skill	National Social Studies Standards
The Earliest Humans	hominid, prehistoric, ancestors, fire, tools, migration	Even though my grandmother and I are from different **generations**, we enjoy the same movies and music.	Prefixes: *pre-*	Hunters and Gatherers Tools and Culture The Agricultural Revolution	Comparing and Contrasting Relating to Your Own Experiences	Reading a Migration Map	Time, Continuity, and Change People, Places, and Environments Culture
The Earliest Societies	civilization, Fertile Crescent, alphabet, soil, trade routes, Indus Valley, wheel	The **symbol** $ stands for the word "dollar."	Word Origins: civilization	Mesopotamia and the Phoenicians The First Writing The Indus Valley	Visualizing Hypothesizing	Analyzing Archaeological Artifacts	Time, Continuity, and Change People, Places, and Environments Culture Science, Technology, and Society
Ancient Civilizations	pyramid, hieroglyph, social classes, pharaoh, Tutankhamen, Cleopatra, archaeologist, mummy, dynasty	The ancient Egyptians **preserved** the bodies of the dead through mummification.	Word Origins: hieroglyphics	Ancient Egypt The Pyramids of Ancient Egypt Ancient China	Comparing and Contrasting Paraphrasing	Interpreting Charts	Time, Continuity, and Change People, Places, and Environments Culture Individuals, Groups, and Institutions
Classical Civilizations	ancient Greece, democracy, Roman Empire, citizens, Parthenon, philosophy, columns, Olympic Games	The United States basketball team will **participate** in the next Olympic Games.	Word Origins: philosophy	Ancient Greece The Roman Empire The Rise of Christianity and the Decline of Rome	Making Inferences Comparing and Contrasting	Reading a Historical Map	Time, Continuity, and Change People, Places, and Environments Power, Authority, and Governance Civic Ideals and Practices
Europe in the Middle Ages	king, noble, knight, feudalism, Viking, castle, serf	In the feudal **hierarchy**, the king was at the top and serfs were at the bottom.	Homonyms: knight, night	The Catholic Church in Feudal Times Life on the Manor The Vikings	Comparing and Contrasting Making Inferences	Interpreting a Painting	Time, Continuity, and Change People, Places, and Environments Individuals, Groups, and Institutions Power, Authority, and Governance

World History

Lesson title	Social Studies Vocabulary	Academic Vocabulary	Word Study	Concepts	Critical Thinking	Social Studies Skill	National Social Studies Standards
The Later Middle Ages	Venice, silk, jade, medicine, Marco Polo, pepper, cinnamon, spices, market	Wei saw a **decline** in her grades after she stopped studying.	Multiple-Meaning Words: China / china	Muslims and Christians; Marco Polo in China; The Later Middle Ages	Making Inferences; Making Inferences	Reading a Map	Time, Continuity, and Change; People, Places, and Environments; Production, Distribution, and Consumption; Global Connections
Early African and American Civilizations	salt, Timbuktu, gold, empire, Maya, Aztec, Inca, Yucatán Peninsula	Historians do not know why the Maya **abandoned** their cities.	Antonyms: rise, decline	African Civilizations; Maya and Aztec Civilizations; Inca Civilization	Hypothesizing; Comparing and Contrasting	Reading a Venn Diagram	Time, Continuity, and Change; People, Places, and Environments; Culture; Power, Authority, and Governance
The Age of Exploration	New World, Christopher Columbus, explorer, voyage, Queen Isabella, King Ferdinand, disease	The indigenous people had never seen the deadly **weapons** of war used by the Europeans.	Syllabification: exploration	Exploration and Exchange; Conquest; Colonization	Paraphrasing; Summarizing	Interpreting Graphic Information	Time, Continuity, and Change; People, Places, and Environments; Culture; Global Connections
The Renaissance	architecture, painting, Michelangelo, sculpture, Leonardo da Vinci, William Shakespeare, Queen Elizabeth I, literature, printing press, microscope, telescope	Nadia liked to **create** works of art with oil paints.	Word Origins: renaissance	Art of the Renaissance; Science during the Renaissance; Inventions of the Renaissance	Hypothesizing; Relating to Your Own Experiences	Distinguishing Fact from Opinion	Time, Continuity, and Change; Culture; Science, Technology, and Society
The Reformation	pope, Catholic Church, Reformation, Protestant, Henry VIII, monk, Martin Luther	The students **opposed** the new school fees.	Prefixes: re-	Complaints against the Church; The Church Responds; Effects of the Protestant Reformation	Recognizing Cause and Effect; Making Inferences	Reading a Tree Diagram	Time, Continuity, and Change; Individuals, Groups, and Institutions; Power, Authority, and Governance

World History

Lesson title	Social Studies Vocabulary	Academic Vocabulary	Word Study	Concepts	Critical Thinking	Social Studies Skill	National Social Studies Standards
Enlightenment and Revolution	The Enlightenment, science, reason, revolution, monarchy, Louis XVI, Marie Antoinette	The piece of cake and the apple are **equal** in weight.	Prefixes: *mon-* / *mono-*	Enlightenment Thinking The American Revolution The French Revolution	Recognizing Cause and Effect Summarizing	Interpreting a Concept Map	Time, Continuity, and Change Power, Authority, and Governance Civic Ideals and Practices Science, Technology, and Society Global Connections
European Imperialism	imperialism, coffee, plantation, crops, sugar, missionary, silver, mission	The children **controlled** the puppets' movements.	Word Families: trade	What Is Imperialism? Power over Distant Lands Imperialism and Christianity	Paraphrasing Comparing and Contrasting	Reading a Historical Map	Time, Continuity, and Change People, Places, and Environments Individuals, Groups, and Institutions Power, Authority, and Governance Global Connections
The Industrial Revolution	spinning wheel, industry, factory, thread, locomotive, cotton, steam engine	Sarah worked hard and saw an **improvement** in her grades.	Word Parts: locomotive	Industrial Landscapes Advances in Transportation People in Industrial Cities	Hypothesizing Making Inferences	Interpreting a Visual Image	Time, Continuity, and Change People, Places, and Environments Production, Distribution, and Consumption Science, Technology, and Society
The Rise of Nationalism	Napoleon Bonaparte, nationalism, German Empire, Prussia, defeat, Otto von Bismarck, troops, unite, hostility	Tom **challenged** Nick to an arm wrestling competition.	Word Families: hostile hostility	Napoleon and the Rise of Nationalism Nationalism and Germany European Nations Compete Overseas	Hypothesizing Making Inferences	Reading a Chart	Time, Continuity, and Change Individuals, Groups, and Institutions Power, Authority, and Governance Global Connections

World History

Lesson title	Social Studies Vocabulary	Academic Vocabulary	Word Study	Concepts	Critical Thinking	Social Studies Skill	National Social Studies Standards
Reform and Revolution	suffragist, voting rights, socialist, Karl Marx, Vladimir Lenin, equality, Czar Nicholas II, abdicate, throne	Suffragists held **marches** to gain voting rights.	Word Meanings: czar	Voting Reforms / Women Get the Vote / Revolution in Russia	Comparing and Contrasting / Inferring from Evidence	Interpreting a Photograph	Time, Continuity, and Change / Individuals, Groups, and Institutions / Power, Authority, and Governance / Civic Ideals and Practices
World War I	Allied Powers, Central Powers, machine gun, tank, submarine, weapons, ally, League of Nations, war	Students **reduced** the school's garbage by recycling.	Word Parts: submarine	New Weapons of War / The War Comes to an End / The Rise of Adolf Hitler	Hypothesizing / Hypothesizing	Reading a Map	Time, Continuity, and Change / Power, Authority, and Governance / Global Connections
World War II	fascism, dictator, Benito Mussolini, Adolf Hitler, Soviet Union, Nazi, bomb, Holocaust	After a long battle, the soldiers **surrendered**.	Word Families: aggressive aggression	The War in Europe / Italy, Germany, and Japan Surrender / The Holocaust	Hypothesizing / Recognizing Cause and Effect	Interpreting a Pie Chart	Time, Continuity, and Change / Power, Authority, and Governance / Global Connections
Post–World War II	United Nations, colonized, independence, superpower, totalitarian, communism, Cold War	After years of fighting, Israel and Egypt agreed to **peace** between the two countries in 1979.	Prefixes: *post-*	The Cold War / Asia and the Middle East / African Independence	Paraphrasing / Paraphrasing	Analyzing Political Cartoons	Time, Continuity, and Change / Power, Authority, and Governance / Individuals, Groups, and Institutions / Global Connections
Globalization	multinational corporation, globalization, international trade, technology, cell phone, Internet, e-mail, computer, human rights	When apartheid was **legal** in South Africa, white people and non-white people were separated from each other.	Prefixes: *multi-*	The Global Economy and Environment / Global Politics / The Information Age	Relating to Your Own Experiences / Recognizing Cause and Effect	Comparing Historical Maps	Time, Continuity, and Change / Power, Authority, and Governance / Global Connections

American History

Lesson title	Social Studies Vocabulary	Academic Vocabulary	Word Study	Concepts	Critical Thinking	Social Studies Skill	National Social Studies Standards
Early Native Americans	land bridge, society, Native Americans, pottery, petroglyph, Americas, hunting, mound, weaving	The Southwest **region** of the United States does not get much rainfall.	Word Origins: petroglyph	Native Americans of the Arctic and Pacific Northwest; Native Americans of the Southwest and Great Plains; Native Americans of the Northeast and Southeast	Making Inferences; Integrating Information	Interpreting a Photograph	Time, Continuity, and Change; People, Places, and Environments; Culture; Science, Technology, and Society
Early Explorers and Settlers	Jamestown, colony, *Mayflower*, religious freedom, Pilgrim, Plymouth, harvest, Thanksgiving	Spanish explorers **claimed** Florida for Spain.	Synonyms: voyage, journey	Early Spanish Explorers; Jamestown and Plymouth; The Colonists and the Native Americans	Analyzing Information; Recognizing Cause and Effect	Reading a Map Key	Time, Continuity, and Change; People, Places, and Environments; Power, Authority, and Governance; Civic Ideals and Practices
Colonial America	original 13 colonies, New England Colonies, Middle Colonies, Southern Colonies, town meeting, tobacco, fur, slavery	The two men signed a **contract** when they became business partners.	Noncount Nouns: rice, tobacco, cotton	Slavery in the Southern Colonies; French and Indian War; Protest in the Colonies	Comparing and Contrasting; Recognizing Cause and Effect	Analyzing Political Cartoons	Time, Continuity, and Change; People, Places, and Environments; Power, Authority, and Governance
The American Revolution	tax, tea, boycott, Thomas Jefferson, Declaration of Independence, George Washington, Minuteman, Redcoat	British soldiers killed colonists in the event known as the Boston **Massacre**.	Word History: boycott	Rising Tensions between Great Britain and the Colonies; The First and Second Continental Congress; The American Revolution	Making Inferences; Hypothesizing	Reading a Cause and Effect Diagram	Time, Continuity, and Change; Power, Authority, and Governance; Civic Ideals and Practices

American History

Lesson title	Social Studies Vocabulary	Academic Vocabulary	Word Study	Concepts	Critical Thinking	Social Studies Skill	National Social Studies Standards
The New Nation	Articles of Confederation, delegate, Benjamin Franklin, James Madison, Constitutional Convention, constitution, debate	The balloon **expanded**.	Syllabification: constitution	The Constitutional Convention; The First Presidents; Thomas Jefferson and the Louisiana Purchase	Paraphrasing; Comparing and Contrasting	Reading a Historical Map	Time, Continuity, and Change; Civic Ideals and Practices; Power, Authority, and Governance
The Nation Grows	Meriwether Lewis, William Clark, Sacajawea, frontier, prairie, Mississippi River, woodlands, buffalo, pioneer, log cabin, Trail of Tears	The cars have to **pass through** the toll plaza to cross the bridge.	Suffixes: -less	The Lewis and Clark Expedition; Frontier Life; Native Americans on the Plains	Making a Prediction; Comparing and Contrasting	Reading a Route Map	Culture; Time, Continuity, and Change; People, Places, and Environments
Expansion and Reform	expansion, border, Missouri Compromise, harbor, ranch, Elizabeth Cady Stanton, Lucretia Mott, suffrage	Dolores **divided** the pie into eight pieces.	Loan Words: ranch / rancho	The Missouri Compromise; War with Mexico; Women's Rights	Paraphrasing; Comparing and Contrasting	Reading a Map Key	Time, Continuity, and Change; People, Places, and Environment; Power, Authority, and Governance; Civic Ideals
The End of the Frontier	gold rush, trail, wagon train, transcontinental railroad, Sierra Nevada Mountains, Rocky Mountains, Great Plains, cattle, reservation	Adriana's new haircut **transformed** her appearance.	Multiple-Meaning Words: reservation	Crossing the Continent; The Transcontinental Railroad; Transforming the Great Plains	Comparing and Contrasting; Making Inferences	Comparing and Contrasting Visual Images	Culture; Time, Continuity, and Change; People, Places, and Environments; Production, Distribution, and Consumption
A Nation Divided	abolitionist, free state, slave state, fugitive, Harriett Tubman, Frederick Douglass, Underground Railroad, civil war	Sindhu's backpack is her personal **property**.	Multiple-Meaning Words: state	Slavery and the *Dred Scott* Decision; The Abolitionists; The Election of Abraham Lincoln	Recognizing Cause and Effect; Comparing and Contrasting	Interpreting Primary Source Documents	Time, Continuity, and Change; Individuals, Groups, and Institutions; People, Places, and Environments; Power, Authority, and Governance
The Civil War	secede, Union, Confederacy, Jefferson Davis, Battle of Gettysburg, Abraham Lincoln	The barrier **prevented** us from driving on the road.	Irregular Plurals: -fe / -ves	A Long and Difficult War; The South Surrenders; The Assassination of President Lincoln	Comparing and Contrasting; Recognizing Cause and Effect	Readings Double Bar Graphs	Time, Continuity, and Change; People, Places, and Environments; Power, Authority, and Governance

American History

Lesson title	Social Studies Vocabulary	Academic Vocabulary	Word Study	Concepts	Critical Thinking	Social Studies Skill	National Social Studies Standards
Reconstruction and the New South	Andrew Johnson, Emancipation Proclamation, 13th Amendment, sharecropper, Freedmen's Bureau, Ku Klux Klan	People call 911 when there is an **emergency**.	Suffixes: -ize	The South after the War The Freedmen's Bureau Black Codes and Jim Crow	Making Inferences Summarizing	Interpreting a Photograph	Time, Continuity, and Change People, Places, and Environments Individuals, Groups, and Institutions Power, Authority, and Governance
The Industrial Revolution in the United States	invention, transportation, factory, industry, assembly line, union, strike, urban, immigrants	Discount sales often encourage **consumers** to buy more.	Prefixes: trans-	The Rise of Big Business Urban Areas Grow Problems with City Life	Making Inferences Making Inferences	Interpreting Bar Graphs	Time, Continuity, and Change People, Places, and Environments Production, Distribution, and Consumption Science, Technology, and Society
The Spanish-American War and the United States as a World Power	U.S.S. *Maine*, Cuba, Carribbean, Puerto Rico, Philippines, Buffalo Soliders, Rough Riders, Panama Canal	The bridge **connects** the island to the mainland.	Multiple-Meaning Words: rule	Yellow Journalism Rough Riders, Buffalo Soldiers, and Yellow Fever The Panama Canal	Hypothesizing Summarizing	Analyzing Historical Photographs	Time, Continuity, and Change People, Places, and Environments Science, Technology, and Society
Inventors, Reformers, and the New Americans	light bulb, camera, telephone, sweatshop, Jane Addams, Ellis Island, Theodore Roosevelt, muckraker	Firefighters use special **equipment** to put out fires.	Compound Words: sweatshop muckrakers	Inventors and Inventions of the Industrial Revolution Reformers The New Americans	Hypothesizing Recognizing Cause and Effect	Studying Primary and Secondary Sources	Time, Continuity, and Change Individuals, Groups, and Institutions Science, Technology, and Society Power, Authority, and Governance
The United States in World War I	Woodrow Wilson, invasion, neutral, *Lusitania*, army, propaganda, peace	Angela agreed with only one of the three **points** on the page.	Syllabification: propaganda	The United States Remains Neutral The United States in World War I Wilson and the Fourteen Points	Analyzing Information Summarizing	Interpreting a Timeline	Time, Continuity, and Change Individuals, Groups, and Institutions Power, Authority, and Governance

Lesson title	Social Studies Vocabulary	Academic Vocabulary	Word Study	Concepts	Critical Thinking	Social Studies Skill	National Social Studies Standards
The 1920s	prosperity, radio, Model T, 19th Amendment, jazz, stock market, Herbert Hoover	After Lourdes saw the **advertisement** for the bicycles, she wanted to buy one.	Homonyms: by, buy	A Time of Business Changes in Society The Stock Market Crash	Paraphrasing Recognizing Evidence	Reading a Graph	Time, Continuity, and Change Culture Production, Distribution, and Consumption Science, Technology, and Society
The Great Depression and the New Deal	economic depression, unemployment, Great Depression, Dust Bowl, Franklin D. Roosevelt, New Deal, Social Security	By cycling hard, Anna **generated** enough power to finish the bike race.	Antonyms: temporary, permanent	The Great Depression New Deal Programs Effects of the New Deal	Comparing and Contrasting Summarizing	Interpreting Historical Photographs	Time, Continuity, and Change People, Places, and Environments Production, Distribution, and Consumption
The United States in World War II	Pearl Harbor, D-Day, internment camp, Dwight D. Eisenhower, atomic bomb, Harry Truman, Hiroshima, Nagasaki	In **response** to the gift, Rafael smiled.	Nouns Used as Verbs: bomb	The Road to Pearl Harbor The War at Home Defeat of Germany and Japan	Analyzing Information Comparing and Contrasting	Analyzing Primary Sources	Culture Time, Continuity, and Change Power, Authority, and Governance Individuals, Groups, and Institutions Global Connections
Suburbanization and the Cold War	college, suburb, highway, drive-in movie theater, shopping mall, Korean War, Nikita Khrushchev, John F. Kennedy, nuclear missile, Fidel Castro	Traffic **congestion** became a problem after World War II because so many people bought cars.	Word Families: prosperous prosper prosperity	Prosperity and Suburban Living The Cold War The Cuban Missile Crisis	Making Inferences Summarizing	Analyzing a Primary Source	Time, Continuity, and Change Individuals, Groups, and Institutions Power, Authority, and Governance Production, Distribution, and Consumption Global Connections

Lesson title	Social Studies Vocabulary	Academic Vocabulary	Word Study	Concepts	Critical Thinking	Social Studies Skill	National Social Studies Standards
The Civil Rights Era	discrimination, civil rights, segregation, Rosa Parks, Dr. Martin Luther King, Jr., sit-in, march, César Chávez, Betty Friedan	President Johnson signed the Civil Rights Act of 1964, which **guaranteed** equal rights for all citizens.	Antonyms: integration, segregation	African Americans and Civil Rights; The Law Is Challenged; Other Groups Struggle for Rights	Hypothesizing; Relating to Your Own Experiences	Analyzing Historical Photographs	Time, Continuity, and Change; Civic Ideals; Individuals, Groups, and Institutions; Power, Authority, and Governance
The Vietnam War	Ho Chi Minh, domino theory, North Vietnam, South Vietnam, advisor, containment, Lyndon B. Johnson	Some Americans protested the draft by burning their **draft** cards.	Prefixes: un-	A Long and Different Kind of War; Protests Against the War; The War Comes to an End	Paraphrasing; Analyzing Information	Interpreting a Political Cartoon	Time, Continuity, and Change; Power, Authority, and Governance; Global Connections
The United States in the Twenty-first Century	global, imports, exports, terrorism, natural resource, fossil fuels, renewable energy	We have a **multicultural** classroom.	Nouns Used as Verbs: export / import	A Changing Population; Challenges Facing the United States; Breakthroughs in the Twenty-first Century	Comparing and Contrasting; Recognizing Cause and Effect	Analyzing Line Graphs	Time, Continuity, and Change; Production, Distribution, and Consumption; Science, Technology, and Society; Global Connections
Origins and Structure of Our Government	republic, citizens, Magna Carta, Jean-Jacques Rousseau, John Locke, United States Constitution, separation of powers	In the nineteenth century, boys and girls often sat on **separate** sides of the classroom.	Multiple-Meaning Words: right	The Foundations of Government; The United States Constitution; The Separation of Powers	Summarizing; Making Inferences	Reading a Table	Time, Continuity, and Change; Power, Authority, and Governance; Civic Ideals and Practices; Individuals, Groups, and Institutions
The Legislative Branch	Congress, House of Representatives, Senate, bill, law, elect, representative, committee	The **majority** of the class voted to take a class trip to Washington, D.C.	Prefixes: con- / com-	The Senate; The House of Representatives; Bills and Congressional Committees	Comparing and Contrasting; Comparing and Contrasting	Reading a Flow Chart	Power, Authority, and Governance; Civic Ideals and Practices

Civics and Government

Welcome to
GATEWAY TO SOCIAL STUDIES

Each lesson begins with a **Focus Question** and a list of key **Vocabulary** words related to the lesson topic to help direct student learning.

The **Word Study** demonstrates useful and important characteristics of key words. Features may include explaining how prefixes and suffixes function in vocabulary words or that some words have multiple meanings.

The **Timeline** feature found in the World and American History sections provide students with a visual map of key historical dates.

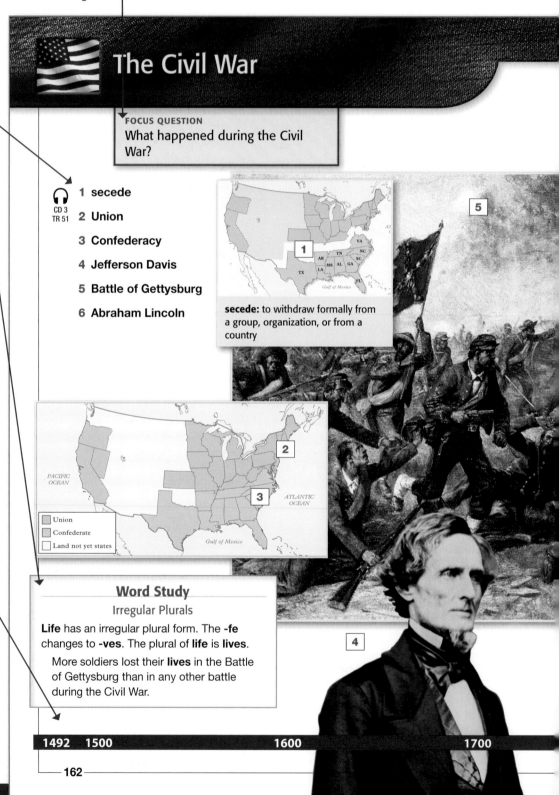

The Civil War

FOCUS QUESTION
What happened during the Civil War?

CD 3
TR 51

1 **secede**

2 **Union**

3 **Confederacy**

4 **Jefferson Davis**

5 **Battle of Gettysburg**

6 **Abraham Lincoln**

secede: to withdraw formally from a group, organization, or from a country

Union
Confederate
Land not yet states

Word Study
Irregular Plurals

Life has an irregular plural form. The **-fe** changes to **-ves**. The plural of **life** is **lives**.

More soldiers lost their **lives** in the Battle of Gettysburg than in any other battle during the Civil War.

1492   1500   1600   1700

162

Vocabulary in Context contextualizes words from the vocabulary list with an informational reading that provides an overview of the topic.

6

Vocabulary in Context CD 3 TR 52

By mid-1861, eleven Southern slave states had **seceded** from the **Union**. The Southern states formed a new government called the **Confederacy** with **Jefferson Davis** as their president. United States president **Abraham Lincoln** faced the greatest crisis in the nation's history.

The Civil War began when the Confederacy attacked Fort Sumter, South Carolina, on April 12, 1861. At first, each side thought it would win the war. Southerners had more experience with guns and horses. Since most of the fighting took place in the South, Southerners were fighting in familiar surroundings and they had less distance to travel. However, the North had a larger population and army. The North also had more factories, a strong navy, and railroads to transport supplies and people.

The Confederacy grew weaker after the **Battle of Gettysburg** in July 1863. In 1864, the Union army destroyed cities, railroads, and plantations across much of the South. The war ended soon after the main Confederate army surrendered on April 9, 1865.

Battle of Gettysburg: an important battle fought July 1–3, 1863, that resulted in the most deaths during the Civil War

✔ Check Your Understanding

1. What was the new government in the South called?
2. Where did the first battle occur?
3. How many years did the Civil War last?

Critical Thinking Comparing and Contrasting
4. What strengths did each side have in fighting the war?

Check Your Understanding questions assess vocabulary and reading comprehension and provide the opportunity to apply knowledge to **Critical Thinking** questions.

1861	1863	1864	1865
The Civil War begins	The Battle of Gettysburg is fought	Lincoln is reelected president	Lincoln is assassinated; The Civil War ends

1861 | 1865

| 1800 | 1900 | 2000 | 2010 | Present |

📖 Workbook page 157

The Civil War

Many soldiers died because of harsh living conditions during the Civil War.

A Long and Difficult War 🎧 CD 3 TR 53

More Americans died in the Civil War than in all other wars involving the United States. In addition to dying from **wounds**, many soldiers died because of the harsh living conditions and from disease. Soldiers often did not have medicine, clean water, or fresh food.

The South had difficulty getting food, medicine, and weapons because the Union **blockaded** Southern **ports**. The blockade also affected the economy of the South. It **prevented** Southerners from selling cotton, a major source of income, **overseas**.

Academic Vocabulary

Word	Explanation	Sample Sentence	Visual Cue
prevent (verb)	to stop something from happening	The barrier **prevented** us from driving on the road.	ROAD CLOSED

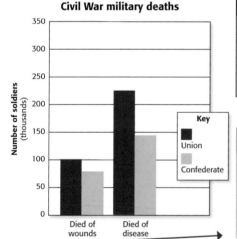

Civil War military deaths

Number of soldiers (thousands)

Key
Union
Confederate

Died of wounds   Died of disease

Social Studies Skill Reading Double Bar Graphs

This double bar graph shows the number of soldiers who died during the Civil War.

1. Which side had more deaths due to wounds?
2. Did more soldiers die of wounds or disease?
3. Overall, which side suffered more deaths?

General Lee (seated on left) surrendered to General Grant (seated on right) in 1865.

The South Surrenders 🎧 CD 3 TR 54

Ulysses S. Grant, a Union soldier, had been a strong leader in several battles. In 1864, Lincoln made Grant commander of the Union forces.

On April 2, 1865, Grant's soldiers took control of Richmond, Virginia, an important economic center and capital of the Confederacy. A week later, the main Confederate army led by **Robert E. Lee** surrendered at Appomattox Court House, Virginia.

After four years of fighting and the loss of more than 630,000 lives, the Civil War was finally over.

—— 164 ——

Feature boxes such as **Primary Sources, Kids Around the World,** and **Kids in History** showcase excerpts from authentic sources like the Declaration of Independence or real-life stories from the youth of a particular time period. These features help students make real-world connections and gain perspective of a particular time and place.

CONCEPTS

The Assassination of President Lincoln CD 3 TR 55

After General Lee surrendered, there was hope that the divided nation would **reunite**. However, days later, President Lincoln was **assassinated**.

John Wilkes Booth, a Confederate supporter, shot Lincoln while he was watching a play in a theater. Lincoln died the next morning. Booth escaped, but he was caught and killed two weeks later.

Vice President Andrew Johnson became president. He now had to rebuild the nation.

President Lincoln was assassinated while watching a play at Ford's Theater in Washington, D.C.

✔ Check Your Understanding

1. Who did President Lincoln make commander of the Union forces in 1864?
2. What happened at Appomattox Court House, Virginia, in 1865?
3. What happened to President Lincoln just a few days after General Lee surrendered?

Critical Thinking Recognizing Cause and Effect
4. How did the Union's blockade make the South weaker?

Research and Inquiry Use the Internet, the library, or your social studies book to answer these questions.

1. Who was the commanding general of the Confederate army?
2. Who was Clara Barton?
3. What was the Gettysburg Address?

 Writing Imagine you are a soldier in the Union or the Confederate army at the beginning of the Civil War. Write a letter to a family member explaining why you think your side will win the war.

Kids in History

By some estimates, as many as a half a million boys under the age of 18 fought in the Civil War. Some were as young as ten years old.

Edward Francis Jemison was just seventeen years old when he was killed fighting as a Confederate soldier.

▶ Why do you think so many boys fought in the Civil War?

The **Research and Inquiry** section provides additional questions for students to research by using the Internet, the library, or their social studies textbooks.

The **Writing** prompts give students the opportunity to demonstrate what they've learned from the lesson while practicing writing skills.

Social Studies Resources: Understanding Globes

FOCUS QUESTION
What does a globe show?

CD 1
TR 1

1 equator
2 North Pole
3 South Pole
4 Arctic Circle
5 Antarctic Circle

6 Northern Hemisphere
7 Southern Hemisphere
8 continent
9 globe

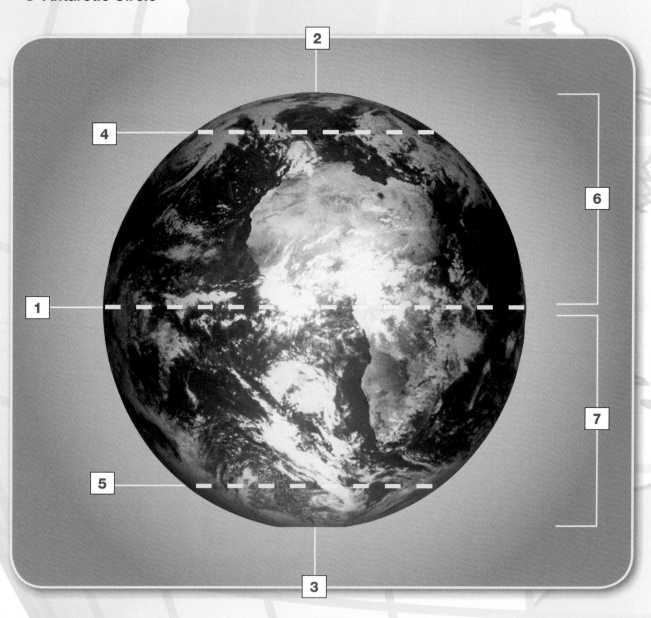

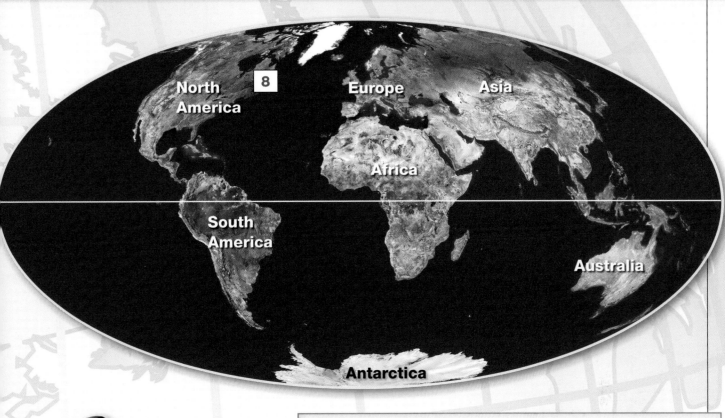

North America 8

Europe

Asia

Africa

South America

Australia

Antarctica

9

Globes CD 1 TR 2

A **globe** is a ball-shaped object that represents Earth. An imaginary line around the middle of the globe is called the **equator**.

The equator divides Earth into the **Northern Hemisphere** and the **Southern Hemisphere**. The northern tip of the earth is called the **North Pole**. The southern tip is called the **South Pole**. The Northern Hemisphere extends from the equator across the **Arctic Circle** to the North Pole. The Southern Hemisphere extends from the equator across the **Antarctic Circle** to the South Pole. About two-thirds of the land on Earth is in the Northern Hemisphere. Very large areas of land are called **continents**.

✔ Check Your Understanding

1. What shape are globes?
2. What is the equator?
3. In which hemisphere is most of the land on Earth located?

Workbook page 1

Social Studies Resources: Understanding Maps

CD 1
TR 3

FOCUS QUESTION
What does a map show?

1 location
2 physical map
3 compass rose
4 north
5 south
6 east
7 west

8 key
9 scale
10 political map
11 longitude line
12 latitude line

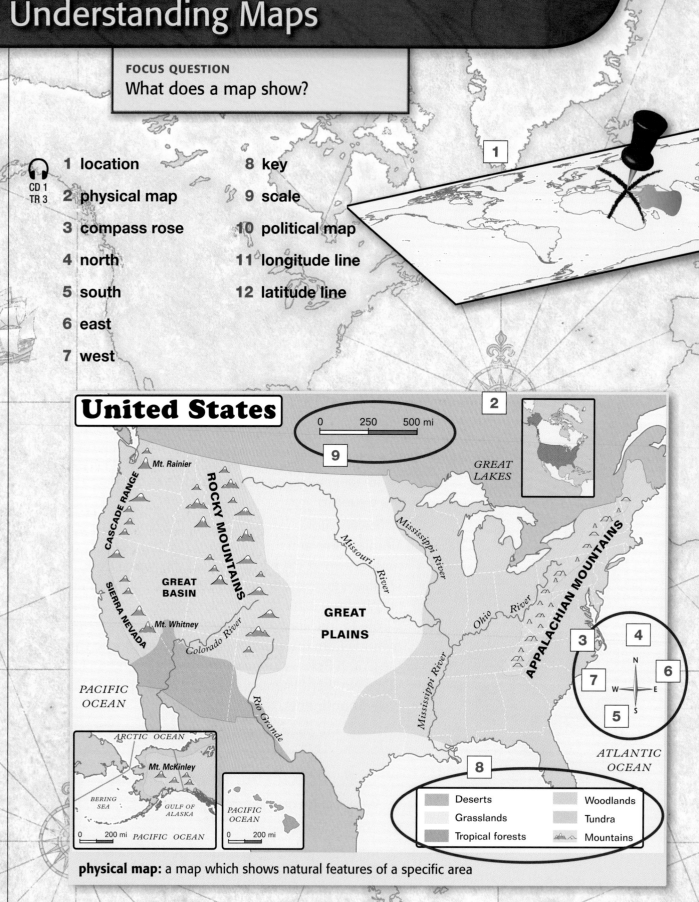

United States

0   250   500 mi

GREAT LAKES

Mt. Rainier

CASCADE RANGE

ROCKY MOUNTAINS

GREAT BASIN

SIERRA NEVADA

Mt. Whitney

Colorado River

Missouri River

Mississippi River

GREAT PLAINS

Ohio River

APPALACHIAN MOUNTAINS

Mississippi River

Rio Grande

PACIFIC OCEAN

N
W   E
S

ATLANTIC OCEAN

ARCTIC OCEAN

Mt. McKinley

BERING SEA

GULF OF ALASKA

PACIFIC OCEAN

PACIFIC OCEAN

0   200 mi   PACIFIC OCEAN

0   200 mi

Deserts
Grasslands
Tropical forests
Woodlands
Tundra
Mountains

physical map: a map which shows natural features of a specific area

Maps CD 1 TR 4

10 United States

○ National capital

CANADA
WASHINGTON
MONTANA
NORTH DAKOTA
MINNESOTA
NEW HAMPSHIRE
VERMONT
MAINE
OREGON
IDAHO
WISCONSIN
MICHIGAN
NEW YORK
MASSACHUSETTS
RHODE ISLAND
CONNECTICUT
WYOMING
SOUTH DAKOTA
NEBRASKA
IOWA
PENNSYLVANIA
NEW JERSEY
DELAWARE
NEVADA
UTAH
COLORADO
ILLINOIS
INDIANA
OHIO
MARYLAND
WEST VIRGINIA
Washington D.C.
CALIFORNIA
KANSAS
MISSOURI
KENTUCKY
VIRGINIA
NORTH CAROLINA
ARIZONA
NEW MEXICO
OKLAHOMA
ARKANSAS
TENNESSEE
SOUTH CAROLINA
PACIFIC OCEAN
MISSISSIPPI
ALABAMA
GEORGIA
ATLANTIC OCEAN
TEXAS
LOUISIANA
MEXICO
FLORIDA
GULF OF MEXICO

RUSSIA
ALASKA CANADA
PACIFIC OCEAN
HAWAII
0 200 mi PACIFIC OCEAN
0 200 mi

0 250 500 mi

N E S W

political map: a map which shows countries, states, or regions

Like globes, maps show the **location** of places on Earth. However, while globes are the same round shape as Earth, maps are flat and do not show Earth's true shape. Different types of maps show different information about Earth. For example, **political maps** show place names, such as states and capital cities. These maps also show borders. **Physical maps** show natural features on Earth. These features, such as continents and oceans, are not created by humans. Many maps contain both physical and political information.

Most maps include a **compass rose**. A compass rose shows the directions **north, east, south,** and **west** on a map. Many maps also include a **scale** and a **key**. The scale shows the relationship between the distance on a map and the same distance on Earth. A key shows what information on a map means.

Each place on Earth is located where a **latitude line** meets a **longitude line**. Latitude lines such as the Arctic and Antarctic Circles are parallel to the equator. These lines show distance north or south of the equator. Longitude lines show distance east or west of an imaginary line that runs from the North Pole to the South Pole.

11

12

✔ Check Your Understanding

1. Look at the political map. With which states does Florida share a border?

2 About how many miles is it across Colorado from east to west?

3 Look at the physical map. Are there more areas of mountains in the east or the west of the United States?

📖 Workbook page 2

Social Studies Resources: Understanding Timelines

FOCUS QUESTION
What is a timeline?

CD 1
TR 5

1 **chronological order**

2 **decade**

3 **century**

4 **horizontal timeline**

5 **vertical timeline**

6 **B.C.E./B.C.**

7 **C.E./A.D.**

1

Event 1   Event 3

Event 2   Event 4

chronological order: the arrangement of a list or description of events in the order in which they happened

2   **decade:** a period of ten years   **3**

1800 1810 1820 1830 1840 1850 1860 1870 1880 1890 1900 1910 1920 1930 1940 1950 1960 1970 1980 1990 2000

century: a period of 100 years

4

1908: First Ford automobile is made

1928: The first helicopter is flown

1961: The first spacecraft carrying a human is launched

| 1900 | 1910 | 1920 | 1930 | 1940 | 1950 | 1960 | 1970 |

1903: The Wright brothers fly their first airplane

1939: The first jet airplane is flown

The Development of Twentieth-Century Transportation

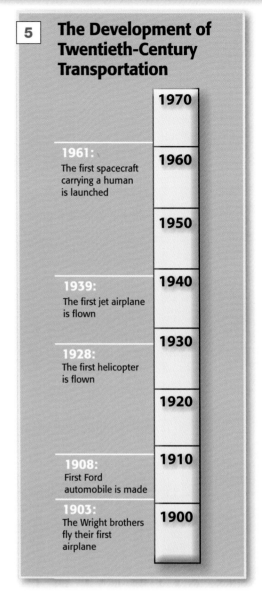

5 **The Development of Twentieth-Century Transportation**

	1970
1961: The first spacecraft carrying a human is launched	**1960**
	1950
1939: The first jet airplane is flown	**1940**
	1930
1928: The first helicopter is flown	
	1920
1908: First Ford automobile is made	**1910**
1903: The Wright brothers fly their first airplane	**1900**

Timelines

CD 1 TR 6

Timelines show the **chronological order** in which events happened. You can use them to see how much time passed between events. Timelines can also show how things change over time. A timeline helps to focus on the events of a certain time period, of a person's life, or of a particular development over time.

There are two basic types of timelines. **Horizontal timelines** have the earliest or first event on the left and the more recent times on the right. **Vertical timelines** often have the earliest or first event on the bottom and the more recent events toward the top. Timelines can span any period of time. They can show events within a year, a **decade**, a **century**, or longer.

Dates in the long-ago past are often followed by **B.C.E.,** which stands for "Before the Common Era." Sometimes you will see **B.C.,** which means "Before Christ." Dates after Christ's birth are often followed by **C.E.,** which means "Common Era," or by **A.D.** When an exact date is not known, the word "circa" is used to indicate approximately when something occurred. The abbreviation for "circa" is "c." or "ca."

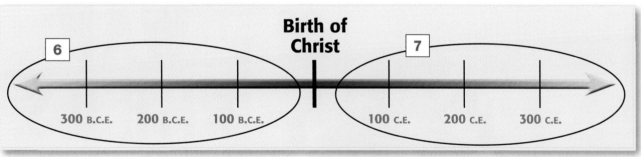

6 / **Birth of Christ** / **7**

300 B.C.E.   200 B.C.E.   100 B.C.E.   100 C.E.   200 C.E.   300 C.E.

✔ Check Your Understanding

1. What do timelines show?
2. What does "B.C.E." stand for?
3. Where does the earliest event on a horizontal timeline appear?

Workbook page 3

Social Studies Resources: Understanding Primary Sources

FOCUS QUESTION
What is a primary source?

CD 1
TR 7

1 document
2 diary
3 object
4 newspaper article

5 legal record
6 letter
7 photograph

document: the United States Constitution

diary: a page from Anne Frank's diary

object: a Greek vase

JAPAN AT WAR WITH U.S.

Hawaii, Philippines And Guam Bombed

FLEET HITS BACK

newspaper article: the front page of a newspaper from December 8, 1941

5 *An invoice of ten negroes sent this day to John B Williamson by Geo Kremer named & cost as follows*

To wit Betsey Tackley $410.00
Nancy Aulick 515.00
Harry & Helen Miller 1200.00
Mary Kootz 600.00
Betsey Ott 560.00
Isaac & Fanny Brent 992.00
Lucinda Luckett 467.50
George Smith 510.00
Amount of my traveling expences & boarding 5254.50
of lot Nᵒ 9 not included in the other bills .39.50
Kremers expences transporting lot Nᵒ 9 to Richmᵈ 51.00
Carryall hire 6.00
$ 5351.00

I have this day delivered the above named negroes costing including my expences and other expences five thousand three hundred & fifty dollars this May 25ᵗʰ 1835

John. W. Pittman

I did intend to leave Nancy child but she made such a damnd fuss I had to let her take it I could of got fifty Dollars or so you must add forty Dollars to the above

legal record: a nineteenth-century receipt for slaves

Primary Sources 🎧 CD 1 TR 8

Primary sources are records of the past that have survived into the present. They are created by people who lived at the time and witnessed or experienced the events themselves.

Primary sources include **documents**, such as the United States Constitution, and **objects**, like a vase from ancient Greece. They can be visual, such as **photographs**, maps, and art.

Some primary sources, like **legal records** and **newspaper articles**, tell about public matters. Others, like **diaries** and **letters**, tell about personal lives.

✔ Check Your Understanding

1. What is a primary source?
2. What are some examples of primary sources?
3. Look at the pages from Anne Frank's diary. How can you tell that this is a personal primary source?

6 Head-Quarters, Appomattox C. H. Va.

Apl. 9ᵗʰ 1865, 4.30 o'clock, P. M.

Hon. E. M. Stanton, Sec. of War Washington

Gen. Lee surrendered the Army of Northern Va this afternoon on terms proposed by myself. The accompanying additional correspondence will show the condition fully.

U. S. Grant
Lt. Gn.

letter: a letter written by a soldier during the United States Civil War

photograph: a photograph of students in 1900

Physical Geography

FOCUS QUESTION
What natural features are found on Earth?

CD 1
TR 9

1 geography
2 ocean
3 lake
4 stream
5 river
6 cliff
7 waterfall

8 valley
9 canyon
10 mountain
11 forest
12 desert
13 grassland

Word Study
Word Origins

The word **geography** comes from two Greek words.

- **Geo** means "earth."
- **Graphia** means "description."

Geography is the study and description of features on Earth.

Vocabulary in Context CD 1 TR 10

Physical **geography** is the study of the natural features on Earth's surface. It includes the study of water and landforms and how they interact.

The United States has many types of land and water features. For example, most of the nation's borders are formed by **oceans**. In the interior, there are also many **lakes**, which are bodies of water surrounded by land.

In the eastern United States, the lowlands and **mountains** get rain all year. Heavy amounts of rainfall have given rise to many **forests** in the region. The Midwest, however, gets less rain, making **grasslands** more widespread. The far West receives very little rain. **Deserts** are commonly found there because there is so little rainfall.

The interaction between water and land also shapes the environment. For example, **streams** and **rivers** flowing over **cliffs** make **waterfalls**. In the Midwest, rivers create shallow **valleys** through grasslands. In the highlands of the West, rivers create steep **canyons**.

✅ Check Your Understanding

1. What is a body of water surrounded by land called?
2. What does a stream or a river make by flowing over a cliff?
3. What do rivers create when they flow through the grasslands?

Critical Thinking Making Inferences
4. How does water affect plant life?

12

9

5

13

6

2

Workbook page 5

A waterfall in a canyon

Water on Earth 🎧 CD 1 TR 11

Most of Earth is covered with water, which can exist in many different forms such as **snow**, **ice**, lakes, and streams to mention a few.

Most of the water on Earth is found in its oceans and **seas**. Water located there makes up 97.25 percent of the water found on Earth and is called **saltwater**. Humans cannot drink or use saltwater to grow plants on land.

The water in lakes, rivers, streams, and **glaciers** and under the ground is **freshwater**. Water flows in rivers, streams, and waterfalls.

Academic Vocabulary

Word	Explanation	Sample Sentence	Visual Cue
percent (noun)	a part of a whole expressed in hundredths	Only 29 **percent** of Earth is made up of land.	29% land / 71% water

The coast and nearby mountains

Landforms on Earth 🎧 CD 1 TR 12

Most of the land on Earth is part of one of the seven **continents**. Earth also has thousands of **islands**, which are small areas of land surrounded by water.

The **elevation** of Earth's **surface** changes from place to place. Land near the coast is at **sea level**. Mountains can be miles above sea level.

Social Studies Skill Comparing Photographs

Look at the photographs of the coast and grassland. These photographs show two different kinds of places. Compare the photographs and then answer the questions.

1. Describe the elevation of the land in the picture of the coast with the nearby mountains.
2. What is the land like in the picture of the grassland?

A grassland

Interactions between Water and Land

 CD 1 TR 13

The amount of water in a place affects the land. Places that get a lot of rain have more plant growth. The **roots** of plants hold the soil together when it rains.

There is little rain in deserts. As a result, few plants grow there. When it does rain in the desert, streams cut into the land, forming canyons over time. A low area in the desert that flows with water when it rains is called an **arroyo**.

A river cut a canyon into this desert land.

✔ Check Your Understanding

1. What type of water is found in oceans and seas?
2. What is a small area of land surrounded by water called?
3. What effect do plant roots have on the land when it rains?

Critical Thinking Analyzing Information
4. Why does rain cut into the soil in deserts?

 Research and Inquiry Use the Internet, the library, or your social studies book to answer these questions.

1. What is the largest body of saltwater? What is the largest body of freshwater?
2. Where on Earth are glaciers generally found?
3. What river flows through the Grand Canyon in the Southwest of the United States?

 Writing Write a paragraph describing the physical geography of your neighborhood. What is the elevation of the land like? What are the closest bodies of water?

Kids Around the World

In 2009, seventeen-year-old Mike Perham became one of the youngest people to sail alone around the world. Starting in England, Mike sailed thousands of miles south, crossing the equator. Then he turned east and then north. His trip crossed three oceans and took nine months.

▶ How would you feel being alone for nine months?

Human and Cultural Geography

CD 1
TR 14

FOCUS QUESTION
What is human and cultural geography?

1. human
2. religion
3. culture
4. language
5. economics
6. government
7. city
8. built environment
9. monument

human: related to or typical of people

culture: culture is the behaviors and beliefs that are passed from one generation to the next

歡迎
Welcome
Bienvenue
Bienvenido
Willkommen
Benvenuto
Boas-Vindas
환영
ようこそ

Word Study
Prefixes

The prefix **inter-** means "between" or "among."

The word **act** means "do."

The word **interact** refers to an action between two or more things.

Planting crops is just one way humans **interact** with the earth.

economics: the making, buying, and selling of goods and services

government: a system of political and social representation and control

Vocabulary in Context CD 1 TR 15

While physical geography focuses on the natural environment, **human** and **cultural** geography look at how humans interact with the earth and help shape the world they live in.

Humans interact with the earth by farming it, using its natural resources, moving across it, and building on it. Humans shape their world through the creation of things like **language**, **religion**, **economics**, and **government**. Humans also shape their world by creating the **built environment**, which includes all human-made structures such as houses, **cities**, and **monuments**.

✅ Check Your Understanding

1. Look at the picture for culture. Describe what the people are doing.
2. How is human and cultural geography different from physical geography?
3. How do humans shape their world?

Critical Thinking Relating to Your Own Experiences
4. What is an example of the built environment in your neighborhood?

The American tradition of the Thanksgiving dinner is an example of culture.

Culture, Language, and Religion 🎧 CD 1 TR 16

Culture is the behaviors and beliefs that are passed from one **generation** to the next.

Language is an important part of culture. There are thousands of languages spoken in the world today. Religion is another important aspect of culture. While the world's largest religions include Christianity, Islam, Hinduism, Buddhism, and Judaism, there are over 4,000 religions in the world.

Other aspects of culture include food, clothing, housing, and government.

The World's Religions and the Percentages of Their Followers

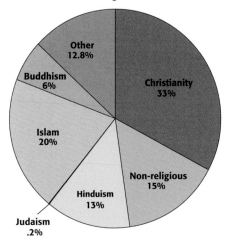

Other 12.8%
Buddhism 6%
Christianity 33%
Islam 20%
Non-religious 15%
Hinduism 13%
Judaism .2%

| **Social Studies Skill** | Reading a Pie Chart |

A pie chart shows a circle divided into parts. A pie chart is used to compare the size of the parts. A pie chart is a good way to show information in percentages. Look at the pie chart on the world's largest religions.

1. Which religion has the most followers?
2. What percentage of people in the world are followers of this religion?
3. Which is the second largest religion in the world?

Government and Economics 🎧 CD 1 TR 17

Humans create social and economic systems to live by. For example, humans create governments. Governments are systems that provide rules for humans to live together. In a **democracy** like the United States, the people elect their leaders. Humans also create economic systems in which they produce, sell, and use **goods** and **services**. Payment with money is just one way that people pay for goods and services. In some **societies,** people also **barter** or **exchange** things as forms of payment.

Money is created by governments. It is used to buy goods and services.

Academic Vocabulary

Word	Explanation	Sample Sentence	Visual Cue
exchange (verb)	to trade one thing for another	People **exchange** money for the things they want or need.	

The Built Environment CD 1 TR 18

Humans shape their environment to meet their needs. The **structures** that humans build to live in and use are all part of the built environment.

The built environment includes buildings, from private homes to skyscrapers and public places, from parks to cities. It also includes transportation systems such as roads, railroads, and bridges.

Public roads such as this highway are examples of the built environment.

✅ Check Your Understanding

1. What do governments provide for people?
2. What different things do people do as part of an economic system?
3. What is one example of the built environment?

Critical Thinking Relating to Your Own Experiences

4. What is something you have bought with money? What is something you have gotten through barter?

 Research and Inquiry Use the Internet, the library, or your social studies book to answer these questions.

1. Human languages are organized into "families." What are some language families, and which languages do they contain?
2. Write a description of three forms of government and an example of a country that has each one.
3. Research a religion. How old is the religion? How many people follow this religion? What do the followers believe?

Writing Think about the human and cultural geography features that are part of your daily life, such as language, clothing, government, or the built environment. Select one of these features and write about why human beings need it.

Kids Around the World

Students around the world go to school in different kinds of buildings. For example, in some places schools are one-room, open-air buildings that can hold only a few students. In other places, they are large structures with thousands of students.

▶ What is your school like? Describe some of its features.

A one-room school in a rural African town

A public high school in the United States

North America

FOCUS QUESTION
What are some geographic features of North America?

CD 1
TR 19

1 North America

2 Atlantic Ocean

3 Pacific Ocean

4 Arctic Ocean

5 isthmus

6 strait

7 settlement

8 indigenous people

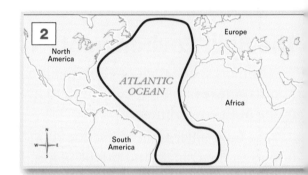

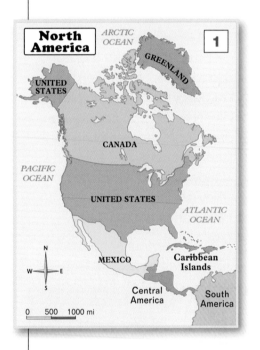

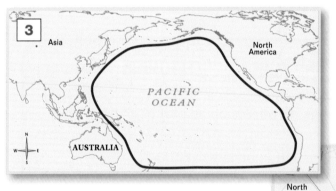

Word Study

Parts of Speech

Settle is a verb.

The Pilgrims hoped to **settle** near the Hudson River.

Settler and **settlement** are nouns.

John Smith was a **settler** in one of the first American colonies.

Many years ago, French people made a **settlement** at St. Louis on the Mississippi River.

5

isthmus: a narrow strip of land connecting two larger pieces of land

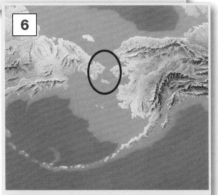

6

strait: a narrow area of water joining two larger areas of water

7

settlement: a new area where a group of people decide to live permanently

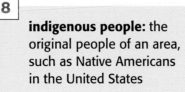

8

indigenous people: the original people of an area, such as Native Americans in the United States

Vocabulary in Context CD 1 TR 20

North America is the third largest continent in the world. It is surrounded by the **Arctic Ocean** to the north, the **Pacific Ocean** to the west, and the **Atlantic Ocean** to the east. The land is connected to South America by an **isthmus** called the Isthmus of Panama.

Between North America and Asia is a body of water called the Bering Strait. This **strait** was not always there. Thousands of years ago, it was an isthmus of dry land. People and animals probably walked across the land from Asia into North America. Those who moved from Asia became the **indigenous people** of North and South America.

Europeans began settling in North America during the 1500s. Spain, France, and England created the greatest number of **settlements**. As a result, today Spanish, French, and English are the languages with the most speakers in North America.

✓ Check Your Understanding

1. Look at the picture of a settlement. What are the people doing?
2. What connects North America to South America?
3. What continent did the indigenous people of North and South America probably come from?

Critical Thinking Making Inferences
4. What do you think might have happened to the indigenous people in the areas where Europeans settled?

Workbook page 13

A physical map of North America

Physical Geography CD 1 TR 21

North America extends from areas with **polar climates** to areas with **tropical climates**. Polar areas are cold and tropical areas are hot. In between the polar and tropical climates are areas with **temperate climates**. In temperate areas, the climate changes with the seasons. Much of the Mexican **highlands**, southern Canada, and the United States have temperate climates.

Social Studies Skill Reading a Physical Map

A physical map shows the physical features of an area. Look at the physical map of North America. The "key" explains the kinds of land found in different areas of North America.

1. What is the land like north of the Sonora Desert?
2. What kind of land is found to the west of the Mississippi River?

Human and Cultural Geography CD 1 TR 22

Christopher Columbus arrived in the Americas in 1492. Other European explorers soon followed. The Europeans took land from the indigenous people.

Settlers from Spain created a **colony** in Mexico and grew rich off its **natural resources**. Spanish settlers also went to Florida, New Mexico, California, and Texas.

The French made colonies in Canada and along the Mississippi River. The English settled along the Atlantic **coast**. Most of these colonies were **developed** to trade and sell resources such as fish and furs.

Quebec City, one of the areas the French colonized

Academic Vocabulary

Word	Explanation	Sample Sentence	Visual Cue
develop (verb)	to turn into something complete, better, or bigger	Seeds **develop** into plants that have roots and leaves.	

North America Today CD 1 TR 23

Most people in North America live in or near a city.

Manufacturing is important in the United States, Canada, and Mexico. These countries are also rich in natural resources such as **minerals** and **farmland**.

Central America and the Caribbean have fewer natural resources. Some people from these areas move to the United States and Canada for greater opportunities.

Many aircraft are manufactured in the United States.

✔ Check Your Understanding

1. What is a temperate climate?
2. Name some parts of the present-day United States that were once Spanish colonies.
3. What are the main manufacturing countries in North America?

Critical Thinking Making Inferences

4. Do you think there are more speakers of Spanish in California and Florida or in Canada? Explain.

 Research and Inquiry Use the Internet, the library, or your social studies book to answer these questions.

1. In addition to New Orleans, what are some places along the Mississippi River that have French names?
2. Aside from England, France, and Spain, what other European countries made colonies in the United States?
3. Research the resources, language, and government of a country in Central America or the Caribbean.

 Writing What if Columbus had not introduced Europeans to the Americas? How do you think North America would be different today? Write a paragraph about your ideas.

Primary Source

"Canada, the United States, and Mexico are good neighbors and good friends. As sovereign countries in the modern world, we are both independent and interdependent."
Stephen Harper,
Prime Minister of Canada, 2008

▶ Why do you think it is important for Canada, the United States, and Mexico to be good friends?

South America

FOCUS QUESTION
What are some geographic features of South America?

CD 1
TR 24

1	**South America**	4	**Spanish**	6	**rainforest**
2	**Andes Mountains**	5	**Portuguese**	7	**volcano**
3	**Amazon River**				

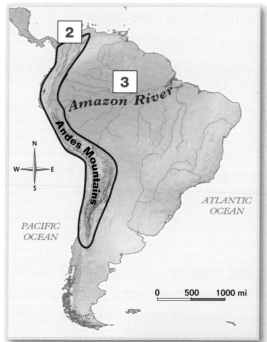

Word Study

Superlative Adjectives

We use superlative adjectives to compare three or more things. Superlative adjectives often have the ending **–est**.

The Andes Mountains make up the **longest** mountain range in the world.

Some superlative adjectives are formed with **the most**.

The Amazon River has **the most** water of any river in the world.

6

Vocabulary in Context
CD 1
TR 25

South America is the world's fourth largest continent. Three of its special physical features are the **Andes Mountains**, the **Amazon River**, and the Amazon **Rainforest**. The Andes Mountains make up the longest mountain range in the world. They extend 4,500 miles from Venezuela to Chile and include more than 30 **volcanoes**. The Amazon River is the largest river in the world, and the Amazon Rainforest is the largest rainforest in the world.

Before the sixteenth century, the Inca were the main inhabitants of South America. Then the European countries of Spain and Portugal took control of much of the continent. Most countries in South America gained their independence from Europe in the nineteenth century. However, **Spanish** and **Portuguese** remained the main languages. Today, the population of South America reflects the cultures of Europe, Africa, Asia, and indigenous people.

✅ Check Your Understanding

1. Look at South America on the map. Which ocean is to the west? Which ocean is to the east?
2. What are three of South America's special physical features?
3. What is the largest river in the world?

Critical Thinking Making Inferences
4. Why do most people in South America speak Spanish or Portuguese?

7

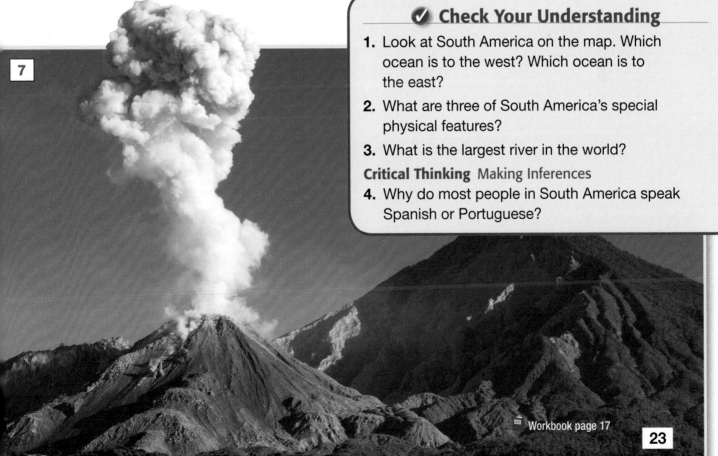

Workbook page 17

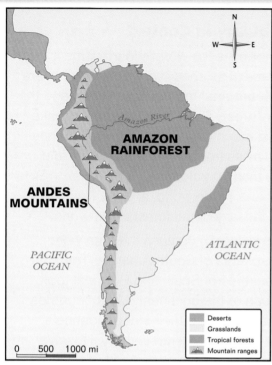

A physical map of South America

Population Pyramid of Brazil

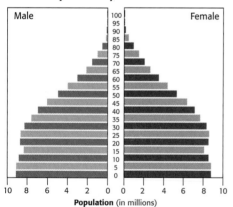

Male	100	Female

Population (in millions)

The Spanish conquered the Inca in South America.

Physical Geography CD 1 TR 26

South America is a continent of **contrasts**. The continent has both highlands and low plains, very high and very low temperatures, and very rainy and very dry areas.

The rainforests of South America are the largest in the world. The Amazon Rainforest covers 40 percent of the South American continent. It contains unique plants and animals.

South America has many natural resources. Brazil produces wood, rubber, and gold, and Venezuela has much natural gas and oil. Tourism is also an important part of the economy of South America.

Social Studies Skill Reading a Population Pyramid

A population pyramid includes two bar graphs. It shows how many males and females there are in different age groups in a country.

Look at the population pyramid for Brazil.

1. Are there more people over 50 or under 50 in Brazil?
2. Are there more males or females in the 65–69 age group?

Human and Cultural Geography CD 1 TR 27

Before the Spanish arrived in South America in the sixteenth century, the Inca had a great civilization. At the height of this **empire**, there were 12 million Inca.

Portugal **colonized** a large area of what is now Brazil, and forced the indigenous people to work for them. When disease and overwork killed many of the indigenous people, the Europeans brought slaves from Africa to do the work.

The mixture of indigenous people, Europeans, Africans, and Asians has made Brazil a **diverse** country.

Academic Vocabulary

Word	Explanation	Sample Sentence	Visual Cue
diverse (adjective)	different from one another	There are many **diverse** cultures in South America.	

South America Today CD 1 TR 28

In the 1800s, all the Spanish and Portuguese colonies won their **independence**. Today, most countries in South America are **democracies**.

South America faces some great challenges. The gap between the rich and the poor is large. Some cities are very crowded. There are not always enough jobs.

Despite the challenges, people in South America enjoy a rich culture. People around the world admire South American literature, music, and sports.

Soccer, or *fútbol*, is the most popular sport in South America.

✔ Check Your Understanding

1. What is the name of the rainforest that covers 40 percent of the South American continent?

2. Why did Europeans bring Africans to work as slaves in South America?

3. What kind of government do most countries in South America have?

Critical Thinking Recognizing Cause and Effect

4. How did colonization impact the indigenous people of South America?

 Research and Inquiry Use the Internet, the library, or your social studies book to answer these questions.

1. Why are these South American places famous?

   a. Angel Falls, Venezuela; b. Atacama Desert, Chile; c. La Paz, Bolivia

2. Who was the last Inca ruler? How did he try to escape from the Spanish?

3. What are some musical traditions that originated in South America?

 Writing Imagine you are a sixteenth-century Portuguese explorer. Write a diary entry about your first day exploring the continent of South America.

Primary Source

Inca Musical Instruments

The ancient Inca used wind instruments. They decorated panpipes and flutes to play beautiful music. Archaeologists continue to find these instruments in the highlands of Peru.

▶ What is an example of a musical instrument that is not a "wind" instrument?

An Inca Panpipe

Europe

CD 1
TR 29

FOCUS QUESTION
What are some geographic features of Europe?

1 **Europe**	4 **European Union**	7 **peninsula**
2 **Eurasia**	5 **currency**	8 **landlocked**
3 **Alps**	6 **euro**	

Word Study

Word Origins

The word **peninsula** comes from two Latin words.

- **Paene** means "almost."

- **Insula** means "island."

A **peninsula** is an area of land that is almost completely surrounded by water, so it is almost an island.

European Union: a group of countries in Europe that work together to create a stronger European political and economic system

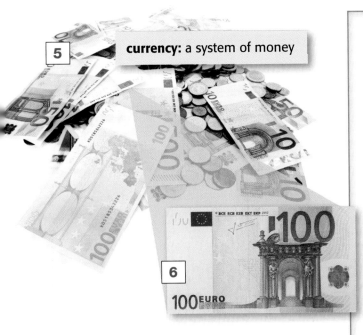

currency: a system of money

5

6

7

peninsula: a long strip of land surrounded by water and connected to the mainland

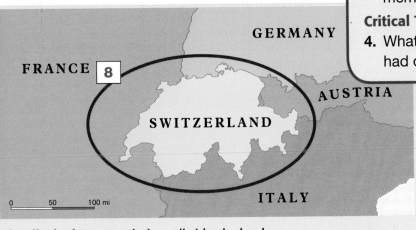

GERMANY

FRANCE

8

AUSTRIA

SWITZERLAND

0   50   100 mi

ITALY

landlocked: surrounded on all sides by land

Vocabulary in Context CD 1 TR 30

The continent of **Europe** is made up of several **peninsulas** and islands. It is connected to Asia on a landmass called **Eurasia**. There are almost fifty countries in Europe.

Most European countries border an ocean or sea. Many of Europe's **landlocked** countries have rivers that flow into a larger body of water.

The North European Plain is an area of rich farmlands. It runs through Belgium, the Netherlands, Germany, Denmark, and Poland.

Europe is also home to a large mountain range called the **Alps**. The Alps extend from Austria in the northeast to southern France in the west.

In 1993, several European countries created a political and economic union called the **European Union**. Some of the countries share a common **currency**, a system of money, called the **euro**.

✔ Check Your Understanding

1. Look at the map of Europe. Point to some of the peninsulas that make up the continent.
2. What are the Alps?
3. What is the currency shared by most of the members of the European Union?

Critical Thinking Making Inferences

4. What impact do you think being close to water had on the development of Europe?

📖 Workbook page 21

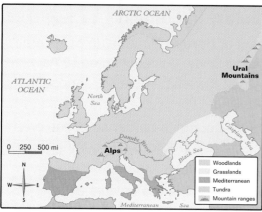
A physical map of Europe

Physical Geography CD 1 TR 31

Europe's access to water has been very important to the continent's development. Sailing and **trade** brought Europeans in contact with Africa, Asia, and the Americas, and helped the European economy grow.

Aside from its numerous bodies of water, Europe also has many mountainous areas. Historically, water and mountains kept people apart. Individual languages and cultures developed as separate societies grew.

Human and Cultural Geography CD 1 TR 32

Europe was the center of both the **Renaissance** and the **Enlightenment**. These were periods of great advances in the arts and in science.

Europe is home to many **ethnic groups** with different backgrounds, lifestyles, and beliefs. At times throughout European history, these differences have led to conflicts between some groups.

European countries value education highly and have some of the highest **literacy** rates in the world.

The Roma are one of the many minority ethnic groups in Europe.

Academic Vocabulary

Word	Explanation	Sample Sentence	Visual Cue
literacy (noun)	the ability to read and write	**Literacy** is developed through instruction in reading and writing.	

Europe Today CD 1 TR 33

Europeans enjoy a high **standard of living**. Workers are generally paid well and have more time off than workers who live on other continents.

Europe is one of the most highly populated places on Earth. Immigrants come to Europe from all over the world.

In 1993, many European countries joined together to form the European Union (EU). The EU countries work together to create a stronger European political and economic system.

A café in Europe

Social Studies Skill — Reading a Line Graph

A line graph shows how two pieces of information are related to each other. This line graph shows the population of Europe through different years.

1. What happened to the population of Europe between 1950 and 2000?

2. What happened to the population in 2010?

3. How is population growth predicted to change between now and 2050?

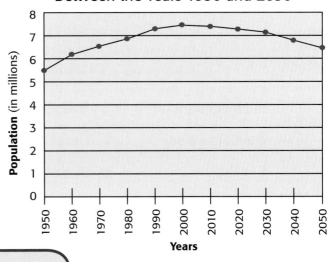

Population of Europe
Between the Years 1950 and 2050

✓ Check Your Understanding

1. How did being close to water affect the development of Europe?

2. What were the Renaissance and the Enlightenment?

3. Why are Europeans considered to have a high standard of living?

Critical Thinking Making Inferences

4. Why do you think that having different lifestyles and beliefs can sometimes lead to conflict between people?

 Research and Inquiry Use the Internet, the library, or your social studies book to answer these questions.

1. What are some of the languages spoken in Europe?

2. Research one of the many ethnic groups in Europe. Describe the group's history, lifestyle, and beliefs.

3. What countries are members of the European Union?

 Writing If you could travel to any country in Europe, where would you go? What would you do? Explain.

Primary Source

The Maastricht Treaty

In 1992, the *Maastricht Treaty* was signed. This treaty led to the creation of the European Union.

"This Treaty marks a new stage in the process of creating an ever closer union among the peoples of Europe."

—from the *Maastricht Treaty*

▶ Why is it important for the people of Europe to work closely with each other?

North Africa and the Middle East

FOCUS QUESTION
What are some geographic features of North Africa and the Middle East?

CD 1
TR 34

1 North Africa

2 Middle East

3 Arab

4 oasis

5 desert

6 Nile River

7 Dead Sea

8 Suez Canal

9 camel

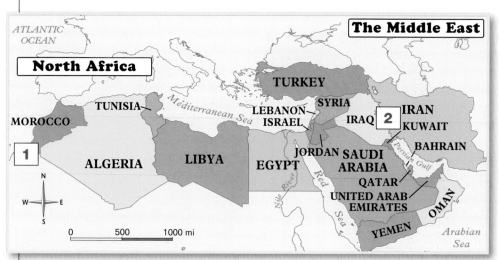

Word Study

Commonly Confused Words

Certain English words are frequently confused because their spellings are similar.

Most **deserts** are dry, hot, and sandy places.

Animals that live in the **desert** do not need much water.

A **dessert** is a usually sweet dish served as the last course of a meal.

Chocolate cake is my favorite **dessert**.

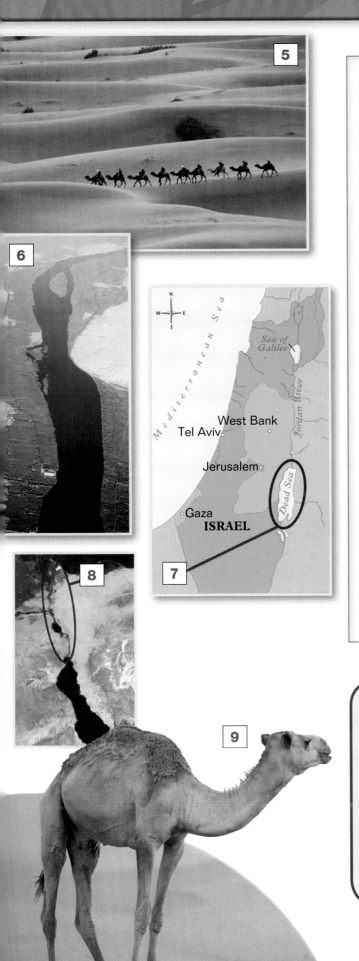

Vocabulary in Context CD 1 TR 35

North Africa and the **Middle East** are geographic areas that are grouped together because they share many of the same characteristics. The majority of the land in these areas is **desert** where very little rain falls. **Camels** do well in the desert because they can travel long distances without water. Even though deserts are dry regions, travelers might come upon an **oasis**, which is an area of the desert with trees and water.

The countries of North Africa are separated from the rest of the African continent by the world's largest desert, the Sahara Desert.

The Middle East is made up of the southwestern countries of Asia, as well as Egypt. Most of the people in this region are **Arabs**. Most Arabs are Muslims who speak Arabic.

The Middle East has the longest river in the world, the **Nile River**. It also has the lowest point on the surface of the earth, the **Dead Sea**. The Dead Sea got its name because it is too salty for animal life. The Middle East also contains one of the world's most important human-made waterways, the **Suez Canal**. The canal connects the Mediterranean Sea and the Red Sea. This makes water travel between Asia and Europe possible without having to sail around Africa.

✔ Check Your Understanding

1. Look at the map of North Africa and the Middle East. Name five countries in this part of the world.

2. What is the Suez Canal?

3. What is the world's largest desert?

Critical Thinking Making Inferences

4. What do you think are the most populated areas of North Africa and the Middle East? Why?

Workbook page 25

Physical Geography

CD 1
TR 36

There are three types of **climate** in North Africa and the Middle East. Some countries that border the Mediterranean have mild, rainy winters and hot, dry summers. People in countries with a Mediterranean climate can farm and raise crops.

The other climates are **arid** and **semi-arid**. Arid areas receive little rain and are very dry. Semi-arid areas get only a bit more rain. It is difficult to grow plants and raise animals in these climates. Most people in these areas live along rivers and by the coasts.

Many cities in North Africa and the Middle East are near bodies of water.

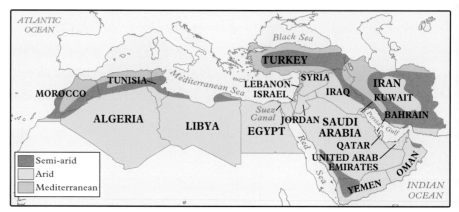

Social Studies Skill Reading a Climate Map

Climate refers to the weather patterns of an area over a long period of time. A climate map identifies the different climates of a specific region. Look at the map of North Africa and the Middle East.

1. What areas have an arid climate?
2. What areas are semi-arid?
3. Which areas have a Mediterranean climate?
4. Which climate is most common in the region?

Human and Cultural Geography

CD 1
TR 37

Three major world religions started in the Middle East: Judaism, Christianity, and Islam. This area is also where some of the great, early civilizations like ancient Mesopotamia and Egypt developed.

Most people in the Middle East and North Africa live and work in urban areas. In the desert, where crops do not grow, the **Bedouins** continually move to find **vegetation** for their animals to eat.

The Wailing Wall in Jerusalem is one of the holiest sites in the region.

North Africa and the Middle East Today CD 1 TR 38

For much of the past century, areas of the Middle East have been in **conflict** over land and religion. After World War II, Israel was created as a Jewish homeland. The Arabs who live there call the area **Palestine** and believe it belongs to them. As a result, there has been a great deal of conflict. Many of these Arabs live on the West Bank and in Gaza.

There is also an unequal division of wealth in the area. Countries that have oil, like Saudi Arabia in the Middle East and Libya in North Africa, are very rich, while countries without oil are not.

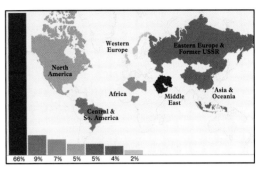

Oil reserves around the world

Academic Vocabulary

Word	Explanation	Sample Sentence	Visual Cue
conflict (noun)	a fight or struggle	The friends had a **conflict** that they worked to resolve.	

✔ Check Your Understanding

1. What are three types of climate in North Africa and the Middle East?
2. What three major world religions began in the region?
3. Name one North African country and one Middle East country that has oil.

Critical Thinking Recognizing Cause and Effect

4. How have land and religion led to conflict in the region?

 Research and Inquiry Use the Internet, the library, or your social studies book to answer these questions.

1. What crops are grown in places with a Mediterranean climate?
2. What are the names of the main religious books of Islam, Judaism, and Christianity?
3. What is OPEC? What nations make up OPEC?

Writing What kind of climate would you most want to live in: arid, semi-arid, or Mediterranean? Write a paragraph to explain.

The Dead Sea Scrolls

The Dead Sea Scrolls are 2,000-year-old documents that were found in caves near the Dead Sea in 1947. The scrolls described religious and daily life in the early Middle East.

▶ Why do you think the scrolls survived?

Sub-Saharan Africa

FOCUS QUESTION
What are some geographic features of Sub-Saharan Africa?

CD 1
TR 39

1 Sub-Saharan Africa
2 Sahel
3 drought
4 savanna
5 vegetation
6 refugee

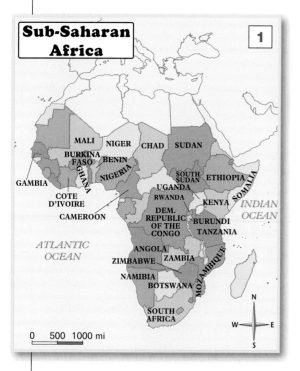

Sub-Saharan Africa 1

MALI NIGER CHAD SUDAN
BURKINA BENIN
FASO
GAMBIA NIGERIA SOUTH ETHIOPIA
GHANA SUDAN SOMALIA
COTE UGANDA
D'IVOIRE RWANDA KENYA INDIAN
CAMEROON DEM. OCEAN
REPUBLIC BURUNDI
OF THE TANZANIA
CONGO
ATLANTIC ANGOLA
OCEAN ZIMBABWE ZAMBIA
NAMIBIA MOZAMBIQUE
BOTSWANA
SOUTH
AFRICA

0 500 1000 mi

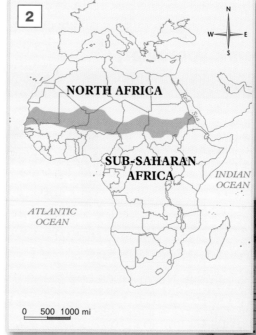

2

NORTH AFRICA

SUB-SAHARAN
AFRICA INDIAN
OCEAN
ATLANTIC
OCEAN

0 500 1000 mi

3

Word Study
Compound Words

A compound word is made when two words are joined to form a new word.

The word **grasslands** is a compound word made up of the words **grass** and **lands.**

Grasslands are an important feature of Africa south of the Sahara.

4

savanna: large area of tall grasslands with few trees

vegetation: the plant life of a region

Vocabulary in Context 🎧 CD 1 TR 40

Sub-Saharan Africa is the area of the African continent south of the Sahara Desert. The **Sahel** is a wide stretch of land that runs between North Africa and Sub-Saharan Africa. The Sahel divides the dry areas of the north from the **savannas** in the south. Savannas usually have rainfall only one season of each year.

There are also a number of tropical rainforests in Sub-Saharan Africa. Rainforests receive rainfall most of the year and have thick **vegetation**. However, there are also very dry areas south of the savannas, such as the large Kalahari Desert.

Sub-Saharan Africa faces a number of challenges. Frequent **droughts** ruin crops. Fewer crops lead to hunger. Another problem is that many Sub-Saharan governments are not stable. Sometimes countries become violent and unsafe. People become **refugees** when they leave their homes to escape the danger.

✔ Check Your Understanding

1. What separates the Sahara Desert in the north and the savannas in the south of Africa?
2. What is the name of the desert in southern Africa?
3. What are some challenges facing Sub-Saharan Africa today?

Critical Thinking Making Inferences

4. Look at the picture representing "drought" and the sentence in the Vocabulary in Context. What do you think "drought" means?

refugee: a person who leaves a country or home to escape dangers, such as war or political oppression

📖 Workbook page 29

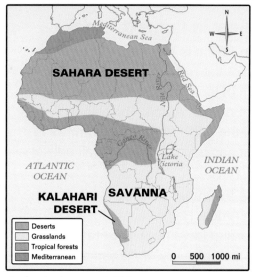

A physical map of Africa

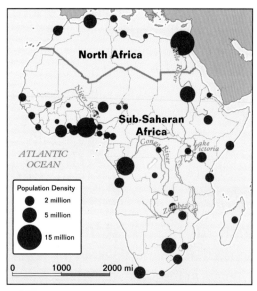

Population density map of Africa

African ethnic groups weave different patterns in their cloth.

Physical Geography 🎧 CD 1 TR 41

Sub-Saharan Africa has **lowlands** made up of grasslands and forests. It also has high peaks such as Mount Kilimanjaro, the highest mountain in Africa. The river valleys and **freshwater lakes** support the many population centers in the region.

Millions of years ago, **earthquakes** and volcanic **eruptions** created the Great Rift Valley. The valley is about 5,000 miles long and most of Africa's freshwater lakes are located there. The valley is also home to many different animals. Sub-Saharan Africa has many national parks where animals such as zebras, giraffes, and elephants live and are protected from illegal hunting.

Social Studies Skill — Reading a Population Density Map

A population density map shows where people live in a particular area. Look at the Population Density Map of Africa. The larger the circle, the greater the number of people who live in the area.

1. Which area of Africa has more people: North Africa or Sub-Saharan Africa?

2. Do you see any connections between water and population density?

Human and Cultural Geography 🎧 CD 1 TR 42

Much of Sub-Saharan Africa is still very **rural**. Many people are farmers. Farmers and their families **consume** most of the crops they grow and do not have much left over to sell. This kind of farming is called **subsistence farming**.

The region is home to many different **ethnic groups**, such as the Ashanti and the Masai. These groups have their own customs and languages.

Academic Vocabulary

Word	Explanation	Sample Sentence	Visual Cue
consume (verb)	to eat, drink, or use up	Lions **consume** an average of 5,500 pounds of meat a year.	

Sub-Saharan Africa Today CD 1 TR 43

Africa south of the Sahara is rich in natural resources such as gold, copper, and diamonds. However, Sub-Saharan Africa is the poorest region in the world. Many people do not have access to clean water, especially in times of drought. The region has a very high **child mortality** rate as a result of illness, drought, and **malnutrition**.

But this diverse continent also has a rich tradition of art, craft, and music. African music is at the root of many kinds of modern music such as rock and roll, samba, jazz, rap, and salsa.

✔ Check Your Understanding

1. Where are most freshwater lakes in Africa located?
2. What is subsistence farming?
3. What are some of the natural resources found in Africa south of the Sahara?

Critical Thinking Relating to Your Own Experiences
4. Can you think of any music, clothing, or food you enjoy that may have African roots?

 Research and Inquiry Use the Internet, the library, or your social studies book to answer these questions.

1. Research one of the ethnic groups that live in Sub-Saharan Africa. How do they live? What are their traditions?
2. Learn about refugees from a particular African country. Why did these people leave this country? Where have most of them gone?
3. Research some African proverbs (short, popular sayings) and share them with your classmates.

 Writing Imagine you are a tour guide in Sub-Saharan Africa. What area would you show visitors? What would you tell them about this area?

Primary Source

African Tribal Masks

In Sub-Saharan Africa, tribal masks have been used in ceremonies and celebrations for centuries. The colors, patterns, and decorations of the masks are unique to different cultures and time periods.

▶ Think of a ceremony or celebration that you participate in. Are there any special decorations or clothing used?

A traditional African Drummer

South Asia

CD 1
TR 44

1 **Himalaya Mountains**

2 **South Asia**

3 **Taj Mahal**

4 **monsoon**

5 **Ganges**

6 **Hindu**

7 **Hindu temple**

8 **Muslim**

9 **mosque**

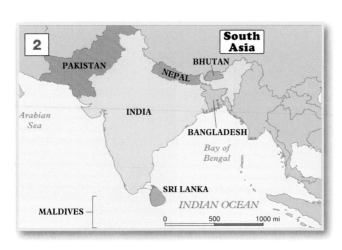

Taj Mahal: a famous monument in India

monsoon: seasonal winds that bring heavy rainstorms

Word Study

Suffixes

A suffix is a word part that is added to the end of a word. Adding the suffix **-ous** or **-ious** to a noun changes it to an adjective.

fame + **ous** = **famous**

The Taj Mahal is a **famous** building.

religion + **ious** = **religious**

Mosques and temples are two kinds of **religious** buildings.

Hindu: a follower of Hinduism, a religion that began in India

Vocabulary in Context

CD 1
TR 45

The **Himalaya Mountains** separate **South Asia** from the rest of Asia. This helps explain why South Asian peoples developed religious ideas, cultures, and languages that differ from other parts of Asia. South Asia is home to one of the most famous buildings in the world, the **Taj Mahal**. A ruler built it in the 1600s to honor his wife.

Most people in South Asia work as farmers. They depend on the seasonal **monsoon** for water for their crops. Rivers such as the **Ganges** also provide an important source of water.

Most people living in South Asia are **Hindus**. Hindus follow the religion of Hinduism and pray at **Hindu temples**. Many **Muslims** also live in South Asia. Muslims follow the religion of Islam and pray at **mosques**.

✔ Check Your Understanding

1. What separates South Asia from the rest of Asia?
2. What river is an important source of water for South Asia?
3. What are two major religions in South Asia?

Critical Thinking Comparing and Contrasting

4. Look at the photos of the Hindu temple and Muslim mosque. How are they alike? How are they different?

Muslim: a believer of Islam, a religion that began in the Middle East

📖 Workbook page 33

39

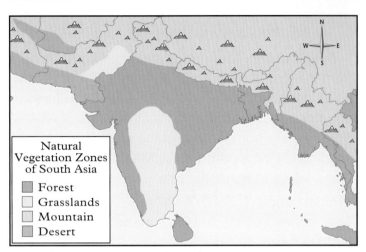

Natural vegetation zones of South Asia

Physical Geography CD 1 TR 46

Most of South Asia has a tropical climate. The Himalaya Mountains protect South Asia from cold northern **winds**.

Rain and snow on the Himalaya Mountains created the Ganges and other large rivers. During the months of June through September, parts of South Asia are hit by monsoon rains. The amount of rain that falls is different from area to area. Partly for this reason, various regions of South Asia have different kinds of **vegetation**.

Social Studies Skill   Reading a Natural Vegetation Map

The natural vegetation of an area refers to the plants living there that have not been brought in by humans. Generally, more vegetation grows in wet climates than dry climates. Look at the map above and answer the following questions.

1. In what part of South Asia is the mountain vegetation zone?

2. Are there more dry areas in the northeastern part or northwestern part of South Asia?

A Christian church in South Asia

Human and Cultural Geography   CD 1 TR 47

Throughout history, many groups of people have **invaded** South Asia and each invading group has brought changes to the area. During the 900s, Muslims built the first mosques. In the 1500s, Portuguese Catholics built the first Christian churches.

In the 1800s, the British ruled South Asia. When the British left in 1947, India was divided into two countries—India and Pakistan. Most Indians were Hindu. Most Pakistanis were Muslim. India and Pakistan have disagreed for many years about the border between their countries.

South Asia Today CD 1 TR 48

South Asia today faces old and new issues. Most people still work as farmers and depend on the monsoons to provide water for their crops.

Increasingly, however, South Asia is becoming **modern**. Many people now work in cities. India has become an industrial country. Because the people of South Asia speak different languages, English has become an important way to **communicate** across language groups.

Workers in an Indian city

Academic Vocabulary

Word	Explanation	Sample Sentence	Visual Cue
communicate (verb)	to exchange information	Deaf people often use sign language to **communicate** with others.	

✔ Check Your Understanding

1. What do the Himalaya Mountains protect most of South Asia from?
2. What two religions did invaders bring to South Asia?
3. Which South Asian country has become an industrial country?

Critical Thinking Hypothesizing
4. How do you think English was introduced to South Asia?

 Research and Inquiry Use the Internet, the library, or your social studies book to answer these questions.

1. How did Mohandas Gandhi convince the British to leave India?
2. Why was British India divided into two countries?
3. What does the term "Bollywood" refer to?

 Writing Write a paragraph that tells how geography affects people in South Asia.

Kids Around the World

Each spring, Hindus in South Asia celebrate Holi, the Hindu Festival of Colors. Holi celebrates the beginning of spring. During Holi, people of all ages go out onto the street and playfully splash paint, powder, and water on one another.

▶ Do you know other holidays that happen in spring? What are they?

CD 1
TR 49

FOCUS QUESTION
What are some geographic features of East Asia?

1 emperor

2 East Asia

3 walled city

4 herder

5 nomads

6 Chinese characters

7 Great Wall

8 steppe

emperor: a person who rules an empire

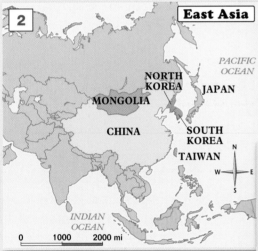

East Asia

PACIFIC OCEAN

NORTH KOREA

JAPAN

MONGOLIA

CHINA

SOUTH KOREA

TAIWAN

N W E S

INDIAN OCEAN

0   1000   2000 mi

Word Study

Suffixes

A **suffix** is a word part that is added to the end of a word. Adding the suffix **-er** to a verb changes it to a noun. It also names the person who performs the action.

People who **herd** are called **herders**.

People who **invade** are called **invaders**.

People who **rule** are called **rulers**.

herder: someone who takes care of a group of animals such as cows, goats, or sheep

5

nomads: people who do not have a permanent home, but travel from place to place setting up temporary camps

6

您好

7

Vocabulary in Context
CD 1
TR 50

Most of the area and population of **East Asia** is in China. Around 1600 B.C.E., cities developed in China. In some places, the Chinese built **walled cities** for protection from invaders. Some of these invaders were **herders** who lived on the dry grasslands, or **steppe**, northwest of China. Herders lived as **nomads**. They did not have permanent homes and sometimes attacked Chinese towns and cities to steal goods.

Over time, Chinese **emperors** built a 4,000-mile-long wall called the **Great Wall**. The Great Wall kept the nomads from attacking China. It also cut them off from learning about Chinese culture. However, Chinese culture greatly influenced people in the lands east of China such as Japan and Korea. For example, the Japanese adapted **Chinese characters** to write the Japanese language. Ideas about Chinese art and architecture influenced the people of Korea.

✔ Check Your Understanding

1. Look at the picture of the steppe. Describe it.
2. Why did the Chinese build walls around cities in China?
3. What idea from Chinese culture spread to Japan? What ideas from Chinese culture spread to Korea?

Critical Thinking Hypothesizing

4. How do you think life for the nomads differed from that of people living in Chinese cities?

steppe: a dry grassland, usually in Asia or Europe

8

Workbook page 37

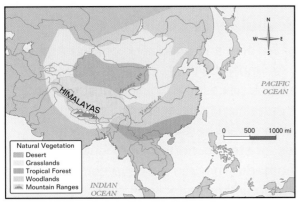

A physical map of East Asia

Physical Geography

CD 1
TR 51

Two great rivers run through China—the Huang Hu and the Yangtze. These long rivers flow slowly through wide **lowlands** toward the eastern coast of China.

In **contrast**, Korea and Japan have only short rivers and a few small lowlands. Both countries are very mountainous. The **elevation** of the land falls quickly from the mountains to the sea, which makes rivers flow fast.

Social Studies Skill — Reading a Physical Map

Physical maps show natural features, including where different types of land are located. Physical maps also show where bodies of water are located. The map key tells you how to read the map.

1. The key shows that there are five types of land in East Asia. What are these five types?

2. Which river flows through a large area of grassland?

Academic Vocabulary

Word	Explanation	Sample Sentence	Visual Cue
contrast (noun)	a comparison between two things to show a difference	Mongolia is surrounded by land. Japan, in **contrast**, is surrounded by water.	

Human and Cultural Geography

CD 1
TR 52

From 221 B.C.E. to 1912 C.E., Chinese emperors led a strong central government. These emperors built and enlarged the Great Wall to keep out nomads. They also built roads connecting walled cities across China. The emperor's **officials** and **soldiers** lived in the cities and carried out the laws.

In Japan, mountains separated people and cities. Different **nobles** governed each part of Japan, which led to a weak central government. The Japanese emperor had little **power**.

A fast-flowing river in Japan

East Asia Today CD 1 TR 53

There are different types of governments in the countries of East Asia. For example, Japan and South Korea became democracies after World War II. About the same time, China and North Korea became **communist** countries.

In the 1950s, North Korea invaded South Korea. The invaders were pushed back, but the two Koreas are still not at peace.

Japan and China are very important industrial countries. Cities such as Tokyo and Shanghai are major trading centers.

Shanghai, the industrial center of China

✔ Check Your Understanding

1. Where are China's wide lowlands?
2. Why are most rivers in Korea and Japan fast flowing?
3. Name two types of government in East Asia today.

Critical Thinking Comparing and Contrasting
4. How did the power of the emperor of China differ from the power of the emperor of Japan?

 Research and Inquiry Use the Internet, the library, or your social studies book to answer these questions.

1. When was Korea divided into two countries, North Korea and South Korea?
2. Why is the Huang Hu River also known as the Yellow River?
3. What government power does the Japanese emperor have today?

 Writing Is the land where you live low and flat like the lowlands of China or more mountainous like the land in Japan and Korea? Write a paragraph describing the land where you live.

Kids Around the World

Twenty-year-olds in Japan observe Coming of Age Day to celebrate becoming adults. Traditionally, women wear *kimonos,* long tight-fitting robes. Men wear *hakamas,* ankle-length clothes that tie at the waist.

▶ What special event do you observe to celebrate becoming an adult?

Southeast Asia and Australia

FOCUS QUESTION

What are some geographic features of Southeast Asia and Australia?

CD 1
TR 54

1 **Southeast Asia**

2 **Australia**

3 **rice paddy**

4 **water buffalo**

5 **kangaroo**

6 **Aborigine**

7 **Outback**

Word Study

Compound Words

Compound words are two or more words combined to make one word. The words below are open compounds. Each pair of words names one thing, but is written as two words. When you say these words, put the stress on the first word.

rice paddy

water buffalo

5

6

Aborigine: one of the original people of Australia

Vocabulary in Context CD 1 TR 55

Although **Southeast Asia** and **Australia** are close to each other, they are very different regions. Southeast Asia includes the land between China and India. It is tropical, wet, and mountainous. Tropical forests cover much of the area. The region also has rich farmland to grow food for its large population. Although there are big cities in Southeast Asia, most people are farmers. **Water buffalo** and **rice paddies** are commonly seen in this region, too.

Australia has tropical areas, as well as areas with temperate climates. Most Australians live in cities along the coastline. Much of Australia is called the **Outback**, which is a dry, flat area located in the middle of the country. It is home to animals such as **kangaroos**. Many of the people who live there are **Aborigines**. Aborigines have lived in the Outback for thousands of years.

✔ Check Your Understanding

1. Look at the picture of the Australian Outback. How can you tell that the Australian Outback is dry?
2. What type of work do most people do in Southeast Asia?
3. Name one Asian animal and one Australian animal.

Critical Thinking Comparing and Contrasting
4. What do Southeast Asia and Australia have in common? How are they different?

7

Outback: the isolated area of land in Australia where few people live

📖 Workbook page 41

47

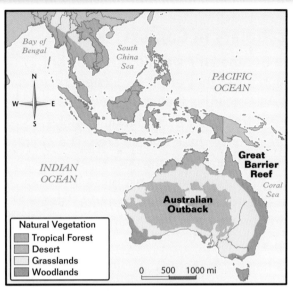

A physical map of Southeast Asia and Australia

A river in Southeast Asia

A river in Australia

A Hindu teenager on the island of Bali, Indonesia

Physical Geography CD 1 TR 56

The geography of Southeast Asia changes a lot from place to place. Tropical forests, mountains, and farmlands are commonly found in this part of the world. However, because of its closeness to the sea, people are often concerned about **tsunamis**. Tsunamis are giant waves that occur after earthquakes. The area also has several active **volcanoes**. The soil of Southeast Asia is rich because of the volcanic ash and the **silt** from the region's many rivers.

Australia does not have any active volcanoes or large rivers. Generally, Australia has poor soil.

Social Studies Skill Making Observations

When you make an observation, you look at something and learn something from it. Look at the two photographs. One shows a river in Southeast Asia. The other shows a river in Australia.

1. Describe the vegetation along each river.
2. Do you think the area along the Southeast Asian river or the Australian river receives more rainfall? Why?

Human and Cultural Geography CD 1 TR 57

For centuries, Southeast Asia has been a **crossroads** where travelers from other areas exchanged new ideas. Some of the most important ideas were religious beliefs. For example, traders from across the Indian Ocean brought Islam. Other groups brought **Buddhism**, Christianity, and Hinduism.

The Aborigines are the native people of Australia. The British arrived in Australia in the 1700s. At first, Australia was a British colony, however over the years, many people from Asia have also come to Australia to live.

Southeast Asia and Australia Today 🎧 CD 1 TR 58

Southeast Asia has raw materials such as **tin**, oil, and **rubber** as well as large areas of rice paddies and tropical forests. However, people have cut down many forests for wood or for farmland.

Like Southeast Asia, Australia produces raw materials such as coal and wool. **Tourists** travel long distances to visit Australia. They want to see kangaroos and visit **isolated** natural sights such as the Outback and the **Great Barrier Reef**. Sadly, pollution is damaging the reef.

The Great Barrier Reef is along the northeast coast of Australia.

Academic Vocabulary

Word	Explanation	Sample Sentence	Visual Cue
isolated (adjective)	the state of being alone, completely separate from others	Marisela felt **isolated** when her friends left the island.	

✓ Check Your Understanding

1. What makes land good for farming in Southeast Asia?
2. Who are the native people of Australia?
3. What is happening to tropical forests in Southeast Asia?

Critical Thinking Analyzing Information

4. Volcanoes and rivers make new land. Do you think Australia or Southeast Asia has more new land?

 Research and Inquiry Use the Internet, the library, or your social studies book to answer these questions.

1. What were the first European visitors to Southeast Asia looking for?
2. What are some of the major rivers in Southeast Asia? What do people use these rivers for?
3. Research the Great Barrier Reef. Describe where it is, how big it is, and what it is made of.

 Writing Imagine you are going on vacation to a small tropical island in Southeast Asia. Write a paragraph telling what you plan to do there.

Kids Around the World

In 2004, a ten-year-old English girl, Tilly Smith, was on vacation with her family. They were staying on an island in Southeast Asia. One morning, Tilly saw the water start to bubble and boats begin to bob up and down. She had just studied tsunamis in school. Tilly said, "I had a feeling there was going to be a tsunami." She told her mother, and her mother warned other people. This saved many people from being killed.

▶ What made Tilly feel there might be a tsunami?

CD 1
TR 59

1 hominid   4 fire

2 prehistoric   5 tools

3 ancestors   6 migration

3

ancestors: all the people in a family who lived before a person's grandparents

1

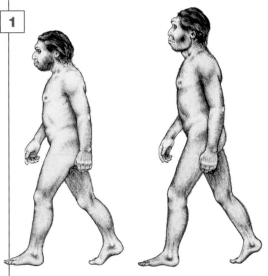

2

prehistoric: time before history was recorded through pictures or writing

Word Study
Prefixes

The prefix **pre-** means "before."

The word **history** means "a written account of past events."

The word **prehistoric** means "before recorded history."

The wooly mammoth was a **prehistoric** animal.

4

3 million B.C.E.

5

6

migration: movement from one area to settle in another

Vocabulary in Context CD 1 TR 60

About three million years ago, human-like **hominids** first appeared on Earth. Hominids, **ancestors** of humans, could walk standing up and used sticks and bones as **tools**. They ate plants and the remains of dead animals that they found.

The first humans appeared about two million years ago. They were taller than their ancestors and had larger brains. During **prehistoric** times, early humans used stones to make tools. Much later they discovered **fire** and used it in their daily lives.

Early humans first lived in Africa. Over time, they **migrated** to other parts of the world. Millions of years ago, narrow pieces of land called land bridges connected one continent to another. These bridges allowed people to travel to and settle in parts of Asia and the Americas.

✔ Check Your Understanding

1. Look at the first picture of the human-like man. In what ways does he look like a human?
2. What are the ancestors of humans called?
3. On which continent did the first humans live?

Critical Thinking Comparing and Contrasting

4. How were the hominids and the first true humans different?

ca. 3 million B.C.E.	**ca. 2 million** B.C.E.	**ca. 500,000** B.C.E.	**ca. 100,000** B.C.E.	**ca. 85,000** B.C.E.	**ca. 8,000** B.C.E.
Hominids appear	First true humans appear	Humans make and use fire	Language develops	Humans begin to use land bridges to migrate outside of Africa	Humans begin to keep animals and grow crops

100,000 B.C.E.	85,000 B.C.E.	8,000 B.C.E.	Present

📖 Workbook page 45

Early humans hunted animals and gathered plants for food.

Hunters and Gatherers

CD 1
TR 61

Early humans were **hunters** and **gatherers**. In their search for food, they often killed animals and collected plants. Early humans never stayed in one place for a long period of time. They moved constantly in search of food.

Some early humans lived in caves, while others built homes using branches, leaves, and animal skins. Much later, they cut down trees and used them for **shelter**.

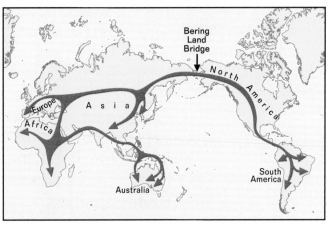

Map of Early Human Migration
(150,000 B.C.E –10,000 B.C.E.)

Social Studies Skill   Reading a Migration Map

Migration maps show how people move from one area to another. Arrows are often used to show direction.

According to history, the first humans appeared in Africa. Look at the map of early human migration.

1. After humans left Africa, which continent do you think they arrived at first?
2. What made it possible for humans to cross from Asia to North America?

Early humans used fire for light, warmth, and to cook food.

Tools and Culture

CD 1
TR 62

Early humans used tools for hunting, building, and farming. Using tools for these purposes was a **milestone** for humans. Making and controlling fire was also an important development. Not only did they use fire to cook food, but fire also provided light at night and gave warmth during the winter.

The development of **language** allowed humans to communicate with one another. Through language, one **generation** could teach the beliefs and culture of a group to the next generation.

Academic Vocabulary

Word	Explanation	Sample Sentence	Visual Cue
generation (noun)	any of the different age groups in a family, such as grandparents, children, and grandchildren	Even though my grandmother and I are from different **generations**, we enjoy the same movies and music.	

The Agricultural Revolution 🎧 CD 1 TR 63

During the period called the Agricultural Revolution, humans began to get their food more by farming and raising animals than by hunting and gathering. For the first time, humans planted seeds and grew crops. They also **domesticated** animals.

Humans settling in one area led to new ways of life. Because more food was produced, fewer people had to be farmers. This made it possible for some people to take on new roles, such as craftsmen and leaders. As a result, societies grew more complex.

Farming provided more food for humans.

✅ Check Your Understanding

1. How did early humans get their food?
2. Why was the development of language important?
3. What is the "Agricultural Revolution"?

Critical Thinking Relating to Your Own Experiences
4. What kind of tools do you use in your own life?

 Research and Inquiry Use the Internet, the library, or your social studies book to answer these questions.

1. Explain what the names of these three types of hominids mean: *Homo habilis, Homo erectus,* and *Homo sapiens.*
2. Who were the Neanderthals? Where did they live?
3. What animals were domesticated by humans first?

 Writing The people who lived inside the Lascaux caves drew images from their daily life. If someone asked you to draw pictures about your daily life, what would you draw? What would these pictures tell about your daily life?

Primary Source

Lascaux Cave Paintings

The Lascaux cave paintings in France were created 17,000 years ago by our early ancestors. The caves include almost 2,000 images of the people and animals that lived at the time. Other drawings are less clear, and their meaning remains a mystery.

▶ What animal do you think is shown in this cave painting?

A **Lascaux** cave painting

FOCUS QUESTION
What were the earliest societies and where were they located?

civilization: an advanced human society in which the people have a common culture, economy, and government

CD 1
TR 64

1 civilization
2 Fertile Crescent
3 alphabet
4 soil

5 trade routes
6 Indus Valley
7 wheel

2

Mediterranean Sea
Asia
FERTILE CRESCENT
Africa
Red Sea
Arabian Sea
Nile River
Euphrates River
Tigris River

3
ABCDEFG HIJKLMN OPQRST UVWXYZ

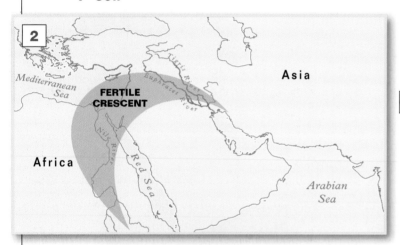

4

Word Study
Word Origins

The word **civilization** comes from the Latin word *civis*. Civis means "citizen."

A **citizen** is a member of a city, town, or nation.

A **civilization** is an advanced human society.

5
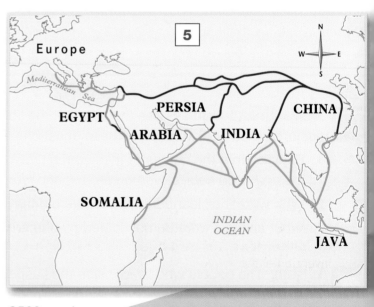

Europe
Mediterranean Sea
EGYPT
PERSIA
ARABIA
INDIA
CHINA
SOMALIA
INDIAN OCEAN
JAVA

3500 B.C.E

| 4500 B.C.E. | 4000 B.C.E. | 3500 B.C.E. | 3000 B.C.E. |

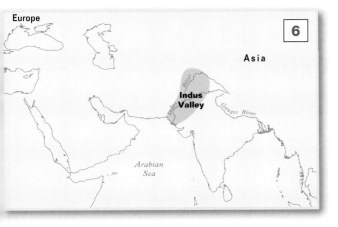

Europe

Asia

Indus Valley

Ganges River

Arabian Sea

6

Vocabulary in Context
CD 1
TR 65

About 7,000 years ago, as humans began living in settlements, they developed larger and more complex societies. These early **civilizations** were located in river valleys.

In southwest Asia and northeast Africa, a region known as the **Fertile Crescent** provided rich **soil** and water for farming. This area was home to the first civilizations. It was also the birthplace of important inventions such as the **wheel** and the **alphabet**.

Civilization also developed in the **Indus Valley**. Seas, deserts, and mountains surrounded these civilizations, protecting them from attack. Later, **trade routes** developed between civilizations. This allowed for the exchange of ideas, cultures, inventions, and goods. This exchange transformed civilizations.

7

✔ Check Your Understanding

1. Look at the map of the Indus Valley. On which continent is the Indus Valley?

2. Why was the Fertile Crescent a good place to settle?

3. How did trade routes change civilizations?

Critical Thinking Visualizing

4. Imagine what life was like for humans before the invention of the wheel. How might people have transported things before the wheel?

ca. 3500 B.C.E.	**ca. 3000** B.C.E.	**ca. 2500** B.C.E.	**ca. 2000** B.C.E.	**ca. 1800** B.C.E.
Sumerian civilization grows. Invention of the wheel	Writing is developed	Indus Valley civilizations grow	Phoenicians trade throughout the Mediterranean	Code of Hammurabi is introduced

2500 B.C.E.   **2000** B.C.E.

1800 B.C.E.

Present

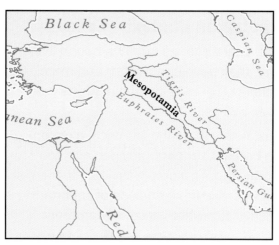

Mesopotamia was located between the Tigris and Euphrates Rivers.

Mesopotamia and the Phoenicians

CD 1 TR 66

The earliest civilizations began in Mesopotamia, between the Tigris and Euphrates Rivers.

Sumer was an area in the southern part of Mesopotamia. Many believe that this was the birthplace of the first civilization. Sumerians kept records of their crops and trading. They also developed a calendar.

The Phoenicians developed a society on the eastern side of the Mediterranean. The Phoenicians were skilled sailors and traders.

Artifact from an early society

Social Studies Skill Analyzing Archaeological Artifacts

Much of the information we have about early societies comes from **artifacts** that have been found deep in the earth. By analyzing these artifacts, we can learn about early societies.

Look at the artifact (*left*) that was found in the Indus Valley.

1. Describe the artifact. What do you think it is?
2. What does this object tell you about the people who created it?

The First Writing

CD 1 TR 67

As cultures became more complex, people needed to keep records. For example, traders needed to record business **transactions**, and rulers needed to record laws.

One of first systems of writing was **cuneiform**. It was invented by the Sumerians, and it had hundreds of **symbols**. Using cuneiform allowed **scribes** to record the society's history. Today, we know a great deal about the ancient Sumerians because of these records.

The Phoenicians also developed an alphabet made up of twenty-two single letters. This alphabet is an ancestor of most modern alphabets.

Cuneiform was written on clay tablets.

Academic Vocabulary

Word	Explanation	Sample Sentence	Visual Cue
symbol (noun)	a sign, mark, or picture that represents something else	The **symbol** $ stands for the word "dollar."	

The Indus Valley   CD 1 TR 68

Like Mesopotamian society in the Fertile Crescent, societies in the Indus River Valley developed near water on land good for farming.

The Harappan civilization began to grow in this area in about 2500 B.C.E. It was one of the first societies to plan cities in a **grid**. The Harappan people were also well known for their ability to measure and weigh things accurately.

✔ Check Your Understanding

1. Between which two rivers was Mesopotamia located?
2. What was cuneiform?
3. What was the name of the civilization that began to grow in the Indus Valley about 2500 B.C.E.?

Critical Thinking Hypothesizing
4. The Sumerians and Phoenicians both had systems of writing. Which do you think was easier to use? Explain.

Research and Inquiry Use the Internet, the library, or your social studies book to answer these questions.

1. This time period discussed in this lesson is sometimes called the Bronze Age. Why?
2. Learn more about the ancient civilization of the Harappa in the Indus River Valley. Describe the society that developed there.
3. How was cuneiform script made? What materials were used? How were these symbols written on the tablets?

Writing Choose one of the laws from Hammurabi's Code in the Primary Source. Do you think this law is fair? Why or why not? Write a paragraph.

The Harappan people were one of the first to plan cities in a grid.

Primary Source

Hammurabi's Code

Hammurabi was a ruler in Mesopotamia who created a set of 282 written laws, as well as punishments for breaking those laws. The laws, known as the Code of Hammurabi, dealt with property, business, and personal relationships. Here are examples:

#6: If someone steals the property of a temple or of the court, he shall be put to death.

#196: If a man takes out the eye of another man, his eye shall be taken out.

▶ Write your own legal code. What two laws would you create?

Ancient Civilizations

1

FOCUS QUESTION
What were the ancient civilizations of Egypt and China like?

CD 2
TR 1

1 pyramid
2 hieroglyph
3 social class
4 pharaoh
5 Tutankhamen

6 Cleopatra
7 archaeologist
8 mummy
9 dynasty

2

3
4

social class: a group of people of the same economic level and position in society
pharaoh: a ruler of ancient Egypt

Word Study
Word Origins

Hieroglyphs are symbols ancient Egyptians used to develop their system of writing. Hieroglyphs were often carved into stone.

The word **hieroglyph** is made up of two Greek words.

- **Hieros** means "holy."
- **Glyphe** means "carving."

5
6

3000 B.C.E.

4 million B.C.E.   **3 million B.C.E.**   **2 million B.C.E.**

7

archaeologist: someone who studies the past through objects left by the people in the past

8

9

dynasty: a series of rulers from the same family or group

Vocabulary in Context CD 2 TR 2

The ancient Egyptians in the Nile River Valley developed a great civilization beginning about 3000 B.C.E. They built **pyramids** for their rulers. These rulers were called **pharaohs**. Two of the most famous pharaohs are **Tutankhamen** and **Cleopatra**.

Ancient Egypt was a complex society with a number of different **social classes**. We know a lot about ancient Egypt from **hieroglyphs**, the Egyptian writing system discovered by **archaeologists**. The discovery of Egyptian **mummies** has also provided information about life in ancient Egypt.

During the time that Egyptian civilization was developing, the Chinese were building a great civilization as well. Family **dynasties** ruled China for generations. Each dynasty brought new ideas about things like government, art, and religion to Chinese society.

✔ Check Your Understanding

1. Look at and describe the Egyptian hieroglyphics. What objects do you see?
2. How was ancient China ruled?
3. What are the names of two famous Egyptian pharaohs?

Critical Thinking Comparing and Contrasting
4. How do you think hieroglyphs is like the English alphabet? How is it different?

ca. 3000 B.C.E.	**ca. 2560** B.C.E.	**ca. 1800** B.C.E.	**1333** B.C.E.	**206** B.C.E.	**51** B.C.E.
First hieroglyphic script is developed	Great Pyramid of Giza is completed	First dynasty of China, the Shang Dynasty, begins	Tutankhamen becomes pharaoh of Egypt at age 9	Great Wall of China is completed	Cleopatra becomes the last pharaoh of Egypt

51 B.C.E.

2000 B.C.E.	**1500** B.C.E.	**1000** B.C.E.	**500** B.C.E.	**Present**

Workbook page 53

Egyptian scribes wrote hieroglyphs on papyrus.

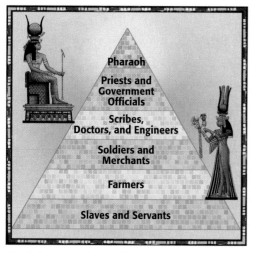

Social classes in Ancient Egypt

Tutankhamen's tomb

Ancient Egypt CD 2 TR 3

Scribes were educated people who used a hieroglyphic writing system based on pictures. The hieroglyphs were sometimes carved in stone, and sometimes written in ink on a paperlike material called **papyrus**.

People in Egyptian society were arranged into social classes according to their jobs. Some people were farmers. Others were **merchants**. Still others were government **officials** or **priests**.

The ancient Egyptians believed in many gods. They also believed in an **afterlife**. For this reason, they buried their dead with objects to use in the next life.

Social Studies Skill Interpreting Charts

Charts present information visually. This chart shows the social classes of ancient Egypt, within a pyramid shape. The lowest class is at the bottom, and the highest class is at the top.

Look at the chart:

1. Which groups made up the bottom social class?
2. Which groups are closest to the pharaoh?
3. Why do you think scribes, doctors, and engineers were higher on the chart than soldiers and farmers?

The Pyramids of Ancient Egypt CD 2 TR 4

The belief in an afterlife was important to the ancient Egyptians. The Egyptians built huge pyramids as **tombs** for the pharaohs. Before burial, Egyptians **preserved** the body through **mummification**. They then buried the pharaohs in the tombs. These tombs were beautifully decorated and filled with riches. The Egyptians believed that the pharaohs would need the **treasures** even after death.

Academic Vocabulary

Word	Explanation	Sample Sentence	Visual Cue
preserve (verb)	to keep in good condition	The ancient Egyptians **preserved** the bodies of the dead through mummification.	

Ancient China CD 2 TR 5

While Egyptian civilization was developing, the Chinese were developing an advanced civilization in Asia. During this time, the Chinese invented many things we use today, such as paper, silk, and fireworks.

Around 200 B.C.E., China began to trade with other regions. One of the Chinese goods in greatest demand was silk cloth. For this reason, the trade routes between China and the rest of Asia were known as the Silk Road.

As the Chinese became richer, they were often attacked. One of the Chinese emperors ordered that the Great Wall be built to keep out **invaders**.

The Great Wall of China was built to keep out invaders.

✔ Check Your Understanding

1. What is the name of the paperlike material that scribes used?
2. Why did the Egyptians build pyramids?
3. What was the Silk Road?

Critical Thinking Paraphrasing
4. How were pharaohs buried?

 Research and Inquiry Use the Internet, the library, or your social studies book to answer these questions.

1. Research Egyptian hieroglyphs. Find the symbols that correspond to the letters in your name and write your name using hieroglyphs.
2. Learn more about one of the pharaohs of Egypt. When did the pharaoh rule? What kind of ruler was this pharaoh? Has the pharaoh's tomb been discovered?
3. Research and write about five things invented by the Chinese.

 Writing Select a social class from Egyptian society. Write a paragraph describing what life might be like if you lived in ancient Egypt as a member of that social class.

Primary Source

The Rosetta Stone

An important artifact from ancient Egypt is the Rosetta Stone.

For thousands of years, no one understood hieroglyphs. Then in 1799 the Rosetta Stone was found in Egypt. This stone had hieroglyphs, as well as writing in ancient Greek. Scholars were able to use the ancient Greek to understand the meaning of the hieroglyphs.

▶ Why do you think historians think the Rosetta Stone is such an important artifact?

FOCUS QUESTION

What was life like in ancient Greece and the Roman Empire?

CD 2
TR 6

1 ancient Greece

2 democracy

3 Roman Empire

4 citizens

5 Parthenon

6 philosophy

7 columns

8 Olympic Games

1

2

BALLOT BOX

democracy: government in which citizens elect their political leaders

3

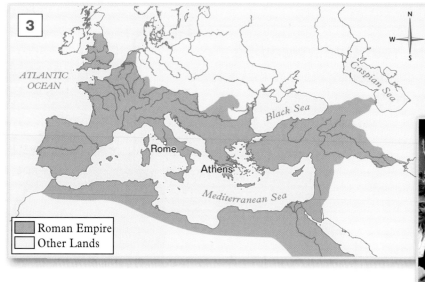

Roman Empire
Other Lands

4

citizens: legal members of a country, state, or city

Word Study

Word Origins

The word **philosophy** comes from two Greek words.

• **Philo** means "loving."

• **Sophy** means "wisdom."

Because ancient Greeks valued wisdom, they studied **philosophy**.

5

3500 B.C.E.	3000 B.C.E.	2500 B.C.E.	2000 B.C.E.

philosophy: the study of knowledge, truth, and life

Vocabulary in Context
CD 2
TR 7

The classical civilizations of **ancient Greece** and the **Roman Empire** gave birth to some of the most important ideas in history. For example, the ancient Greeks laid the foundations for theater, math, science, **philosophy**, and engineering. They were the first to have **citizens** participate in their government through **democracy**. The ancient Greeks also began the **Olympic Games**. The ancient Romans laid the foundations for law, art, music, and religion.

The design of Greek and Roman buildings has also influenced modern buildings. For example, like the Greek **Parthenon**, many modern government buildings, university buildings, and libraries have **columns** and are made of marble.

✓ Check Your Understanding

1. Look at and describe the picture of the Parthenon.
2. What things did the ancient Romans lay the foundations for?
3. What kinds of modern buildings often have columns?

Critical Thinking Making Inferences

4. How might life be different today if the Greek and Roman cultures had not existed?

Olympic Games: international sports competitions held every four years

776 B.C.E.	**438** B.C.E.	**146** B.C.E.	**44** B.C.E.	**117** C.E.	**392** C.E.	**476** C.E.
The first Olympic Games are held	The Parthenon is built in Athens	Greece becomes part of the Roman Empire	Julius Caesar is killed	The Roman Empire reaches its greatest size	Christianity is made the official religion of the Roman Empire	The last Roman Emperor is removed

		776 B.C.E.		476 C.E.	
1500 B.C.E.	**1000** B.C.E.	**500** B.C.E.			**Present**

 Workbook page 57

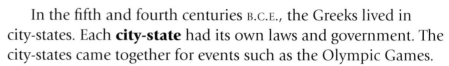

Citizens in Ancient Athens

Ancient Greece 🎧 CD 2 TR 8

In the fifth and fourth centuries B.C.E., the Greeks lived in city-states. Each **city-state** had its own laws and government. The city-states came together for events such as the Olympic Games.

The leading Greek city-state was Athens. In most other civilizations at that time, a king or a small group of people ruled. However, in Athens all male citizens could vote and **participate** in government. This was an early example of democracy. Athens was also known for its philosophers and buildings such as the Parthenon.

Academic Vocabulary

Word	Explanation	Sample Sentence	Visual Cue
participate (verb)	to take part in an activity or event	The United States basketball team will **participate** in the next Olympic Games.	

A Roman soldier

The Roman Empire 🎧 CD 2 TR 9

In 146 B.C.E., Greece was conquered by a new empire centered on Rome, a city on the Italian peninsula. Great Roman leaders such as **Julius Caesar** conquered many lands. By the time Caesar died in 44 B.C.E., Rome ruled most of the lands around the Mediterranean Sea.

For two centuries, Rome's strong army and walls kept out invaders. The empire was safe and **prosperous**. This time became known as the **Roman Peace**.

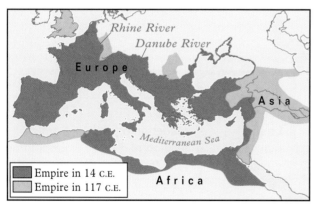

The Roman Empire 14 C.E. to 117 C.E.

Social Studies Skill Reading a Historical Map

Historical maps show an area at a time in the past. This map shows the land included in the Roman Empire during two different periods of time.

1. Look at the lands included in the Roman Empire in 14 C.E. What two rivers formed part of the northern border of the empire in 14 C.E.?

2. Look at the areas that made up the Roman Empire in 117 C.E. On which three continents did the empire expand between 14 C.E. and 117 C.E.?

The Rise of Christianity and the Decline of Rome 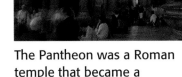 CD 2 TR 10

During the Roman Peace, a new religion spread in the empire. This religion, based on **Judaism**, was called **Christianity**. Roman emperors tried to stop the new religion. They did not succeed, and Rome became the center of Christianity. It became the official religion of the empire in 392 C.E.

By this time, the empire had grown weaker. Romans fought among themselves. They could no longer stop German tribes from coming into the empire. In 476 C.E., Germans removed the last Roman emperor.

The Pantheon was a Roman temple that became a Christian church.

✔ Check Your Understanding

1. Why was the government of Athens considered to be an early kind of democracy?

2. What areas did the Roman Empire cover by the time of Julius Caesar's death?

3. What, at first, did Roman emperors do about the growth of Christianity?

Critical Thinking Comparing and Contrasting

4. How are modern democracies similar to the kind of democracy that existed in ancient Athens? How are they different?

 Research and Inquiry Use the Internet, the library, or your social studies book to answer these questions.

1. What are some events from the ancient Olympic Games that are still part of the modern Olympics?

2. Research Hadrian's Wall. What is it? Why was it built? Where was it built?

3. Emperor Constantine moved the capital of the Roman Empire. Where did he move it? Why did he move it? What did he call this city?

 Writing Think about how the ideas formed in ancient Greece and Rome have an impact on your own life. In what ways are the ideas of these ancient civilizations a part of your daily life? Write a paragraph.

Primary Source

Roman Coins

The Romans used coins as currency from around the middle of the third century B.C.E. Having a common currency made trade in the empire easier.

▶ Compare a coin that you use today with the Roman coins. How are they similar? How are they different?

A Roman coin showing Julius Caesar.

Europe in the Middle Ages

FOCUS QUESTION

What was life like in Europe during the Middle Ages?

CD 2
TR 11

1 **king**   5 **Viking**

2 **noble**   6 **castle**

3 **knight**   7 **serf**

4 **feudalism**

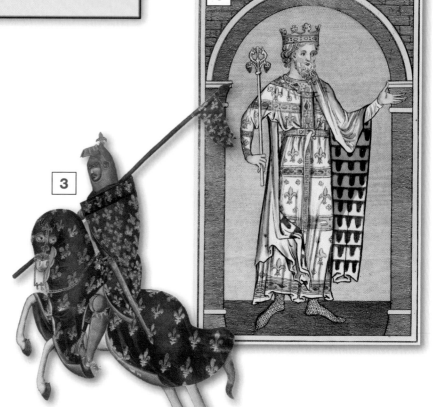

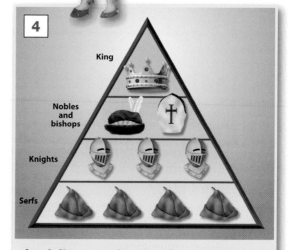

Word Study

Homonyms

The words **knight** and **night** are homonyms. Homonyms are words that have the same pronunciation, but different meanings.

A **knight** was a soldier hundreds of years ago who fought on horseback for a noble or a king.

Night is the time between when the sun sets and the sun rises.

King

Nobles
and
bishops

Knights

Serfs

feudalism: a political and social system in which a king and the people of the upper classes owned the land, and people of the lower classes worked on it

3500 B.C.E.	3000 B.C.E.	2500 B.C.E.	2000 B.C.E.	1500 B.C.E.	1000 B.C.E.

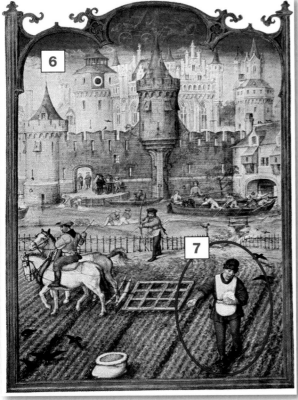

Vocabulary in Context CD 2 TR 12

The period from about 500 to 1500 C.E. is known as the Middle Ages. During much of this time, Europeans lived under the threat of attack and war. This made peoples' lives unsafe, and they needed protection.

A new way of life called **feudalism** developed during the Middle Ages to help protect people. In feudalism, **kings** and powerful **nobles** gave protection and land to lesser nobles and **knights**. In return, the lesser nobles and knights gave military assistance to the kings and the more powerful nobles. **Serfs**, members of the lowest feudal class, lived on a manor and worked for a lord. They also served nobles and knights. In return for their service, they were given protection and work.

Knights fought to protect the people of an area. Nobles' **castles** also provided protection to the people when attackers came. However, feudalism could not always offer protection from **Vikings**, who attacked much of Europe from about 800 C.E. to about 1100 C.E.

✅ Check Your Understanding

1. Look at the picture of a castle and describe it.
2. Who did serfs serve?
3. When did Vikings attack many parts of Europe?

Critical Thinking Comparing and Contrasting
4. In what ways were knights and serfs similar? In what ways were they different?

476 C.E.	**793** C.E.	**800** C.E.	**982** C.E.	**1215** C.E.
Last Roman emperor loses his throne	First Viking raid on England	Charlemagne is crowned emperor of the Romans by the pope	Vikings settle Greenland	King John signs the Magna Carta

		476		1215			
500 B.C.E.		**500 C.E.**		**1000 C.E.**	**1500**	**2000**	**Present**

📖 Workbook page 61

Charlemagne being crowned
emperor of the Romans by the pope

The Catholic Church in Feudal Times CD 2 TR 13

By about 1000 C.E., Christianity had spread throughout Europe. Kings accepted the head of the Catholic Church, called the **pope**, as Europe's religious leader. In all areas of Europe **bishops**, who were the pope's officials, governed the church.

In 800 C.E., a German king named **Charlemagne** tried to bring back the Roman Empire. The pope crowned him emperor of the Romans and together they worked to unite Europe. But this empire fell apart after Charlemagne died.

Life on the Manor CD 2 TR 14

Feudalism was a system of social **hierarchy**. In return for service to the king or a great noble, each lesser noble and knight was made **lord** of an area of land called a **manor**. The serfs who lived on a manor belonged to the manor. They were not free to leave. Serfs raised crops and sometimes animals. They had to work for the lord and give him part of their crops.

Painting of Serfs Listening to the Lord of the Manor

Social Studies Skill Interpreting a Painting

Studying paintings created at a certain time in history can help give us a better understanding of how people lived at that time. Look at the painting:

1. How can you tell who is the lord and who are the serfs?

2. What do you think the lord is telling the serfs?

Academic Vocabulary

Word	Explanation	Sample Sentence	Visual Cue
hierarchy (noun)	organization from higher to lower by rank or social status	In the feudal **hierarchy**, the king was at the top and serfs were at the bottom.	

The Vikings

In the 800s, the population of **Scandinavia** was growing quickly. Scandinavia's cold climate and shortage of good farmland led some Scandinavians to start sailing to places where life was easier. They attacked people in these places, and took any **treasure** they found. These Scandinavians became known as **Vikings**.

Later, Vikings settled in the lands they had invaded such as England, the Normandy **region** of France, and along the rivers of Russia. They also settled far west across the Atlantic Ocean in places such as Greenland.

Vikings

✔ Check Your Understanding

1. Who was Charlemagne?

2. What was a manor?

3. What are some places Vikings settled?

Critical Thinking Making Inferences

4. What do you think happened to serfs of a manor if the land was granted to a new lord?

 Research and Inquiry Use the Internet, the library, or your social studies book to answer these questions.

   1. What areas did Charlemagne's empire cover?

   2. What is the origin of the name "Normandy"?

   3. Besides growing crops and grazing animals, what other jobs were there on a manor?

 Writing As you've learned, the feudal system was based on a hierarchy. Do you think there are any hierarchies in today's society? Write a paragraph to explain your answer.

Primary Source

The Magna Carta

In 1215 C.E., nobles forced King John of England to sign the Magna Carta. This document put limits on the power of the king. It stated that the king and his officials were not above the law. The Magna Carta states: "To no one will we sell, to no one will we refuse or delay right or justice."

▶ Why would the king agree to have limits placed on his power?

FOCUS QUESTION
How did the lives of Europeans change during the later Middle Ages?

 (CD 2 TR 16)

1 Venice

2 silk

3 jade

4 medicine

5 Marco Polo

6 pepper

7 cinnamon

8 spices

9 market

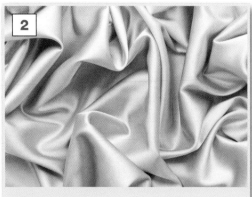

silk: a soft, fine fabric made from fibers produced by silkworms

jade: a stone used for jewelry and carvings

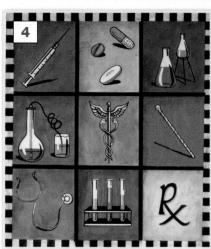

Word Study
Multiple-Meaning Words

The word **china** has different meanings.

China can refer to a country in eastern Asia.

  China has a larger population than any other country.

China can also refer to porcelain dishes.

  Roberto washed the **china** after dinner.

3500 B.C.E.	3000 B.C.E.	2500 B.C.E.	2000 B.C.E.	1500 B.C.E.	1000 B.C.E.

6

7

8

9

Vocabulary in Context
CD 2
TR 17

In the 600s C.E., the religion of Islam started on the Arabian Peninsula. Muslims, followers of Islam, began to spread the ideas of Islam through the Middle East and to Africa. During the 700s C.E., Islam also spread to Europe. Muslims from Africa built kingdoms in Spain. In addition to new foods such as lemons, Muslims also brought new ideas in **medicine** and mathematics to Europe.

During the Middle Ages, traders also brought Asian **silk, jade**, and **spices** to Europe. Spices such as **pepper** and **cinnamon** grew only in tropical areas, but the Europeans wanted them. The demand for spices made European trading centers such as **Venice** rich and powerful. By the 1200s, European traders such as **Marco Polo** reached China.

Trade also grew inside Europe. **Markets** developed in towns. At these markets, people began to use money to buy and sell things.

✓ Check Your Understanding

1. Look at the pictures. What are some things traders brought to Europe during the Middle Ages?
2. When did Islam spread to Europe?
3. What European city was important to the spice trade?

Critical Thinking Making Inferences

4. Why do you think spices such as pepper and cinnamon did not grow in Europe?

1096	1271	1291	1295	1347	1492
The first Crusade begins	Marco Polo travels to China	The Crusades end	Marco Polo returns to Venice	Plague arrives in Europe	The last Muslims are pushed out of Spain

		1096	1492		
500 B.C.E.	500 C.E.	1000 C.E.	1500	2000	Present

Workbook page 65

Muslims built the Alhambra Palace in Spain.

Muslims and Christians

Starting in 711 C.E., Muslims invaded parts of Christian Europe. Muslims from North Africa ruled most of Spain for hundreds of years. Spanish culture and architecture still show their influence.

Muslims also ruled most of the Middle East. In the 1000s, Christians wanted to force Muslims out of Europe and the Middle East. In 1095, the pope called for a **Crusade**. He encouraged Christians to go to **Palestine** to fight against Muslims.

Marco Polo meeting the emperor of China

Marco Polo in China CD 2 TR 19

In 1271, three traders traveled from Venice to China. One of them was seventeen-year-old Marco Polo.

Marco Polo met the Chinese emperor, who invited him to travel through China. He saw markets filled with silk, jade, and spices such as cinnamon and pepper. He also saw many things that did not exist in Europe, including **paper money** and **gunpowder**. Later, Marco Polo wrote a book about his experiences in China.

A market in the Middle Ages

The Later Middle Ages CD 2 TR 20

By the late Middle Ages, the manor system of working the land was in **decline**. Because of a deadly disease called the **plague**, there were fewer workers. People produced more goods in towns. Lords and serfs now wanted to be paid in money, not in goods and services.

Merchants in towns held weekly markets. Farmers sold food and **livestock**. People bought cloth, shoes, and iron pans.

Academic Vocabulary

Word	Explanation	Sample Sentence	Visual Cue
decline (noun)	a move downward	Wei saw a **decline** in her grades after she stopped studying.	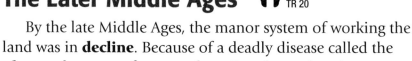

Social Studies Skill Reading a Map

It took time for the plague to spread throughout different parts of Europe. Generally, the plague was brought to new places by travelers following trade routes. This map shows how and when the plague spread.

1. From which continent did the plague spread to Europe?

2. Which southern European city did the plague reach in 1348?

3. In what year did the plague spread far to the north?

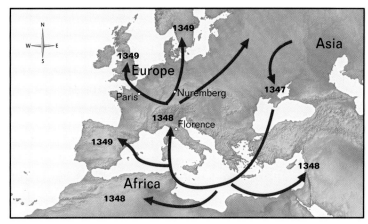

A map of the plague in Europe

✔ Check Your Understanding

1. What still shows that the Muslims were once in Spain?

2. What were two things Marco Polo saw in China that did not exist in Europe at the time?

3. By the late Middle Ages, instead of being paid in goods and services, what did lords and serfs want?

Critical Thinking Making Inferences
4. Why do you think farmers bought cloth, shoes, and iron pans at markets?

Research and Inquiry Use the Internet, the library, or your social studies book to answer these questions.

1. Name two religions that have holy places in Palestine.

2. Which king and queen joined their kingdoms to unite Spain and push the Muslims out of Spain? Whose famous voyage across the Atlantic, in 1492, did this king and queen help pay for?

3. What other group was made to leave Spain at the same time as the Muslims? Why were they made to leave?

Writing Do you eat foods that contain pepper or cinnamon? What other spices are used in foods you eat? Write a paragraph describing how spices are used in the foods you eat.

Kids in History

In 1429, a teenage French girl called Joan of Arc believed God spoke to her. She believed God chose her to help force the English army out of France. Joan convinced the French king to let her lead an army against the English. Joan fought bravely, but was later caught and killed. There are many monuments to Joan of Arc in France and other countries.

▶ Why would Joan have risked her life?

Early African and American Civilizations

FOCUS QUESTION

What early civilizations developed in Africa and the Americas?

CD 2
TR 21

1 salt

2 Timbuktu

3 gold

4 empire

5 Maya

6 Aztec

7 Inca

8 Yucatán Peninsula

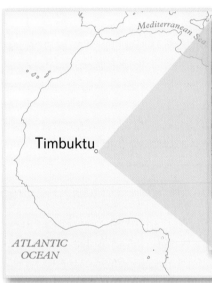

Timbuktu

Mediterranean Sea

ATLANTIC OCEAN

Timbuktu: an early center of trade and culture in Africa

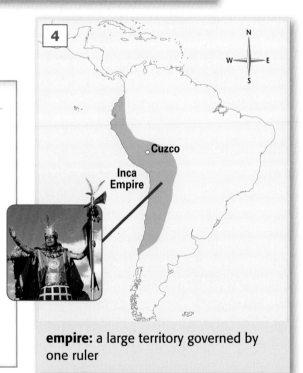

Cuzco

Inca Empire

N
W — E
S

empire: a large territory governed by one ruler

Word Study

Antonyms

Antonyms are words that mean the opposite of each other. **Rise** and **decline** are antonyms.

Rise means "strengthen" or "move upward."

The **rise** of the Aztec civilization started in 1100 C.E.

Decline means "weaken" or "move downward."

The reasons for the **decline** of the Maya civilization are unknown.

| 3500 B.C.E. | 3000 B.C.E. | 2500 B.C.E. | 2000 B.C.E. | 1500 B.C.E. |

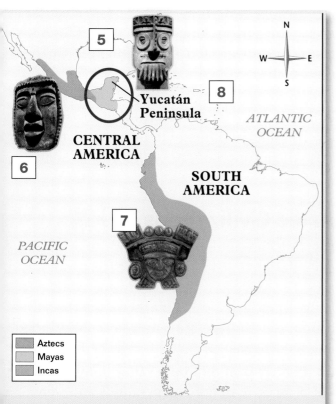

Maya: An indigenous people who lived in what is now Mexico, Guatemala, and Belize whose civilization reached its height between about 250 C.E. and 900 C.E.

Aztec: An indigenous people who lived in what is now central Mexico between about 1100 C.E. and 1520 C.E.

Inca: An indigenous people who lived in South America, from what is now northern Ecuador to central Chile, between about 1200 C.E. and 1533 C.E.

Vocabulary in Context CD 2 TR 22

Starting in 250 C.E., advanced civilizations formed in different regions of Africa and the Americas.

In Africa, **Timbuktu** emerged as a great trading society. **Salt**, **gold**, and cloth were some of the main goods traded across African societies.

In Central America, the **Maya** civilization had built great cities in the **Yucatán Peninsula** by 250 C.E. As that civilization declined, the **Aztecs** rose to power in the area that is now known as Mexico.

In South America, the **Inca** developed the largest **empire** in the Americas starting about 1000 C.E. Their capital, Cuzco, was in the Andes Mountains. At its largest, the empire was home to 12 million people. The language of the Inca, Quechua, is still spoken in the Andes Mountains today.

✔ Check Your Understanding

1. Look at the map of Central and South America. Where were the Aztec, Maya, and Inca civilizations located?
2. What goods were traded in Africa?
3. Where was the capital of the Inca empire located?

Critical Thinking Hypothesizing

4. Why do you think gold was one of the main goods traded in Africa?

ca. 250 C.E.
Maya civilization reaches its height

ca. 700 C.E.
Kingdom of Ghana emerges in West Africa

ca. 1100 C.E.
Aztec civilization emerges

ca. 1200 C.E.
Mali empire emerges; Inca civilization develops in South America

250 C.E.			1200 C.E.

1000 B.C.E.   **500 B.C.E.**   **500 C.E.**   **1000 C.E.**   **Present**

Workbook page 69

Sundiata was the ruler of the empire of Mali.

The Maya built pyramids on the Yucatán Peninsula.

African Civilizations CD 2 TR 23

By the eighth century, the **kingdom** of Ghana had emerged as a great trading society. This African kingdom prospered for 300 years. Muslims from the north spread Islam throughout Ghana, but the kingdom eventually declined.

The next African empire to emerge was in Mali. The popular ruler Sundiata led the people to create an advanced society. He made the city of Timbuktu a center of trade, culture, and education. It was also the location of one of the world's first universities.

Maya and Aztec Civilizations ⌒ CD 2 TR 24

The Maya built great cities on the Yucatán Peninsula starting about 250 C.E. Their cities included buildings such as pyramids, temples, and palaces. The Maya recorded their history with symbols called glyphs. They were skilled **mathematicians** and **astronomers**. In about the ninth century, the Maya **abandoned** their cities for unknown reasons.

The Aztecs built their civilization in the Valley of Mexico. Like the Maya, they built palaces, temples, and pyramids and were skilled astronomers. They developed a calendar of 365 days and recorded their history in books with pictures.

Academic Vocabulary

Word	Explanation	Sample Sentence	Visual Cue
abandon (verb)	leave behind	Historians do not know why the Maya **abandoned** their cities.	

Maya
Yucatán Peninsula, written language, mathematics

built great cities, calendar, astronomy, pyramids, palaces

Aztec
Mexico Valley, books with pictures

Comparing the Maya and Aztec civilizations

Social Studies Skill — Reading a Venn Diagram

A Venn Diagram is used to show relationships between groups. It is made up of two or more overlapping circles. The overlapping portion indicates what the groups have in common.

Look at the Venn Diagram of the Maya and Aztec civilizations.

1. Name something in the Maya civilization that was not in the Aztec civilization.

2. Name something that was only true of the Aztec civilization.

3. What did both civilizations have in common?

Inca Civilization CD 2 TR 25

The Inca had a **system** of communication in which a runner ran a short distance with a message, then handed the message to the next runner. Messages were carried as far as 250 miles each day with this system.

The Inca also developed a system for farming their mountainous land. **Terrace farming** involved cutting steps into the sides of the mountains and planting crops on these steps.

The Inca developed ways to farm in the high mountains of the Andes.

✅ Check Your Understanding

1. What was Timbuktu a center for?
2. Why did the Maya abandon their cities?
3. What is "terrace farming"?

Critical Thinking Comparing and Contrasting
4. How did the Maya and Aztecs differ in the way they recorded their histories?

 Research and Inquiry Use the Internet, the library, or your social studies book to answer these questions.

1. Who was the African leader who came after Sundiata? What did he accomplish?
2. What games or sports were played by the Aztecs?
3. Research the Inca city of Machu Picchu. When was it built? Where is it located?

 Writing Imagine you could go back in time and spend a day in an early African or American civilization. Which one would you choose, and why?

Primary Source

Inca Quipu

The Inca used a system of knots on strings to record messages. They called these knots "quipu" or "talking knots." The Inca created these knots with colored thread or animal hair. Runners would carry messages to and from the king with the quipu. The quipu was used to record messages.

▶ Name two things we use today to record messages.

The Age of Exploration

CD 2
TR 26

1 **New World**

2 **Christopher Columbus**

3 **explorer**

4 **voyage**

5 **Queen Isabella**

6 **King Ferdinand**

7 **disease**

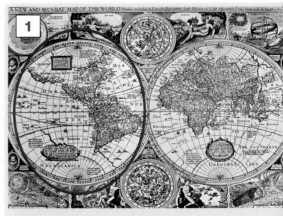

New World: name given to the American continents in the Western Hemisphere

Word Study

Syllabification

You can divide **exploration** into syllables to make it easier to read and say.

exploration = ex · plo · **ra** · tion

The Age of **Exploration** is an important time period in world history.

explorer: someone who travels in order to discover new things
voyage: a long trip

3500 B.C.E.	3000 B.C.E.	2500 B.C.E.	2000 B.C.E.	1500 B.C.E.	1000 B.C.

5

6

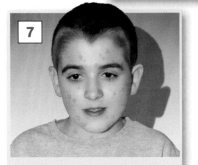

7

disease: sickness that is inherited or caused by infection or bad living conditions

Vocabulary in Context
CD 2
TR 27

Spices were in great demand in Europe during the Middle Ages. Europeans traveled east to buy spices from Asia. In 1492, an Italian sailor named **Christopher Columbus** decided to travel west in search of a shorter route to Asia. **Queen Isabella** and **King Ferdinand** of Spain paid for Columbus's **voyage**.

Columbus and his men thought they had landed in India, but they never reached Asia. Instead they had landed in the Americas. The Americas were soon referred to as the **New World**.

A new period began in which European **explorers** traveled to new lands and traded with people of other cultures. This trade and exploration led to an exchange of goods and ideas. However, the Europeans also took over the land of the indigenous people and spread **disease**.

✔ Check Your Understanding

1. Look at the pictures of the king and queen. How can you tell that they are a king and queen?
2. Why did Columbus want to travel west?
3. Who paid for Columbus's trip?

Critical Thinking Paraphrasing

4. In your own words, what effects did the Age of Exploration have?

| **1492** Columbus first sails to the New World | **1513** Ponce de León explores Florida | **1519** Magellan begins to sail around the world | **1519** Cortés defeats the Aztecs | **1533** Pizarro defeats the Incas | **1619** First Africans arrive in the English colonies in North America |

1492   1619

500 B.C.E.   500 C.E.   1000 C.E.   1500   2000   Present

📖 Workbook page 73

Information can be presented with graphics or pictures. The image below uses graphics and pictures to show the things that Europeans brought to and took from the New World.

1. What are three things that the Europeans took from the Americas?

2. What are three animals that the Europeans brought to the Americas?

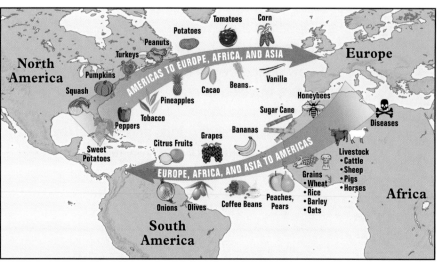

European exploration brought about exchange with the New World.

Exploration and Exchange CD 2 TR 28

When Columbus landed in the New World, he believed he had found a new route to Asia. When he returned to Spain, he told the king and queen about this new land and its people.

As word spread, Spain sent other explorers to the New World such as Juan Ponce de León who explored Florida. Other European countries such as Portugal, France, and England also started sending explorers. In 1519 Portuguese explorer Ferdinand Magellan began to sail around the world.

The European explorers brought back new plants and animals from the Americas, and introduced European ones to the Americas. They also brought diseases that killed many indigenous people.

Conquest CD 2 TR 29

In 1519, Spanish explorer Hernán Cortés arrived in Mexico in search of gold. Cortés took the Aztec emperor, Moctezuma, prisoner. With the help of European **weapons** and the spread of European disease, Cortés **defeated** the Aztecs in 1521 and **claimed** the land for Spain.

Spanish explorer Francisco Pizarro heard of the gold and silver of the Inca empire in South America. In 1531, he led a small army to **conquer** the Inca. After killing the Inca emperor, they defeated the Inca and claimed the land for Spain.

Hernán Cortés led the Spanish army in Mexico.

Academic Vocabulary

Word	Explanation	Sample Sentence	Visual Cue
weapon (noun)	a tool used to harm or kill	The indigenous people had never seen the deadly **weapons** of war used by the Europeans.	

Colonization CD 2 TR 30

The Europeans defeated and then **colonized** the empires in the Americas. They forced the indigenous people to accept their religion and learn their language. The Europeans also forced the indigenous people to work for them on the land they had taken over.

As the indigenous people died from overwork and disease, the Europeans brought **enslaved** Africans to the Americas to work. The enslaved Africans **harvested** crops. These crops were sent to Europe. Europeans used these crops to create **goods**, which they took to Africa in exchange for slaves. This **cycle** was known as the Triangular Trade.

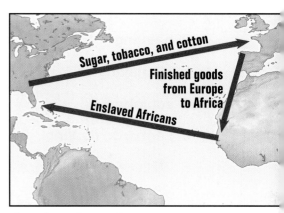

The Triangular Trade

✓ Check Your Understanding

1. What are four European countries that sent explorers to the New World?

2. What were the names of the Spanish explorers who led the conquests of the Aztecs and the Inca?

3. When the indigenous people in the conquered lands died, who did the Europeans bring to the Americas?

Critical Thinking Summarizing

4. Explain the flow of goods and people in the Triangular Trade.

 Research and Inquiry Use the Internet, the library, or your social studies book to answer these questions.

1. What was the Treaty of Tordesillas?

2. Research an explorer. From which country did he travel? What areas did he explore? How long did his voyage take?

3. What was the Middle Passage?

 Writing Imagine you are an Aztec soldier seeing the white Europeans and their weapons of war for the first time. Write a paragraph describing the men and their weapons.

Primary Source

Letter from Pizarro to King of Spain

"This city (Cuzco) is the finest and the most magnificent ever before seen in this land or any place in the Indies."

Francisco Pizarro, Spanish explorer, in a 1534 letter to King Charles I of Spain about Peru

▶ Imagine a "fine and magnificent" city. Describe what it would look like.

The Renaissance

FOCUS QUESTION
How did the Renaissance change the way people thought about art, science, and the world?

CD 2
TR 31

1 architecture

2 painting

3 Michelangelo

4 sculpture

5 Leonardo da Vinci

6 William Shakespeare

7 Queen Elizabeth I

8 literature

9 printing press

10 microscope

11 telescope

architecture: the art and science of designing buildings and other structures

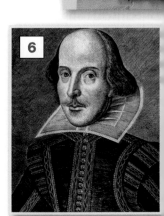

Word Study

Word Origins

Many words used in English are borrowed from other languages.

The word **renaissance** is a French word that means "rebirth."

The **Renaissance** was a time of rebirth in the arts.

3500 B.C.E.	3000 B.C.E.	2500 B.C.E.	2000 B.C.E.	1500 B.C.E.	1000 B.C.E.

7

8

9

10

literature: written works, such as novels, poems, and plays

11

Vocabulary in Context
CD 2
TR 32

The Renaissance began in Italy in the fourteenth century. It was a time of great creativity in Europe. During this time, there was a renewed interest in ancient Greek and Roman art and ideas. Great works of **architecture**, **sculpture**, and **painting** were created. Artists such as **Leonardo da Vinci** and **Michelangelo** created great works of art.

Renaissance writers wrote important works of **literature**. In England, **Queen Elizabeth I** gave financial support to playwrights such as **William Shakespeare**.

There were also advances in science and technology at this time. New machines like the **printing press** were invented. **Telescopes** and **microscopes** allowed scientists to see things that had never been seen before.

✔ Check Your Understanding

1. Look at the pictures of the telescope and microscope. With which instrument can people see stars? With which can people see germs?
2. Where did the Renaissance begin?
3. What were three things invented during the Renaissance?

Critical Thinking Hypothesizing

4. Do you think the Renaissance probably happened at a time of prosperity and peace? Explain.

LATE 1300s	**MID 1400s**	**ca. 1503**	**1508**	**1589**
The Renaissance begins	Gutenberg invents the printing press	Leonardo da Vinci paints the *Mona Lisa*	Michelangelo begins painting the Sistine Chapel	Shakespeare writes his first play

Late 1300s | 1589

500 B.C.E.	500 C.E.	1000 C.E.	1500	2000	Present

Workbook page 77

Leonardo da Vinci's *Mona Lisa*

Art of the Renaissance

Artists such as Michelangelo and Leonardo da Vinci **created** works of art for churches and palaces. This art was more realistic than art had been in the past.

Literature also became popular. For the first time books were written in **modern** languages that many people could read. In England, the **playwright** William Shakespeare wrote plays that were enjoyed by thousands of people at the Globe Theatre in London.

Social Studies Skill Distinguishing Fact from Opinion

A fact can be proven true with evidence. An opinion is what someone believes. It cannot be proven with evidence.

Which of the following statements about the *Mona Lisa* is a fact? Which is an opinion?

1. Leonardo da Vinci painted the *Mona Lisa*.
2. The *Mona Lisa* is the most beautiful Renaissance painting.

Academic Vocabulary

Word	Explanation	Sample Sentence	Visual Cue
create (verb)	to produce or make	Nadia liked to **create** works of art with oil paints.	

Science during the Renaissance

Advancements were made in science during the Renaissance. The Polish astronomer Nicolaus Copernicus said that the sun was at the center of the universe. Before this time, people believed that the earth was the center of the universe.

Advances were also made in medicine. Scientists began to **dissect cadavers** in order to learn more about the human body. These studies led to new discoveries and understandings about the human body. Artists used this new knowledge to create more realistic art.

Da Vinci created detailed drawings of the human body.

Inventions of the Renaissance

 CD 2
TR 35

The Renaissance introduced inventions that changed how people lived. For example, for the first time there were eyeglasses to correct poor eyesight and the flush toilet made it possible to flush **waste** away through a drain pipe.

In Germany, Johannes Gutenberg invented the printing press. This machine made it possible to create many copies of a book more easily and with less expense. The printing press made books more widely available.

The Gutenberg Bible was one of the first books printed with a printing press.

✔ Check Your Understanding

1. Why is William Shakespeare famous?

2. What was astronomer Nicolaus Copernicus's new idea about the sun?

3. What are three things that were invented during the Renaissance?

Critical Thinking Relating to Your Own Experiences

4. Which of the Renaissance inventions do you think it would be hardest to live without? Explain.

Research and Inquiry Use the Internet, the library, or your social studies book to answer these questions.

1. Create a timeline showing the important events in the lives of one of these Renaissance artists: Leonardo da Vinci, Michelangelo, Raphael.

2. What role did the Medici family play in the Renaissance?

3. Tell the title of a Shakespeare play, and give a brief summary of the plot.

 Writing What Renaissance artist, scientist, or ruler would you most like to meet? Write five questions that you would ask this person.

Kids in History

During the Renaissance, if a young boy wanted to be an artist, he became an apprentice to an art master. At around age 12, he began helping the master in his studio. During this time, the boy learned how to paint and sculpt. Renaissance artist Raphael began as an apprentice.

▶ If you could apprentice with an art master, what type of art would you choose to study?

FOCUS QUESTION
What was the Reformation?

CD 2
TR 36

1 pope

2 Catholic Church

3 Reformation

4 Protestant

5 Henry VIII

6 monk

7 Martin Luther

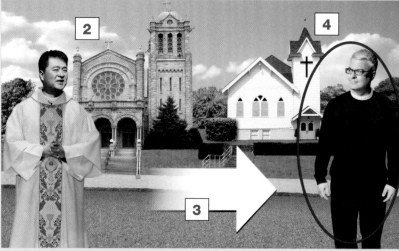

Reformation: a sixteenth-century movement in Western Europe that tried to improve some practices of the Catholic Church
Protestant: referring to a Christian religion that broke away from the Catholic Church in the sixteenth century

Word Study

Prefixes

When the prefix **re-** is added to a word, it means "again."

Reform means to change or improve something that exists.

Martin Luther tried to **reform** the Catholic Church.

3500 B.C.E.	3000 B.C.E.	2500 B.C.E.	2000 B.C.E.	1500 B.C.E.	1000 B.C.E.

Vocabulary in Context 🎧 CD 2 TR 37

By the time of the Renaissance, the **Catholic Church** had become very powerful. Its leader, the **pope**, used church money to build costly churches and to buy expensive art. Soon, more people began to question the church's power and many of its activities.

One of these people was a German Catholic **monk** named **Martin Luther**. He made a list of ninety-five things he believed the Catholic Church was doing wrong. He nailed this list, called *The Ninety-five Theses,* to the door of a church. Many people agreed with Martin Luther. They thought that the church needed reform, or change. This was the beginning of the **Protestant Reformation**.

The Reformation led to the creation of new Christian churches, such as the Baptist, Presbyterian, and Lutheran Churches. In England, King **Henry VIII** created the Church of England.

✔ Check Your Understanding

1. What is the leader of the Catholic Church called?
2. What is the name of the German monk who started the Reformation?
3. How did this monk start the Reformation?

Critical Thinking Recognizing Cause and Effect

4. What was created as a result of the Reformation?

1483	**1513**	**1517**	**1521**	**ca. 1534**
Martin Luther is born	Leo X becomes the pope	Martin Luther publishes *The Ninety-five Theses*	Martin Luther is forced out of the Church	King Henry VIII creates the Church of England

1483 | 1534 |

| 500 B.C.E. | 500 C.E. | 1000 C.E. | 1500 | 2000 | Present |

📖 Workbook page 81

Complaints against the Church 🎧 CD 2 TR 38

The Catholic Church taught that only people without **sin** could get to heaven. To guarantee entrance to heaven, the Church allowed people to pay money in exchange for forgiveness of their sins. This was known as the selling of indulgences.

Martin Luther believed that people should not be able to pay their way into heaven. This was one of the most important ideas of *The Ninety-five Theses*.

Martin Luther nailed his *Ninety-five Theses* to the door of a church.

Social Studies Skill   Reading a Tree Diagram

A tree diagram shows how one thing grows into other things, and how things on the tree are related to each other.

This tree diagram shows how several Christian churches were formed as a result of the Protestant Reformation.

1. Which was the original Christian church?
2. What groups grew out of the Protestant Reformation?

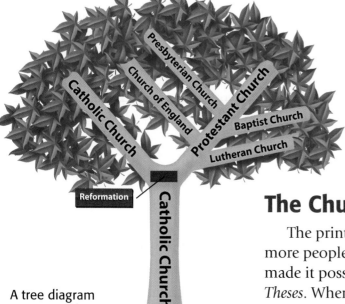

A tree diagram

The Church Responds 🎧 CD 2 TR 39

The printing press, a recent invention, allowed more and more people to learn about Martin Luther's list. This invention made it possible to make thousands of copies of *The Ninety-five Theses*. When Pope Leo X learned about Martin Luther's list, he **excommunicated** Martin Luther from the church.

It was at this time that the Catholic Church started the Inquisition. The Inquisition was a system for finding and punishing people who **opposed** the Catholic Church.

Pope Leo X

Academic Vocabulary

Word	Explanation	Sample Sentence	Visual Cue
oppose (verb)	to be against	The students **opposed** the new school fees.	

Effects of the Protestant Reformation

🎧 CD 2 TR 40

The Reformation led to the creation of new churches. For example, followers of Martin Luther started the Lutheran Church. Followers of John Calvin, a French religious leader, started the Presbyterian Church.

In England, King Henry VIII started the Church of England. He wanted to **divorce** his wife, Catherine of Aragon. When the pope refused to give him a divorce, Henry started a new church. The Church of England was based on Catholicism but was led by the king rather than the pope.

King Henry VIII married six times.

✔ Check Your Understanding

1. What was the selling of indulgences?
2. Why was the printing press important to the Reformation?
3. Why did King Henry VIII start a new church?

Critical Thinking Making Inferences
4. How do you think the creation of the printing press led to the spread of new ideas in Europe?

Research and Inquiry Use the Internet, the library, or your social studies book to answer these questions.
1. When did the Inquisition start? Who started it?
2. Select one of the Protestant groups. When was it started? What are its main beliefs?
3. What were the names of King Henry's wives? Why did he remarry so many times?

Writing Imagine you are Martin Luther. Write a letter to a friend, explaining why you nailed *The Ninety-five Theses* to the church door.

Primary Source

Martin Luther Quote

"I would never have thought that such a storm would rise from Rome over one simple scrap of paper."

Martin Luther, on the posting of his *Ninety-five Theses* on a church door

▷ What is the scrap of paper Martin Luther is referring to?

Enlightenment and Revolution

1

The Enlightenment: a period of time in seventeenth- and eighteenth-century Europe that emphasized science and the ability to think logically

FOCUS QUESTION

How did the ideas of the Enlightenment lead to revolution?

CD 2
TR 41

1 **The Enlightenment**

2 **science**

3 **reason**

4 **Isaac Newton**

5 **revolution**

6 **monarchy**

7 **Louis XVI**

8 **Marie Antoinette**

2

4

3

$$1+1=2$$

reason: the ability to think logically

5

Word Study

Prefixes

The prefixes **mon-** or **mono-** mean "one" or "alone."

A **monarch** is someone such as a king or queen who alone rules a country.

revolution: a big change, sometimes caused by force or war, especially in a government

3500 B.C.E.	3000 B.C.E.	2500 B.C.E.	2000 B.C.E.	1500 B.C.E.	1000 B.C.E.

6

monarchy: a government run by a monarch, such as a king or queen

7

8

Vocabulary in Context CD 2 TR 42

The Enlightenment was a time of great advances in **science** and philosophy. Before this time, people believed that religion could explain nature. Enlightenment thinkers believed that nature could be better understood through **reason** and scientific thought. During the Enlightenment, scientists conducted experiments and made scientific observations. One scientist, **Isaac Newton**, explained the laws of gravity and motion.

Enlightenment thinkers also believed that people had the right to be in charge of their own lives. This new way of thinking led to **revolutions** in North America, France, and Haiti.

In North America, people living in the English colonies fought for independence from Great Britain. The colonists won the war and formed the United States of America. In France, the people also wanted changes in their government. They overthrew the **monarchy** of **Louis XVI**, the ruler of France, and his wife, **Marie Antoinette**. Finally, in Haiti, people fought for their independence from France.

✅ Check Your Understanding

1. Look at the painting of Louis XVI. How can you tell he is a king?
2. What are two places that experienced revolutions?
3. Look at the timeline. Who was executed in France in 1793?

Critical Thinking Recognizing Cause and Effect

4. How did the new way of thinking lead to revolution?

1687	**1762**	**1775**	**1789**	**1791**	**1793**
Isaac Newton publishes his ideas about gravity and motion	Rousseau's *The Social Contract* is published	American Revolution begins	French Revolution begins and *Declaration of the Rights of Man* is adopted	The Haitian Revolution begins	Louis XVI and Marie Antoinette are executed

1687 1793

500 B.C.E.	500 C.E.	1000 C.E.	1500	2000 Present

📖 Workbook page 85

Rousseau wrote that all people are created equal.

Enlightenment Thinking

During the Enlightenment, philosophers such as Jean-Jacques Rousseau said that all people are created **equal** and there should be no **nobility**.

Writers such as Voltaire in France and Jonathan Swift in Ireland criticized social institutions such as government and churches. They used literature to make fun of rich people.

The new ideas of this time led to many changes, including changes in governments.

Academic Vocabulary

Word	Explanation	Sample Sentence	Visual Cue
equal (adjective)	having the same quantity or value	The piece of cake and the apple are **equal** in weight.	

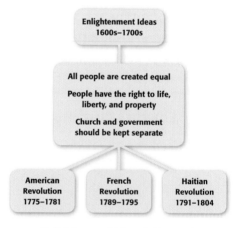

Enlightenment ideas influenced political revolutions.

Social Studies Skill Interpreting a Concept Map

A **concept map** organizes information. The boxes show related ideas. This concept map shows how Enlightenment ideas influenced political revolutions.

1. What are two important ideas of the Enlightenment?
2. Which three revolutions were influenced by Enlightenment ideas?

The American colonists fought for independence from Great Britain.

The American Revolution

CD 2 TR 44

Enlightenment thinkers such as **John Locke** believed that people had the right to life, liberty, and personal property. These ideas later influenced the American colonists. They wanted to be independent from Great Britain. The colonists **rebelled**, resulting in the American Revolution and the writing of the United States Declaration of Independence.

The French Revolution CD 2 TR 45

For many years, most of the people in France were **peasants**. No matter how hard they worked, they would always be poor. They wanted to live in a fairer society. Another group of people living in France were the **middle class**. They too wanted a more equal society as the Enlightenment thinkers had written about.

In 1789, the French people rebelled against the government by attacking a prison called the Bastille. They wanted to free **political prisoners** and get weapons that were stored there.

Soon the rebellion turned into a full-blown revolution. The French people overthrew the king and queen of France and a new government was created. King Louis XVI and his wife, Marie Antoinette, were **convicted** of **treason** and **executed** in 1793.

The Bastille prison was attacked in 1789.

✅ Check Your Understanding

1. What did Jean-Jacques Rousseau believe?

2. Which United States document was influenced by the thinking of John Locke?

3. What was the name of the prison in France that was attacked by the French people?

Critical Thinking Summarizing

4. Why did French people rebel in 1789?

 Research and Inquiry Use the Internet, the library, or your social studies book to answer these questions.

1. What were some scientific discoveries that were made during the Enlightenment?

2. Select one of the Enlightenment thinkers and read a biography of him or her. What was the person's most important achievement?

3. Research the French Revolution and create a timeline with the major events of that time period.

 Writing If you had been living in France in 1789, would you have attacked the Bastille? Give three reasons to support your answer.

Primary Source

"Men are born and remain free and equal in rights."

Excerpt from the *Declaration of the Rights of Man*, approved by the National Assembly of France, August 26, 1789

▶ What are some rights that you think all humans are born with?

European Imperialism

CD 2
TR 46

1 imperialism   5 sugar

2 coffee   6 missionary

3 plantation   7 silver

4 crops   8 mission

imperialism: one country's control over another country or area

plantation: a large farm where crops are grown

Word Study
Word Families

Trade can be a noun, a verb, or an adjective.

Some Europeans became rich from the spice **trade**. (noun)

Europeans still **trade** with people from Asia to get spices. (verb)

Explorers wanted to find new **trade** routes. (adjective)

sugar: a sweet substance that comes from plants

| 3500 B.C.E. | 3000 B.C.E. | 2500 B.C.E. | 2000 B.C.E. | 1500 B.C.E. | 1000 B.C.E. |

6

missionary: a person who teaches religious ideas in a foreign country

7

8

Vocabulary in Context CD 2 TR 47

In the 1400s, Europeans wanted to find new routes to Asia. In 1492, Christopher Columbus tried to sail from Europe to Asia. Instead, he landed in North America. In 1498, Vasco da Gama, a Portuguese explorer, found a sea route to India.

At first, the Europeans traded goods with the people in the new lands they explored. Later, the Europeans wanted power over people in these places. This is one reason why European **imperialism** began to spread around the world. There were other reasons, too.

Europeans wanted riches such as gold and **silver** from the new lands. They set up **plantations** in some areas to grow **crops** such as **sugar** and **coffee**. They could not grow these crops in Europe. In addition, Europeans wanted **missionaries** to spread Christianity. They set up **missions** in the new lands to teach their religious ideas to the native people.

✔ Check Your Understanding

1. Who found a sea route from Europe to India in 1498?
2. Name two crops that were grown on plantations.
3. What riches did Europeans want from the new lands?

Critical Thinking Paraphrasing

4. In your own words, what were three reasons for European imperialism?

1492	**1498**	**1597**	**1690**	**1885**	**1914**
Christopher Columbus sails to North America	Vasco da Gama finds a sea route to India	European missionaries no longer allowed in Japan	British trading settlement starts in Calcutta, India	European countries begin to rule most of Africa	World War I begins

			1492		1914	
500 B.C.E.	**500 C.E.**	**1000 C.E.**	**1500**	**2000**	**Present**

📖 Workbook page 89

Calcutta, an early British trading post in India, became part of Great Britain's empire.

What Is Imperialism?

Imperialism can mean one nation having **political** power over another nation. It also can mean one nation having **economic** power over another nation. Usually, imperialism is part political and part economic.

From the 1400s to the beginning of World War I in 1914, Europeans **controlled** much of the world. At first Spain and Portugal were the main imperial nations. Other European nations such as Great Britain and France later built large empires.

Academic Vocabulary

Word	Explanation	Sample Sentence	Visual Cue
control (verb)	to have power over	The children **controlled** the puppets' movements.	

European imperialism in Africa, 1885–1914

Social Studies Skill Reading a Historical Map

Historical maps help people understand events from the past. This map shows the European countries that controlled parts of Africa in the late 1800s and early 1900s.

1. Which two European nations ruled the largest parts of Africa?
2. Which two African countries were independent (not ruled by a European country)?

A coffee plantation in Central America

Power over Distant Lands

Very few Europeans lived in the far-off countries that European nations controlled. However, the Europeans had great power over the government and economy of these countries. For example, in Central America, Europeans set up coffee plantations where local people did the work. In some places, Europeans moved people from one area to another to work on their plantations. For example, the British brought people from India to work in sugar fields on the Fiji Islands.

Imperialism and Christianity CD 2 TR 50

European imperialism helped spread Christianity to some parts of the world. In **Latin America**, for example, native people came to Christian missions to live, work, or trade. This helped missionaries from Spain and Portugal **convert** native people to Christianity.

Missionaries were generally more successful converting people in Latin America than they were in places such as Africa and Asia. The Japanese government said Christian missionaries were not welcome in their country. In China, the government did not help missionaries. They were sometimes attacked or even killed.

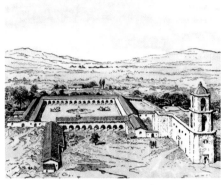

A Spanish mission in North America

✔ Check Your Understanding

1. What were the two main imperial nations when European imperialism first began?
2. Name one place where Europeans set up coffee plantations.
3. In which country were missionaries sometimes attacked or even killed?

Critical Thinking Comparing and Contrasting
4. How was the work of Christian missionaries in Latin America and Asia the same? How was it different?

 Research and Inquiry Use the Internet, the library, or your social studies book to answer these questions.

1. Henry Morton Stanley went to Africa to find a lost explorer. Who was he looking for? What major African river did Stanley explore?
2. In 1914, which European country had the largest empire? What countries were part of its empire?
3. By 1914, which Asian country had also become an imperial power? What other parts of Asia did this country rule?

 Writing Write a paragraph telling what it might be like to live in a place that is controlled by another country.

Primary Source

Historical Photograph

Porters are people hired to help travelers. This photograph shows African porters carrying a European man. The photograph was taken in Southern Rhodesia (now Zimbabwe) around 1900. Great Britain controlled this area at that time.

▶ What do you think the porters felt about carrying this man?

The Industrial Revolution

FOCUS QUESTION
How did the Industrial Revolution affect the modern world?

CD 2
TR 51

1 spinning wheel

2 industry

3 factory

4 thread

5 locomotive

6 cotton

7 steam engine

spinning wheel: a simple machine that twists cotton or wool into thread

industry: the production of goods, especially those made in factories

Word Study
Word Parts

The word **locomotive** includes the word parts "loco" and "moto."

Loco means "from a place."

Mot means "move."

Locomotive is short for "locomotive engine."

A **locomotive** is an engine that moves railroad cars from one place to another.

3500 B.C.E.	3000 B.C.E.	2500 B.C.E.	2000 B.C.E.	1500 B.C.E.	1000 B.C.E.

locomotive: an engine that moves railroad cars from one place to another

Vocabulary in Context
CD 2 TR 52

The Industrial Revolution began in Great Britain in the 1770s. Until that time, most goods were made by hand or by using simple machines. For example, people used the **spinning wheel** to twist **cotton** into **thread**.

The **steam engine** provided power to machines. These machines helped people make goods faster and cheaper. Spinning machines made it possible to quickly spin many threads at once. Steam-powered **locomotives** moved people and goods from one place to another faster than ever before.

Modern **industry** changed how people lived. People began moving to cities to work in big buildings called **factories**. By 1850, Great Britain had become the first nation where more people lived in cities than in the country. Working conditions in the factories were bad. Over time, the government made laws to improve the working conditions for factory workers.

✔ Check Your Understanding

1. In what country did the Industrial Revolution begin?
2. How were most goods made before the Industrial Revolution?
3. What did steam engines provide?

Critical Thinking Hypothesizing

4. How do you think the movement of many people to cities affected Great Britain?

1771	1802	1807	1825	1878
First English cotton factory opens	British law says work areas must have fresh air	Passenger service on steamboats begins in the U.S.	First public railroad opens in Great Britain	British law says children under age 10 cannot work

1771 | 1878

500 B.C.E. — 500 C.E. — 1000 C.E. — 1500 — 2000 — Present

Workbook page 93

99

Industrial Landscapes

An industrial landscape

The Industrial Revolution changed the **landscape** in Great Britain. **Canals** connected towns to rivers and the sea. **Barges** carried **iron**, **coal**, and other raw materials along these waterways. People needed large amounts of iron to build bridges and **railroads**. They needed coal for heat and power.

Workers left ugly piles of waste from the coal and iron **mines** across the countryside. In some places, the air was **polluted** by **smoke** from factories. Factories dumped waste into the waterways.

As the ideas of the Industrial Revolution spread, other countries also experienced these changes.

Social Studies Skill   Interpreting a Visual Image

Visual images can provide important information. Look carefully at the image of an industrial landscape (above left).

1. What do you see in the image? Describe the sky, buildings, and other features of the landscape.

2. What features of the landscape tell you that an artist created this image during or after the Industrial Revolution? Explain your answer.

Advances in Transportation

An early steamboat on the Hudson River, New York

Before the Industrial Revolution, it was **expensive** and difficult to move goods and people over land. During the Industrial Revolution, people made great **improvements** in transportation. For example, barges sailing on canals could easily move heavy raw materials such as iron and coal. Barges also carried goods from factories to faraway cities. Later, railroads and **steamboats** made transportation even faster. The first public railroad began in England in 1825.

Academic Vocabulary

Word	Explanation	Sample Sentence	Visual Cue
improvement (noun)	something that is better or makes something else better	Sarah worked hard and saw an **improvement** in her grades.	

People in Industrial Cities CD 2 TR 55

During the Industrial Revolution, the most successful businessmen were part of the **upper class**. Upper class families lived in large houses and had many **servants** to help them.

Middle class families lived in nice houses. Middle class women stayed at home and raised their children. Many of these women had servants to help them.

Most people, however, were part of the **lower class**. They lived in crowded **cottages** and **apartments**. They usually worked long hours in factories or as servants.

An upper class woman and her servant

✔ Check Your Understanding

1. Name two things that people built out of iron during the Industrial Revolution.
2. Name two types of transportation that made it easier and less expensive to move goods and people during the Industrial Revolution.
3. Where did lower-class people live in industrial cities?

Critical Thinking Making Inferences

4. Why do you think canals became less important once railroads were developed?

 Research and Inquiry Use the Internet, the library, or your social studies book to answer these questions.

1. What was the Great Exhibition of 1851? Why was it held? Where was it located?
2. Select a machine that was invented during the Industrial Revolution. What year was it invented? What did it do?
3. Who is Florence Nightingale and what did she do?

 Writing Imagine you worked in a factory during the Industrial Revolution. Write a letter to a friend telling about your life and how you spend your days.

FOCUS QUESTION
How did nationalism affect Europe?

🎧 CD 2 TR 56

1 **Napoleon Bonaparte**

2 **nationalism**

3 **German Empire**

4 **Prussia**

5 **defeat**

6 **Otto von Bismarck**

7 **troops**

8 **unite**

9 **hostility**

nationalism: a feeling of extreme loyalty to a country

3
GERMAN EMPIRE

4 **PRUSSIA**

North Sea

DENMARK

SCHLESWIG

Baltic Sea

HOLSTEIN

MECKLENBURG

HAMBURG

PRUSSIA

HANOVER

Berlin

BRUNSWICK

NETHERLANDS

ANHALT

Rhine

Elbe

Oder

RUSSIA

BELGIUM

PRUSSIA

HESSE-NASSAU

SAXONY

THURINGIAN STATES

HESSE

HESSE

HESSE

Danube

ALSACE-LORRAINE

WÜRTTEMBERG

AUSTRIAN EMPIRE

Seine

BADEN

BAVARIA

FRANCE

SWITZERLAND

The German Empire, 1871–1918

defeat: loss of a battle or contest

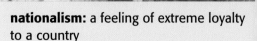

6

Word Study

Word Families

Hostile is an adjective.

The **hostile** driver honked at other drivers.

Hostility is a noun.

The driver's **hostility** made the other drivers uncomfortable.

| 3500 B.C.E. | 3000 B.C.E. | 2500 B.C.E. | 2000 B.C.E. | 1500 B.C.E. | 1000 B.C.E. |

7

8

9

Vocabulary in Context CD 2 TR 57

At the beginning of the nineteenth century, a new political movement called **nationalism** developed in Europe.

France's ruler **Napoleon Bonaparte** spread the idea of nationalism across Europe. He led **troops** in wars against other European countries. After Napoleon's **defeat**, nationalism continued to grow throughout Europe. **Otto von Bismarck**, the main advisor to the king of **Prussia**, wanted to **unite** the small, separate German states into one large empire. He succeeded and the king of Prussia became the emperor of the new **German Empire**.

While strong feelings of nationalism could unite people within a country, it also could lead to **hostility** between nations.

✅ Check Your Understanding

1. Which leader spread the ideas of nationalism across Europe?
2. Which German state wanted to unite German states in one large empire?
3. Who was Otto von Bismarck?

Critical Thinking Hypothesizing

4. Why do you think the king of Prussia became the emperor of the German Empire?

1799	**1815**	**1862**	**1871**	**1888**
Napoleon becomes ruler of France	Napoleon is defeated	Bismarck becomes main advisor to the king of Prussia	German Empire is established	Wilhelm II becomes German emperor

				1799		1888		
500 B.C.E.		**500 C.E.**	**1000 C.E.**	**1500**		**2000**		**Present**

📖 Workbook page 97

Napoleon and the Rise of Nationalism 🎧 CD 2 TR 58

Napoleon was defeated at the Battle of Waterloo, 1815.

Napoleon was ruler of France between 1799 and 1815. During that time, France **conquered** many European countries. The French taxed the people they conquered and made them fight in the French army. Wherever they went, Napoleon and his troops showed their strong loyalty to France.

The conquered people disliked paying taxes and fighting for the French. They started to have nationalistic feelings about their own countries and fought against the French. Napoleon was defeated in 1815.

Nationalism and Germany 🎧 CD 2 TR 59

In the 1860s, Prussia wanted to unite the German states into one large empire. Prussia had grown stronger than the other large German state, Austria. In 1871, all the German states except Austria united with Prussia to form the German Empire. Wilhelm I, who was the king of Prussia, became emperor of Germany. This empire became a strong new European power.

Independence of Selected European Countries

Country	Who ruled the country?	When did the country become independent?
Greece	Ottoman Empire	1823
Italy	Independent States and Austria	1861
Germany	Independent States	1871
Serbia	Ottoman Empire	1878
Norway	Sweden	1905
Poland	Russia, Germany, and Austria	1918

Social Studies Skill Reading a Chart

Charts give information about a topic. First, look carefully at the heads of each column in the chart above. They tell you what information is found in the chart. Then look at the information in the chart.

1. Which two countries did the Ottoman Empire rule?

2. Which country ruled Norway?

3. Which country became independent in 1918?

European Nations Compete Overseas CD 2 TR 60

During the nineteenth century, Great Britain had the biggest **navy**, the most **colonies**, and the largest trading empire.

By 1900, Germany's large new navy **challenged** Great Britain's control of the seas. Germany also competed with Great Britain for colonies in Africa and trade in China. These actions led to hostility between Great Britain and Germany.

German navy ship, ca. 1900

Academic Vocabulary

Word	Explanation	Sample Sentence	Visual Cue
challenge (verb)	to ask another to compete in a contest or fight	Tom **challenged** Nick to an arm wrestling competition.	

✔ Check Your Understanding

1. Why did the people Napoleon conquered begin to fight against the French?

2. Which German state did not become part of the German Empire?

3. What two actions did Germany take to challenge Great Britain?

Critical Thinking Making Inferences

4. Why do you think Germany challenged Great Britain?

 Research and Inquiry Use the Internet, the library, or your social studies book to answer these questions.

1. What was the main purpose of the Congress of Vienna of 1814–1815?

2. What groups of people, other than Germans, lived in the Austrian Empire?

3. When the German Empire was formed, it took some territory from France. After World War I, France took back this territory. What is the name of this territory?

Writing In 1900, Great Britain had colonies around the world and a large trading empire. Imagine you are a citizen of Great Britain. Write a letter to a friend explaining why you are worried about Germany building a large navy.

Primary Source

Newspaper Interview

In 1908, German Emperor Wilhelm II talked to a British newspaper reporter about his plans for his country.

"Germany is a young and growing empire. She has a worldwide commerce which is rapidly expanding. . . . Germany must have a powerful fleet to protect that commerce and her . . . interests."

▶ Why do you think the German emperor said Germany needed a powerful fleet?

Reform and Revolution

FOCUS QUESTION

What is the difference between reform and revolution?

CD 2
TR 61

1 **suffragist**

2 **voting rights**

3 **socialist**

4 **Karl Marx**

5 **Vladimir Lenin**

6 **equality**

7 **Czar Nicholas II**

8 **abdicate**

9 **throne**

suffragist: someone who wants women to have the same voting rights as men

socialist: someone who believes the government should own and control most of the economy to promote equality

Word Study

Word Meanings

A **czar** is a Russian emperor. Over time, however, many English speakers have come to use the word "czar" to mean anyone with a lot of power.

Vinh owned so many buildings that he became known as a real estate **czar**.

3500 B.C.E.	3000 B.C.E.	2500 B.C.E.	2000 B.C.E.	1500 B.C.E.	1000 B.C.E.

7

8

abdicate: to give up power

9

throne: a decorated chair used especially by kings and queens

Vocabulary in Context CD 2 TR 62

After Napoleon's defeat in 1815, many people began to demand changes. Some of these changes included reforms or improvements. In most countries, for example, women were usually not allowed to vote. In many Western countries, **suffragists** began to insist on **voting rights** for women. Reforms that gave more people the right to vote were very important for the rise of democracy.

Some people, however, wanted more reforms. They wanted a complete change or revolution. **Socialists** such as **Karl Marx** and **Vladimir Lenin** thought that people should have economic **equality**. Socialists said the best way to achieve economic equality was for the government to own and control the country's industries, hospitals, schools, and other institutions.

When a revolution started in Russia in 1917, **Czar Nicholas II** was forced to **abdicate** his **throne**. Then, reformers took power. Months later, Lenin forced out the reformers and took over the government.

✓ Check Your Understanding

1. What reforms were important for the rise of democracy?

2. What is a suffragist?

3. What did Lenin think the government needed to do to achieve economic equality?

Critical Thinking Comparing and Contrasting

4. How were suffragists and socialists alike? How were they different?

| **1815** Napoleon is defeated | **1884** Voting rights are extended to most men in Great Britain | **1914** World War I begins | **1917** Revolution begins in Russia | **1918** Russian czar and his family are murdered |

| 500 B.C.E. | | 500 C.E. | 1000 C.E. | 1500 | 1815 | 1918 2000 | Present |

Queen Victoria of Great Britain

Voting Reforms CD 2 TR 63

Between 1815 and 1914, reformers gave voting rights to more people. In Great Britain, for example, nearly all men gained the right to vote by 1884. Many reformers thought that only men were informed enough to vote. Suffragists, however, argued that women were just as capable of voting as men.

In a step toward **democracy**, voters chose the government. **Monarchs** such as Queen Victoria of Great Britain no longer controlled the government.

Women Get the Vote CD 2 TR 64

Before World War I, women had voting rights in only a few countries such as Australia and Norway. Suffragists in Great Britain and the United States held **marches** demanding equality in the right to vote. Sometimes they disobeyed laws to bring attention to the issue.

After World War I, women in many countries gained voting rights. This was partly because women had worked in many jobs outside the home during the war. These jobs showed what women could do if they were allowed.

In London, police stop suffragist Emmeline Pankhurst from sharing her ideas with the king about voting rights for women.

Academic Vocabulary

Word	Explanation	Sample Sentence	Visual Cue
march (noun)	a walk by a group of people to call attention to an issue	Suffragists held **marches** to gain voting rights.	

Social Studies Skill Interpreting a Photograph

Photographs are primary sources that provide information about the time period when they were taken. This photograph shows two women making bombs in a factory during World War I.

1. Look at the photograph. What tells you that this is a factory?

2. Do you think this work is safe? Explain your answer.

Women making bombs at a factory in 1915

Revolution in Russia CD 2 TR 65

When World War I started in 1914, Czar Nicholas II forced Russians to fight. The Russian economy was not strong enough to support a war and meet the basic needs of people at home. Ordinary Russians did not have enough to eat. Although the Russian army was very large, it had poor leadership and lost battle after battle. The Russian people were not happy with the czar's rule. Revolution broke out in 1917, and the czar was forced to abdicate his throne. Promising the people peace and food, Lenin took power from the new Russian government.

People lining up to get food during the Russian Revolution

✔ Check Your Understanding

1. By 1900, who had more control of the British government, the queen or the voters?

2. Name two countries where women had the right to vote before 1914.

3. What happened to the czar in 1917?

Critical Thinking Inferring from Evidence

4. Why do you think Lenin was able to take power from the Russian government in 1917?

 Research and Inquiry Use the Internet, the library, or your social studies book to answer these questions.

1. When did *all* women in Great Britain get the same voting rights as men?

2. In what country was Lenin living when the 1917 revolution broke out in Russia? How did he get to Russia?

3. What methods did suffragists in Great Britain use to draw attention to voting rights in the ten years before 1914?

 Writing What are two reasons why women should have equal rights with men? Write a paragraph explaining your ideas.

Primary Source

Historical Photograph

The czar was forced to abdicate in 1917. He and his family became prisoners of the government. By 1918 Lenin was head of the government. The czar, his wife, and their children were murdered.

▶ Do you think this photograph was taken before or after the czar and his family became prisoners?

FOCUS QUESTION
What were the causes and effects of World War I?

CD 2
TR 66

1 **Allied Powers**

2 **Central Powers**

3 **machine gun**

4 **tank**

5 **submarine**

6 **weapons**

7 **ally**

8 **League of Nations**

9 **war**

3

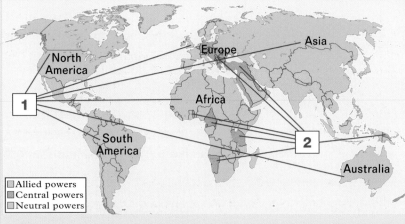

1

2

☐ Allied powers
☐ Central powers
☐ Neutral powers

Allied Powers: a group of countries fighting on the same side in World War I, including Great Britain, France, Russia, and the United States

Central Powers: a group of countries fighting on the same side in World War I, including Germany, Austria-Hungary, Bulgaria, and the Ottoman Empire

4

5

Word Study

Word Parts

The word **submarine** has two parts.

The prefix **sub-** means "under" or "below."

The word **marine** means "water."

A **submarine** is a boat that travels underwater.

6 **weapon:** a tool or machine used to harm or kill

7

ally: a partner or friend

8

League of Nations: an international organization formed in 1919 to prevent future wars

Vocabulary in Context
CD 2
TR 67

In 1914, a small **war** started between Serbia and Austria-Hungary. Germany was an **ally** of Austria-Hungary and supported them in the war. Soon, other countries joined Germany and Austria-Hungary. These countries became known as the **Central Powers**. Serbia's allies—Great Britain, France, and Russia—also joined the war. These countries became known as the **Allied Powers**. The United States later joined the Allied side in what became known as World War I.

During World War I, both sides used new **weapons** such as **submarines**, **tanks**, and **machine guns**. These weapons made the war a long and bloody conflict. The fighting finally stopped in 1918. The Central Powers lost the war. Countries from around the world worked together to form the **League of Nations** to prevent future wars.

9

✅ Check Your Understanding

1. Which alliance included more countries, the Central Powers or the Allied Powers?
2. When did World War I begin?
3. Name three countries that were part of the Allied Powers and three countries that were part of the Central Powers.

Critical Thinking Hypothesizing
4. World War I was also called "The Great War." Why do you think the conflict was called this?

1914	1917	1918	1919	1920
World War I begins	The U.S. enters the war	Fighting in World War I ends	Peace treaty ending World War I is signed	The League of Nations holds first meeting

1914 | 1920

500 B.C.E.	500 C.E.	1000 C.E.	1500	2000	Present

📖 Workbook page 105

American soldier and horse wearing gas masks during World War I

Trenches provided some protection from bullets and bombs, but not from poison gas.

Leaders signing the treaty that officially ended World War I

New Weapons of War CD 2 TR 68

World War I was the first war in history in which tanks, machine guns, submarines, and airplanes were widely used. Tanks could move over rough and uneven land. Bullets did not harm tanks. Machine guns could fire many bullets in a short period of time. Submarines could travel underwater and fire **torpedoes** at **enemy** ships. Airplanes could drop bombs onto cities.

Soldiers dug deep **trenches** to protect themselves from bullets and bombs. Both sides used **poison** gas against each other. Soldiers wore gas masks for protection.

Social Studies Skill   Reading a Map

Look at the map of Europe during World War I. Notice what the different colors mean by looking at the key.

1. Why do you think Germany, Austria-Hungary, Bulgaria, and the Ottoman Empire were called the "Central" Powers?
2. List two neutral countries that had a land border with both a Central Power and an Allied Power.
3. Which two Allied Powers did not have a land border with a Central Power?

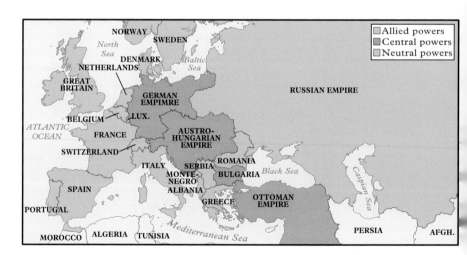

The War Comes to an End CD 2 TR 69

After millions of people were killed and many European cities and towns were destroyed, Germany asked for a **cease-fire**. The two sides agreed to end the fighting in 1918. The Allies won. In 1919, leaders from both sides signed a **treaty** to officially end the war. The treaty also created the League of Nations. This organization worked to keep peace throughout the world.

The Rise of Adolf Hitler CD 2 TR 70

When World War I ended, the Allies forced Germany to give up land and **reduce** the size of its army. Germany also had to pay the Allies for the cost of the war, which put the German government deeply in **debt**.

In 1929, the world went into an economic depression. The **depression** put millions of Germans out of work. During this time, a new politician became Germany's leader. This politician, Adolf Hitler, promised to create jobs and make Germany strong again.

Academic Vocabulary

Word	Explanation	Sample Sentence	Visual Cue
reduce (verb)	to make smaller in size	Students **reduced** the school's garbage by recycling.	

After World War I, Adolf Hitler became the leader of Germany.

✅ Check Your Understanding

1. Name one weapon used during World War I and explain what it could do.
2. Which side won World War I?
3. What happened to Germany after World War I?

Critical Thinking Hypothesizing
4. Why do you think a leader like Adolf Hitler became popular in Germany?

 Research and Inquiry Use the Internet, the library, or your social studies book to answer these questions.

1. How many people were injured during World War I? How many were killed?
2. What was the Battle of Verdun? What did each side want to achieve? Who won?
3. Select one of the weapons of war used during World War I. Who invented it? Which country used it first?

 Writing Imagine you are a soldier fighting in the trenches in World War I. Write a letter to a family member describing your situation and how you are feeling.

Primary Source

War Diary

"At every moment we are sprayed with clouds of earth and stone splinters. How many men are afraid. How many men are weak at the knees! . . . [W]e are no longer in a civilized world."

Henri Desagneaux, *A French Soldier's War Diary 1914–1918*

▶ Why do you think the soldier says that it is no longer a "civilized world"?

FOCUS QUESTION

What caused World War II and how did it end?

CD 2
TR 71

1 fascism

2 dictator

3 Benito Mussolini

4 Adolf Hitler

5 Soviet Union

6 Nazi

7 bomb

8 Holocaust

fascism: a political system, based on the belief that one's country is better than all others, in which one political leader and party have total control over the country

dictator: a ruler who has total power over a country

Europe

Asia

Soviet Union: a group of countries, including Russia, united under one government from 1922 to 1991

Nazi: a member of the National Socialist German Workers' Party, the political party led by Adolf Hitler in Germany before and during World War II

Word Study

Word Families

Aggressive is an adjective.

The **aggressive** nations attacked other countries without a good reason.

Aggression is a noun.

Germany showed **aggression** during World War II.

| 3500 B.C.E. | 3000 B.C.E. | 2500 B.C.E. | 2000 B.C.E. | 1500 B.C.E. | 1000 B.C.E. |

7

8

Holocaust: the mass killing of Jews and others by the Nazis

Vocabulary in Context

CD 2
TR 72

After World War I, people were looking for strong leaders to deal with the problem of unemployment and to bring back national pride. Some people believed that **fascism** was the answer. In Italy and Germany, **dictators** took control. **Benito Mussolini** became the fascist leader of Italy and **Adolf Hitler** became the fascist leader of Germany.

Italy and Germany invaded other countries to get more land and raw materials. Nations in other parts of the world became aggressive, too. In Asia, Japan invaded China, killing millions of people. The three aggressive countries—Italy, Germany, and Japan—became allies. Great Britain, the United States, and the **Soviet Union** became allies to stop fascism from spreading.

New weapons and new forms of fighting developed during World War II. Airplanes dropped more **bombs** on cities than ever before. In Europe, the **Nazis** killed almost 12 million people in what became known as the **Holocaust**.

✔ Check Your Understanding

1. Who were the leaders of Italy and Germany during World War II?
2. Why did Italy and Germany invade other countries?
3. What three nations became allies to stop the fascist aggression?

Critical Thinking Hypothesizing

4. Why do you think people look for strong leaders when they are facing large problems?

1933	**1937**	**1939**	**1943**	**1945**
Hitler becomes leader of Germany	Japan invades China	World War II begins in Europe	Italy surrenders	Germany and Japan surrender

				1933	1945	
500 B.C.E.	500 C.E.	1000 C.E.	1500	2000		Present

Workbook page 109

A European city damaged by bombing

The War in Europe CD 2 TR 73

By the late 1930s, Nazi Germany had become increasingly aggressive. In 1939, after Germany invaded Poland, Great Britain and France declared war on Germany. Germany **defeated** Poland and France, but Great Britain continued to fight. The Soviet Union and the United States eventually joined the war against Germany.

Germany used a new form of fighting known as **blitzkrieg**. Blitzkrieg is a surprise attack from both land and air. Some cities were almost completely destroyed by bombs.

Italy, Germany, and Japan Surrender CD 2 TR 74

In 1943, the **Allies** invaded Italy. Italy soon **surrendered**. Germany and Japan continued to fight, but the Allies were winning the war.

The leaders of Great Britain, the United States, and the Soviet Union met at Yalta.

In February 1945, the leaders of Great Britain, the United States, and the Soviet Union met. They decided to each govern part of Germany after the war. In May 1945, Germany surrendered.

Japan continued to fight until the United States used the new **atomic bomb** in August 1945. Japan surrendered soon after.

Academic Vocabulary

Word	Explanation	Sample Sentence	Visual Cue
surrender (verb)	to give up or admit defeat	After a long battle, the soldiers **surrendered**.	

The Holocaust CD 2 TR 75

During the war, the Nazis forced millions of people into **concentration camps**. When the Allies arrived in 1945, they found that many of the prisoners had been **tortured** and killed. The Nazi **military** had murdered groups of people, including **Jews**, the **disabled**, the **Roma**, and **gays**. This mass killing of almost 12 million people is known as the Holocaust.

People in a Nazi concentration camp during World War II

Social Studies Skill — Interpreting a Pie Chart

We compare and contrast to see the similarities and differences between two or more things. Look at the pie chart showing how many ordinary citizens (civilians) and how many soldiers (military) died during World War II.

1. In total, were there more civilian deaths or military deaths?

2. Which nations suffered the most civilian deaths?

3. Which nations had fewer military deaths?

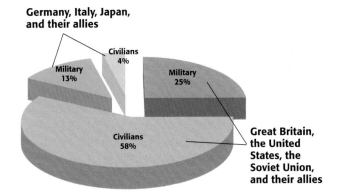

Germany, Italy, Japan, and their allies
Military 13%
Civilians 4%
Military 25%
Civilians 58%
Great Britain, the United States, the Soviet Union, and their allies

---

✔ Check Your Understanding

1. What was the new way of fighting used by Germany?

2. What was the Holocaust?

3. What new weapon was used against Japan in 1945?

Critical Thinking Recognizing Cause and Effect

4. What caused Great Britain and France to declare war on Germany?

Research and Inquiry Use the Internet, the library, or your social studies book to answer these questions.

1. What is the symbol of the Nazi Party called? Where was the symbol displayed?

2. Many cities experienced heavy bombing during World War II. Choose one city that had heavy bombing and describe how everyday life changed for the people in this city.

3. Who were the three Allied leaders who met at Yalta in early 1945? What countries did they represent?

Writing Anne Frank had to hide from the Nazis during World War II. Imagine yourself in this situation. Write a diary entry describing how you feel about having to hide.

Primary Source

The Diary of Anne Frank

Anne Frank was a Jewish girl who kept a diary during the two years that she and her family hid from the Nazis. This is from her diary:

"If I just think of how we live here, . . . it is a paradise compared with how other Jews who are not in hiding must be living."

Saturday, 1 May, 1943

▶ Anne says she is living in a paradise in comparison to other Jews who were not in hiding. Where were the other Jews who were not in hiding living?

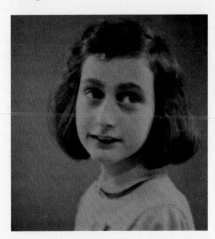

Post–World War II

FOCUS QUESTION
How did the world change after World War II?

CD 2 TR 76

1 **United Nations**
2 **colonized**
3 **independence**
4 **superpower**

5 **totalitarian**
6 **communism**
7 **Cold War**

1

United Nations: an international organization that promotes peace and safety throughout the world

2

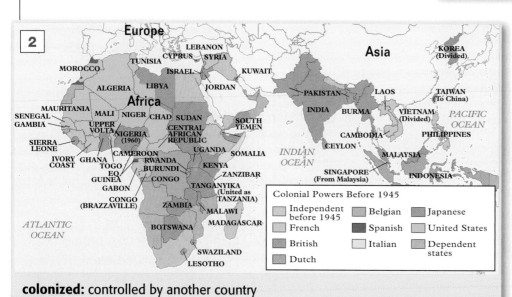

Europe

Asia

Africa

Colonial Powers Before 1945

Independent before 1945	Belgian	Japanese
French	Spanish	United States
British	Italian	Dependent states
Dutch		

colonized: controlled by another country

3

independence: freedom from control by another

Word Study
Prefixes
The prefix **post-** means "later" or "after."

Post–World War II refers to the time that came after World War II.

4 **superpower:** a powerful nation that influences other countries

3500 B.C.E.	3000 B.C.E.	2500 B.C.E.	2000 B.C.E.	1500 B.C.E.	1000 B.C.E.

5

totalitarian: describing a political system in which one person or group has total control over a country

6

communism: an economic and political system in which the government owns all businesses and property

7

Cold War: the conflict between the Soviet Union and the United States from 1947 to 1991

Vocabulary in Context CD 2 TR 77

After World War II, the world experienced a period of conflict and change. To settle conflicts peacefully and to prevent more wars, countries joined together to create the **United Nations**.

Before World War II, most African nations were ruled by other countries. In the years after the war, many **colonized** nations in Africa fought for and won their **independence**. By 1980, most African countries had become independent nations.

Communism became the system of government in many countries, including China, Cuba, Vietnam, East Germany, and North Korea. The Soviet Union supported the **totalitarian** governments of these communist nations. The United States opposed them.

The Soviet Union and the United States soon became competing **superpowers**. The two countries entered a cold war. It was called a "cold" war because it did not involve fighting with weapons. The **Cold War** ended in 1991.

✔ Check Your Understanding

1. What is the name of the organization that helps countries settle conflicts peacefully?
2. Look at the map of colonized nations in Africa and Asia. Which country did the United States colonize?
3. Name two communist countries that existed after World War II.

Critical Thinking Paraphrasing
4. Why was the conflict between the United States and the Soviet Union called a "cold" war?

1947	1949	1957	1961	1969	1980	1991
U.N. proposes creation of a Jewish state and an Arab state in Palestine	Communists take control of China	Soviet Union launches Sputnik 1	Berlin Wall is built	American astronauts land on the moon	Most African nations are independent	The Cold War ends

1947 | 1991

| 500 B.C.E. | 500 C.E. | 1000 C.E. | 1500 | 2000 | Present |

Workbook page 113

119

The Berlin Wall divided the German city into two parts.

The Cold War 🎧 CD 2 TR 78

After World War II, the United States and the Soviet Union entered into a cold war. The United States was worried that communism was spreading to other countries.

Communism had spread to Germany. A wall in Germany divided the city of Berlin into democratic West Berlin and communist East Berlin. The **border** between communist countries and other countries became know as the **Iron Curtain**.

The "Space Race" was another part of the Cold War. In 1957, the Soviet Union launched a **satellite** into space. The Soviet Union and the United States both wanted to be the leader in space exploration. American **astronauts** first landed on the moon in 1969.

A political cartoon

Social Studies Skill Analyzing Political Cartoons

A political cartoon is an illustration or comic strip containing a political or social message. It often uses humor to give an opinion on an issue or event. This political cartoon is about the Space Race between the Soviet Union and the United States during the Cold War.

1. From what country are the astronauts? How can you tell?
2. Where are they?
3. Why do they seem upset?

Mohandas Gandhi helped India gain independence from England.

Asia and the Middle East 🎧 CD 2 TR 79

After World War II, Mao Zedong became leader of a large new communist country, the People's Republic of China. Other Asian countries such as Japan became democratic. In India, Mohandas Gandhi helped his country gain independence from England.

World leaders wanted to bring **peace** to Palestine, an area of the Middle East. The United Nations proposed the creation of a **Jewish** state and an **Arab** state in Palestine. Israel, the newly created Jewish state, declared independence in 1948. Since then, Israel and Arab countries have been in conflict.

Academic Vocabulary

Word	Explanation	Sample Sentence	Visual Cue
peace (noun)	a state of cooperation without fighting or war	After years of fighting, Israel and Egypt agreed to **peace** between the two countries in 1979.	

African Independence CD 2 TR 80

Before World War II, Belgium, France, Great Britain, and other European countries governed many African nations. After World War II, many African nations began to fight for their independence. Starting in the 1950s, most became independent countries.

Nigeria became independent from Great Britain in 1960.

✅ Check Your Understanding

1. Which event in 1957 started the Space Race?

2. Who became the leader of the People's Republic of China when it was created after World War II?

3. Name three countries that colonized African nations.

Critical Thinking Paraphrasing

4. In your own words, what was the Space Race?

 Research and Inquiry Use the Internet, the library, or your social studies book to answer these questions.

1. What was NATO?

2. What were the names of the American astronauts who landed on the moon in 1969? What was the name of the space flight?

3. Research five countries in Africa that were colonized and find the year they gained their independence.

 Writing The Soviet Union launched the first satellite into space. The United States put the first human on the moon. Which achievement was more important? Why?

CD 3
TR 1

1 multinational corporation

2 globalization

3 international trade

4 technology

5 cell phone

6 Internet

7 e-mail

8 computer

9 human rights

multinational corporation: a company that does business in many countries and sells its products around the world

globalization: the connection of countries and peoples around the world through communication, trade, and travel

Word Study

Prefixes

The prefix **multi-** means "many."

Multinational corporations do business in more than one country.

The United States is a **multicultural** nation, made up of people who come from many different cultures.

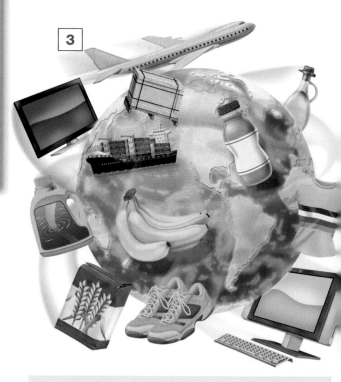

international trade: the exchange of goods and services among countries around the world

3500 B.C.E.	3000 B.C.E.	2500 B.C.E.	2000 B.C.E.	1500 B.C.E.	1000 B.C.E.

Vocabulary in Context

CD 3
TR 2

At the end of the twentieth century, several important events changed the world. The Soviet Union broke apart. The Cold War ended. People in South Africa gained **human rights**, and around the world, more and more people became concerned about the environment.

As the world entered into the twenty-first century, countries became more connected to one another. **International trade** increased. **Cell phones, e-mail**, and other advances in **technology** allowed people to communicate faster and more regularly. **Computers** and the **Internet** made more information available to more people than ever before. **Multinational corporations** began to control more and more of the world's economy. All of these changes led to **globalization**.

✔ Check Your Understanding

1. Look at the picture showing international trade. What are two things that are bought and sold around the world?
2. What happened to the Soviet Union near the end of the twentieth century?
3. What two forms of technology have led to increased global communication?

Critical Thinking Relating to Your Own Experiences
4. Look at the examples of technology. Which ones do you use?

human rights: the basic rights and freedoms of all people

1973	1989	1991	1994	2001
First cell phone call is made	Berlin Wall is torn down	Soviet Union breaks apart	Apartheid ends in South Africa	Terrorists attack New York City and Washington, D.C.

| 500 B.C.E. | 500 C.E. | 1000 C.E. | 1500 | 1973 · 2000 | 2001 · Present |

Sustainable growth is difficult for many developing countries to achieve.

In 1972, United States President Richard M. Nixon opened relations between nations by visiting the People's Republic of China.

Nelson Mandela

The Global Economy and Environment 🎧 CD 3 TR 3

Today, one way countries are connected is through international trade. Countries, especially **developing countries** such as Haiti and Madagascar, must balance their economic growth with the need to protect their **natural resources**. This balancing act is called **sustainable growth**. Achieving sustainable growth is complicated. Countries are looking for new kinds of energy that do not add to global warming.

Global Politics 🎧 CD 3 TR 4

Toward the end of the twentieth century, several important events changed the world.

The first was the end of the Cold War. Relations between the United States and the People's Republic of China improved when President Nixon visited the communist country in 1972. The fall of the Berlin Wall in 1989 and the breakup of the Soviet Union in 1991 marked the end of the Cold War.

In 1994, Nelson Mandela was elected president of South Africa. Mandela ended **apartheid**, a **legal** system of **racial segregation**. In South Africa, it is no longer legal to separate people because of their skin color.

Terrorism also increased. On September 11, 2001, terrorists attacked the United States, killing thousands. Many people around the world continue to fear future terrorist attacks.

Academic Vocabulary

Word	Explanation	Sample Sentence	Visual Cue
legal (adjective)	allowed by law	When apartheid was **legal** in South Africa, white people and non-white people were separated from each other.	

Social Studies Skill — Comparing Historical Maps

Comparing historical maps can show how an area has changed over time. These two maps show the area before and after the Soviet Union broke apart in 1991.

1. Look at the maps. Name three countries that became independent after 1991.

2. Look at the second map. What is the largest new independent country?

The Information Age   CD 3 TR 5

As technology improved, people around the world became more connected to each other. They could watch television programs and movies produced in foreign countries. Cell phones allowed more people to speak to each other from faraway countries. E-mail helped people quickly share new ideas. The Internet made information available to more and more people worldwide.

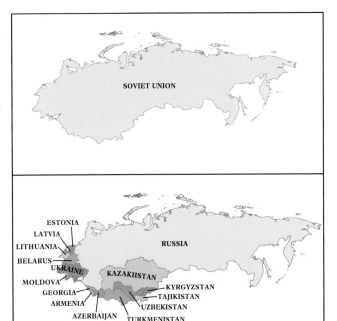

The breakup of the Soviet Union

Young people in Brazil using the Internet

✓ Check Your Understanding

1. What does it mean to have sustainable growth?

2. What was the legal system of racial segregation in South Africa called?

3. How have modern communications helped spread new ideas around the world?

Critical Thinking Recognizing Cause and Effect

4. What led to the end of the Cold War?

 Research and Inquiry Use the Internet, the library, or your social studies book to answer these questions.

1. Identify five multinational corporations that do business in the United States.

2. What does NAFTA stand for? What three countries signed NAFTA?

3. Research Nelson Mandela. How long was he in jail? When did he become president of South Africa? How long did he serve as president?

 Writing Think of a new way to communicate with people in other places. Describe how this new form of communication would work, who would use it, and why it would be useful.

Kids in History

In the past, pen pals wrote letters and mailed them to people who lived far away. With computer technology today, kids communicate with other kids all over the world. Computer technology makes communication fast and easy.

▶ Do you know someone who lives far away? Write a letter or e-mail message and send it.

Early Native Americans

FOCUS QUESTION
What was life like for the early Native Americans?

CD 3
TR 6

1 land bridge
2 society
3 Native Americans
4 pottery
5 petroglyph

6 Americas
7 hunting
8 mound
9 weaving

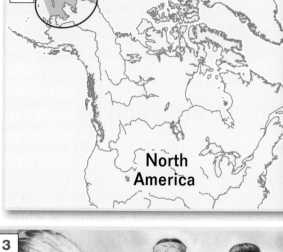

Asia   Bering Strait Land Bridge

1

North America

3

2

society: a large group of people who share the same culture

4

5

Word Study
Word Origins

Petroglyph comes from two Greek words.

• **Petra** means "stone."

• **Glyph** means "carving."

Archaeologists study **petroglyphs** to learn about early Native Americans.

60000 B.C.E.   50000 B.C.E.   40000 B.C.E.   30000 B.C.E.

Vocabulary in Context

CD 3
TR 7

People first came to the **Americas** thousands of years ago. At the time, a drop in sea level in the Bering Strait created a **land bridge** connecting Asia and North America. Early people depended on **hunting** for food, so they probably walked across the land bridge following animals. Over time, people built great **societies** throughout the Americas.

We call the people who first lived in North America **Native Americans** or American Indians. There were many different groups of Native Americans. Each group had its own way of life.

These early people did not have a written language, but they left behind **petroglyphs, pottery**, and **weavings**. They also left behind homes and **mounds**. Historians study these artifacts and sites to learn about the lives of early Native Americans.

mound: a large pile of Earth where people are buried or where buildings were built

✔ Check Your Understanding

1. Look at the map that shows the land bridge. The Bering Strait is between which two continents?
2. How do historians think that the earliest Americans arrived in North America?
3. What artifacts and sites have historians studied to understand the lives of the earliest Americans?

Critical Thinking Making Inferences
4. How might petroglyphs help historians understand the lives of early Native Americans?

ca. 20,000 B.C.E.	**ca. 10,000 B.C.E.**	**ca. 6,000 B.C.E.**	**ca. 200 C.E.**	**ca. 1000 C.E.**	**ca. 1700s C.E.**
People cross land bridge from Asia to North America	Land bridge disappears under the sea	People spread across the Americas	The Anasazi begin to settle in the Southwest	Inuit people begin to travel across the Arctic	The Seminole begin to settle in present-day Florida

20,000 B.C.E.		1700s C.E.
20000 B.C.E.	**10000 B.C.E.**	**Present**

 Workbook page 121

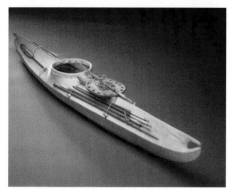

An Inuit Kayak

An Inuit family building an igloo

Teepees are cone-shaped tents made of buffalo skins.

Native Americans of the Arctic and Pacific Northwest 🎧 CD 3 TR 8

The Inuit, Inupiaq, and other peoples who settled in the **Arctic** lived in a very cold environment. These peoples hunted **marine** animals, birds, and large **mammals**. They built homes called **igloos**. They used animal skins to make warm clothes and small boats called kayaks.

The Bella Coola, Nez Perce, and other Native Americans settled in the **Pacific Northwest**. They did not have to grow food. They gathered wild plants, fished, and hunted animals. They made houses with wood **bark**.

Social Studies Skill Interpreting a Photograph

Photographs can provide valuable information about people and places. This photograph shows a modern-day Inuit boy helping his family build an igloo.

1. What are igloos made of?
2. Just like early Native Americans, Inuits today adapt to their environment. How does this picture show Inuits adapting to their environment?

Native Americans of the Southwest and Great Plains 🎧 CD 3 TR 9

The **Southwest** is a dry **region**. Native Americans living there collected water during the rainy season. They needed this water to grow crops. The Pueblo Indians built homes from **adobe,** sun-dried bricks made of clay and straw. Another group, the Anasazi, built their homes on the sides of cliffs.

Native Americans living on the **Great Plains** got most of their food by hunting animals such as buffalo. Some of these Native Americans made homes out of soil, some made homes with wood frames, and others made **teepees**.

Academic Vocabulary

Word	Explanation	Sample Sentence	Visual Cue
region (noun)	a geographical area	The Southwest **region** of the United States does not get much rainfall.	

Native Americans of the Northeast and Southeast CD 3 TR 10

Native Americans such as the Mohawk and Iroquois settled in the **Northeast**. The Mohawks hunted animals and planted crops for food. The Iroquois were also a hunting and farming people. They had a representative form of government that was later used as a model by America's **Founding Fathers**.

The Seminole, Creek, and other Native Americans settled in the **Southeast**. They learned to live in the **swampy** climate. Many lived in houses called **chickees**.

The bottom floor of chickees was raised to protect the house from flooding and animals.

✔ Check Your Understanding

1. How did the Native Americans in the Pacific Northwest get their food?
2. What material did Native Americans use to make teepees?
3. Name two Native American groups that lived in the Southeast.

Critical Thinking Integrating Information
4. How is each type of home related to the natural environment: igloo, adobe, teepee, chickee?

 Research and Inquiry Use the Internet, the library, or your social studies book to answer these questions.

1. Why do historians think the Anasazi built homes on the sides of cliffs? What happened to the Anasazi by 1300 c.e.?
2. Select an early Native American group. Where did they live? How did they dress? What types of food did they eat?
3. Research other forms of Native American housing, such as wigwams and longhouses. Why did Native Americans build these kinds of homes?

Writing Would you prefer to live in an igloo, a house made of adobe, a teepee, or a chickee? Explain your answer.

Kids in History

Early Native American children often played with toys that helped prepare them for the future. Some boys had bows and arrows and slingshots to help them practice hunting. Some girls made clothing for their dolls. This helped them practice sewing and working with beads.

▶ What types of toys did you like playing with when you were a child?

Early Explorers and Settlers

FOCUS QUESTION
Why did European explorers and settlers come to North America?

CD 3
TR 11

1 **Jamestown**

2 **colony**

3 *Mayflower*

4 **religious freedom**

5 **Pilgrim**

6 **Plymouth**

7 **harvest**

8 **Thanksgiving**

1

Jamestown

3

2

colony: an area governed by another country

Word Study

Synonyms

Synonyms are words that have the same meaning. **Voyage** and **journey** are synonyms.

voyage

The *Mayflower*'s **voyage** to the New World took sixty-six days.

journey

Many of the Pilgrims were seasick during the **journey**.

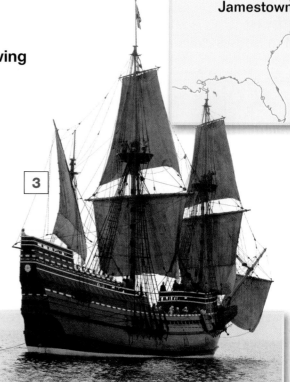

5

4

religious freedom: the right to worship freely

1492			1621	
1492	**1500**	**1600**	**1700**

Vocabulary in Context CD 3 TR 12

After Christopher Columbus's voyage to the New World in 1492, Europeans began setting up **colonies**. The first permanent English colony in North America began at **Jamestown**, Virginia, in 1607.

In 1620, the **Pilgrims** sailed to North America on the *Mayflower* and started a colony at **Plymouth**, Massachusetts. They left England because they wanted **religious freedom**.

During their first winter at Plymouth, half of the Pilgrims died from disease, cold, and hunger. Then they met Native Americans who showed them how to grow New World crops. The Native Americans also showed them which plants could be used for medicine and how to store food for the long winters. In the fall of 1621, the Pilgrims and Native Americans gathered together to give thanks for the **harvest**. Today, we celebrate **Thanksgiving** in honor of this event.

✔ Check Your Understanding

1. Where was the first permanent English settlement in North America?
2. Why did the Pilgrims sail to the New World in 1620?
3. What was the name of the Pilgrims' ship?

Critical Thinking Analyzing Information

4. Why was the Native Americans' knowledge of crops important to the Pilgrims?

1492	1513	1607	1619	1620	1621
Columbus sails to the New World	Ponce de León arrives in Florida	English colonists settle in Jamestown	First Africans are brought to the English colonies	Pilgrims arrive at Plymouth	Pilgrims and Native Americans celebrate the first Thanksgiving

1800	1900	2000	2010	Present

Workbook page 125

Juan Ponce de León explored present-day Florida.

Early Spanish Explorers CD 3 TR 13

After Columbus's journey to the New World, Spain began sending other explorers there to look for **gold** and **spices**. In 1513, Juan Ponce de León and his men arrived in Florida and **claimed** it for Spain. In 1540, Francisco Vásquez de Coronado explored the **American Southwest** and claimed present-day New Mexico for Spain.

Academic Vocabulary

Word	Explanation	Sample Sentence	Visual Cue
claim (verb)	to take something as one's property	Spanish explorers **claimed** Florida for Spain.	

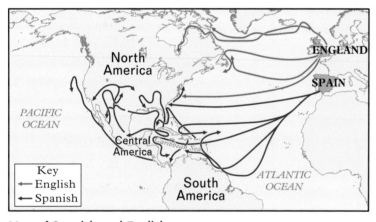

Map of Spanish and English exploration in the Americas, ca. 1400–1500

Social Studies Skill Reading a Map Key

Both England and Spain sent explorers to the New World. This map shows the routes taken by English and Spanish explorers. Look at the map key. The English voyages are shown with a blue line. The Spanish voyages are shown with a red line.

1. Which continent did both the English and Spanish explore?
2. Which country explored the Pacific Coast of North America?
3. Which country explored Central America and the Caribbean?

The Pilgrims signed the Mayflower Compact before they got off the ship.

Jamestown and Plymouth CD 3 TR 14

About 100 Englishmen arrived in Jamestown in 1607. They had a difficult time finding food and many died during the first winter. In 1619, a ship brought Africans to work in the fields in Jamestown.

In 1620, the Pilgrims arrived in Plymouth after a long and difficult sea voyage. Before leaving the ship, all of the men signed the **Mayflower Compact**. This compact, or agreement, allowed the men in the colony to choose their own leader. The compact became the foundation for government in Plymouth Colony.

The Colonists and the Native Americans 🎧 CD 3 TR 15

In 1621, after a hard winter, the Pilgrims became friendly with the Native Americans living in the area. The Native Americans showed the colonists where to fish and how to hunt and grow crops. That fall, they all celebrated the **harvest** with a Thanksgiving feast.

The friendship between the colonists and the Native Americans did not last long. The colonists took land away from the Native Americans and many of them died from European diseases.

At first, the Native Americans welcomed the colonists.

✅ Check Your Understanding

1. Which country sent explorers to the American Southwest?

2. What was the Mayflower Compact?

3. Why didn't the friendship between the colonists and Native Americans last long?

Critical Thinking Recognizing Cause and Effect

4. How did the friendship between the Native Americans and the Pilgrims affect the colonists?

 Research and Inquiry Use the Internet, the library, or your social studies book to answer these questions.

1. Why did Ponce de León name the area he explored in southeastern North America *La Florida*?

2. Why was the *Mayflower* called a "sweet ship"?

3. What foods did the colonists and Native Americans eat at the first Thanksgiving?

 Writing Imagine you were one of the Pilgrims. What three things would you bring with you on your journey to the New World? Explain why you would bring each of these three things.

Kids in History: Children on the Mayflower

The voyage on the *Mayflower* was difficult for the thirty-one children on the ship. Children had a very small space to eat, sleep, read, and play. They played quiet games with each other. They were not allowed to run on the ship and had only the Bible to read.

One baby was born during the trip. He was named Oceanus.

▶ If you had to entertain yourself on such a long voyage, what would you do?

FOCUS QUESTION

What was life like in Colonial America?

🎧
CD 3
TR 16

1 original 13 colonies   6 tobacco

2 New England Colonies   7 fur

3 Middle Colonies   8 slavery

4 Southern Colonies

5 town meeting

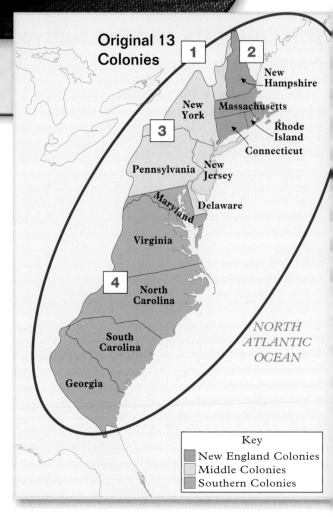

Original 13 Colonies

1   2 New Hampshire

New York   Massachusetts

3   Rhode Island   Connecticut

Pennsylvania   New Jersey

Maryland   Delaware

Virginia

4   North Carolina

South Carolina

Georgia

NORTH ATLANTIC OCEAN

Key
- New England Colonies
- Middle Colonies
- Southern Colonies

5

6

Word Study

Noncount Nouns

Noncount nouns do not form plurals with **s**. The words **rice**, **tobacco**, and **cotton** are noncount nouns. Do not use *a/an* with these words.

People grew **tobacco**, **cotton**, and **rice** on plantations in the Southern Colonies.

| 1492 | 1500 | 1600 | 1733 | 1700 | 1765 | 1800 |

7

8

slavery: a system in which a person can own other people and treat them like property

Vocabulary in Context CD 3 TR 17

After Jamestown and Plymouth, more English colonies were established in the New World. By 1733, there were thirteen English colonies along the east coast of what is the present-day United States. These **original 13 colonies** were divided into three regions.

In the **New England Colonies**, most people lived on farms or in towns. For those who lived in town, many worked in the fishing and shipping industries. Citizens gathered at **town meetings** to discuss current issues and make laws for themselves.

With a temperate climate and large areas of rich soil, farming was an important form of industry in the **Middle Colonies**. However, not everyone farmed in these colonies, some traded goods for **furs**. Others began making products such as paper, tools, and guns.

The **Southern Colonies** were mainly agricultural. People grew **tobacco**, cotton, and rice on plantations. Men, women, and children were taken from Africa, sold into **slavery**, and forced to work on plantations as slaves.

✔ Check Your Understanding

1. Look at the map of the English colonies. Which colonies make up the New England Colonies, Middle Colonies, and Southern Colonies?

2. How many original English colonies were there?

3. Who was forced to work on the Southern plantations?

Critical Thinking Comparing and Contrasting

4. How were the economies of each of the three colonial regions different?

1733	1750	1754–1763	1764	1765
Georgia, the thirteenth English colony, is established	The African slave population makes up one-fifth of the colonial population	The French and Indian War is fought	The Sugar Act is passed	Stamp Act and Quartering Act are passed

1900	2000	2010	Present

📖 Workbook page 129

Kidnapped Africans were packed tightly on ships in cruel conditions.

Land Claims
☐ Spanish
■ English
▨ French
▤ Oregon Territory

Before the French and Indian War

After the French and Indian War

North America before and after the French and Indian War

This teapot was made to celebrate the end of the Stamp Act.

Slavery in the Southern Colonies 🎧 CD 3 TR 18

In the 1500s, more and more Africans were **kidnapped** and forced to become **slaves**. Europeans brought around 12 million Africans to the Americas to work. These people were packed tightly on ships with little food, water, or fresh air. Many of them died on the long sea voyage. Southern colonists used slaves to help them grow **cash crops** on their plantations. The life of a slave was cruel and harsh.

French and Indian War 🎧 CD 3 TR 19

Like Great Britain, France had also claimed land in North America. Both France and Great Britain wanted the land west of the Appalachian Mountains. The Appalachians were the western edge of the thirteen colonies. From 1754 to 1763, Great Britain and France fought the French and Indian War. Both sides asked Native Americans to join them in the fight. Eventually, Great Britain won the war, taking most of the land France claimed in North America.

Protest in the Colonies 🎧 CD 3 TR 20

The French and Indian War left Great Britain in debt. To raise money, Great Britain began **taxing** the colonists directly by passing a series of new acts. The Sugar Act required colonists to pay extra for **molasses**. The Stamp Act taxed printed products like newspapers and legal documents such as **contracts**. The Quartering Act required colonists to let British soldiers stay in their homes.

The colonists **protested** the new taxes. Some colonists began discussing becoming independent from Great Britain.

Academic Vocabulary

Word	Explanation	Sample Sentence	Visual Cue
contract (noun)	an agreement between two or more people or companies	The two men signed a **contract** when they became business partners.	

Social Studies Skill Analyzing Political Cartoons

Benjamin Franklin drew this cartoon during the French and Indian War.

1. Describe the image.
2. What do the initials and the pieces represent?
3. What do you think Franklin was trying to say?

Political cartoon from the
Pennsylvania Gazette, 1754

✓ Check Your Understanding

1. How many Africans were brought to the Americas to work?
2. Why did Great Britain begin taxing the colonists directly?
3. What was the Stamp Act?

Critical Thinking Recognizing Cause and Effect
4. What caused the French and Indian War?

Research and Inquiry Use the Internet, the library, or your social studies book to answer these questions.

1. What was the "Middle Passage"?
2. What did it mean to be an "indentured servant" in Colonial America?
3. Who were the Sons of Liberty?

Writing Imagine that you lived in Colonial America. Write a letter to the king of England telling him why you think the Stamp Act, Sugar Act, or Quartering Act is unfair.

Primary Source

Colonial Newspaper

Benjamin Franklin published the *Pennsylvania Gazette*. This May 30, 1765, issue announced the passage of the Stamp Act.

▶ What is the name of a newspaper in your city?

The American Revolution

CD 3
TR 21

FOCUS QUESTION

What caused the American Revolution?

1 tax

2 tea

3 boycott

4 Thomas Jefferson

5 Declaration of Independence

6 George Washington

7 Minuteman

8 Redcoat

tax: money that people and businesses pay to the government

boycott: a form of protest in which people refuse to buy certain products or services

Word Study

Word History

The word **boycott** comes from Charles C. Boycott's name. Boycott owned an apartment building. Many people thought he was charging too much rent. They expressed their anger by refusing to give him mail, clean his house, or provide him with other important services. Later, people began using the word **boycott** to mean protesting by refusing to buy certain products or services. The word "boycott" can be a noun or a verb.

Declaration of Independence: the document in which the American colonists stated their independence from Great Britain

| 1492 | 1500 | 1600 | 1700 | 1764 | 1781 | 1800 |

6

Vocabulary in Context CD 3 TR 22

After the French and Indian War, Great Britain was in debt. To pay off its debt, Great Britain passed laws requiring American colonists to pay new **taxes**. The colonists were upset that they had to pay these taxes without having someone represent them in the British government.

Colonists responded by organizing **boycotts** of British goods. The boycotts worked. Great Britain removed all taxes except the one on **tea**. Tea was popular, and the tax angered the colonists. The conflict between Great Britain and the colonies became worse.

Colonial leaders met in Philadelphia and discussed becoming independent from Great Britain. **Thomas Jefferson** wrote the **Declaration of Independence**, which colonial leaders signed and sent to the king of England. War broke out between Great Britain and the colonists. **George Washington** led the colonists in the war, while Great Britain sent **Redcoats** to fight. Many colonists became **Minutemen** and fought the British.

7

8

Redcoat: a British soldier who fought in the American Revolution

Minuteman: a soldier in the American colonies who fought against the British

✔ Check Your Understanding

1. Why were the colonists angry with Great Britain?
2. After the boycotts, which tax did Great Britain continue to collect from the colonists?
3. Who led the colonists in their fight against the British?

Critical Thinking Making Inferences

4. Why do boycotts work?

1764	1770	1773	1775	1776	1781
Great Britain begins passing laws requiring colonists to pay new taxes	Five colonists are killed in the Boston Massacre	Colonists protest the tax on tea	The American Revolution begins	Thomas Jefferson writes the Declaration of Independence	The American Revolution ends

1900	2000	2010	Present

 Workbook page 133

The Boston Tea Party

Rising Tensions between Great Britain and the Colonies 🎧 CD 3 TR 23

In 1770, the **tension** between the colonies and Great Britain increased. Great Britain sent **soldiers** to keep the peace in the colonies, which angered the colonists. In Boston, colonists responded by throwing stones and shouting at British soldiers. The soldiers shot into the crowd, killing five people in an event referred to as the Boston **Massacre**.

In 1773, colonists in Boston organized a **protest** against the tax on tea. They threw British tea into the **harbor**. This event became known as the Boston Tea Party.

Academic Vocabulary

Word	Explanation	Sample Sentence	Visual Cue
massacre (noun)	the killing of a large number of innocent people at one time	British soldiers killed colonists in the event known as the Boston **Massacre**.	

Social Studies Skill Reading a Cause and Effect Diagram

The **cause** of something is the reason it happens. The result is the **effect**. A cause and effect diagram shows causes and effects of events.

Look at the events that led to the American Revolution.

1. Why did Great Britain need money?
2. What did Great Britain do to raise money?
3. What was the result of Great Britain's action?

Events leading up to the American Revolution

→ Great Britain fights in French and Indian War → Great Britain needs money → Great Britain taxes the colonists → Colonists fight for independence from Great Britain

The First and Second Continental Congress CD 3 TR 24

In 1774, colonial leaders gathered in Philadelphia at a meeting known as the First Continental Congress. The leaders discussed how they might respond to the unfair laws passed by Great Britain.

The colonial leaders met again the following year at the Second Continental Congress. Some of them said that the colonies should be independent from Great Britain. The delegates asked Thomas Jefferson to write the Declaration of Independence. It was approved and signed on July 4, 1776.

The Declaration of Independence was signed on July 4, 1776.

The American Revolution CD 3 TR 25

The first battles of the American Revolution were fought at Lexington and Concord, Massachusetts, on April 19, 1775. A **poet** described the first gunshot as "the shot heard 'round the world."

General George Washington led the colonial **army**. After six years of fighting, the British finally **surrendered** at Yorktown, Virginia. The colonists won the war and the United States of America became an independent nation.

The first battles of the American Revolution were at Lexington and Concord, Massachusetts.

✔ Check Your Understanding

1. What was the Boston Tea Party?
2. What did the colonists decide to do at the Second Continental Congress?
3. What was "the shot heard 'round the world"?

Critical Thinking Hypothesizing
4. What might have happened if Great Britain had won the war?

 Research and Inquiry Use the Internet, the library, or your social studies book to answer these questions.

1. Why were the American soldiers called "Minutemen"?
2. Who were the Sons of Liberty?
3. Who were the "loyalists"?

 Writing Imagine you live in Colonial America. Write a letter to the king of England explaining why you think the colonies are being treated unfairly.

Primary Source

Declaration of Independence

"We hold these truths to be self-evident, that all men are created equal, that they are endowed by their Creator with certain unalienable Rights, that among these are Life, Liberty and the pursuit of Happiness."

▶ What do you think it means to have the rights of "life, liberty and the pursuit of happiness"?

FOCUS QUESTION

How did the new nation develop?

CD 3
TR 26

1 Articles of Confederation

2 delegate

3 Benjamin Franklin

4 James Madison

5 Constitutional Convention

6 constitution

7 debate

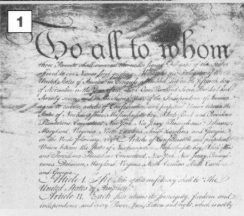

Articles of Confederation: the first governing document of the United States

delegate: a person who represents others at a meeting

Word Study

Syllabification

You can break **constitution** into syllables to make it easier to read and say.

constitution = con · sti · **tu** · tion

The United States **Constitution** was approved in 1789.

Constitutional Convention: the 1787 meeting where delegates wrote the United States Constitution

1492	1500		1600		1700	1776	1800

6

constitution: the written rules governing a country or state

7

debate: to present differing opinions on a topic

Vocabulary in Context CD 3 TR 27

When the American colonies became independent from Great Britain, they were organized as thirteen states under one government. This new government was based on the **Articles of Confederation**, which gave individual states more power than the national government. Leaders of the new nation believed that the Articles of Confederation would not allow the nation to grow strong. They decided to write a new **constitution**.

In 1787, each state sent **delegates** such as **Benjamin Franklin** and **James Madison** to the **Constitutional Convention**. Once there, the delegates began writing the United States Constitution. They **debated** how the new government should work. Some wanted a strong national government. Others thought the states should have more power. After much discussion, they reached an agreement. The states would share power with the national government.

In 1788, the Constitution became the law of the land. George Washington became the nation's first president in 1789 and the country began to grow.

✔ Check Your Understanding

1. Did the Articles of Confederation give more power to individual states or to the national government?
2. What happened at the Constitutional Convention?
3. Who became the nation's first president?

Critical Thinking Paraphrasing
4. In your own words, what was the agreement the delegates reached?

1776 The U.S. declares its independence from Great Britain	**1787** Constitutional Convention is held in Philadelphia	**1788** The Constitution is approved.	**1789** George Washington becomes first president of the U.S.	**1800** Thomas Jefferson is elected president	**1803** Jefferson buys the Louisiana Territory from France

1900	**2000**	**2010**	**Present**

 Workbook page 137

The Founding Fathers at the Constitutional Convention

The Constitutional Convention CD 3 TR 28

In 1787, delegates from the thirteen states went to Philadelphia for the Constitutional Convention. Their goal was to form a new government.

Federalists wanted a strong national government. **Anti-Federalists** believed that the states should have most of the power. After much debate, the delegates reached an agreement. The new government would divide power between the national and state governments. The men who created the new government are known as the **Founding Fathers**.

Presidents Washington (top), Adams (left), and Jefferson (right) led the new nation.

The First Presidents CD 3 TR 29

In 1789, George Washington became the first president of the United States. He asked educated men to advise and help him find solutions to the nation's problems.

John Adams was **elected** president in 1796. His vice president, Thomas Jefferson, was elected the third president of the United States in 1800.

Thomas Jefferson and the Louisiana Purchase CD 3 TR 30

President Jefferson **expanded** the country's **borders** in 1803. The United States paid France $15 million for the Louisiana Territory. This was known as the Louisiana Purchase. The new territory doubled the size of the United States. It extended from the Gulf of Mexico in the south to the British Territories in the north. It stretched from the Mississippi River on the east to the Rocky Mountains on the west. The port of New Orleans, which was part of this territory, was especially important for trade and **commerce**.

The American flag replaced the French flag after the Louisiana Purchase.

Academic Vocabulary

Word	Explanation	Sample Sentence	Visual Cue
expand (verb)	to grow larger	The balloon **expanded**.	

Social Studies Skill Reading a Historical Map

Historical maps help people understand events from the past. This historical map shows the size of the Louisiana Purchase.

1. What body of water is south of the Louisiana Purchase?

2. What area is west of the Louisiana Purchase and north of New Spain?

An 1803 map showing the Louisiana Purchase

✔ Check Your Understanding

1. What did Federalists want?

2. Who were the first three presidents of the United States?

3. What formed the eastern and western borders of the Louisiana Purchase?

Critical Thinking Comparing and Contrasting

4. What did France gain from the Louisiana Purchase? What did it lose?

 Research and Inquiry Use the Internet, the library, or your social studies book to answer these questions.

1. Who are the Founding Fathers of the United States?

2. When George Washington became president, where was the nation's capital?

3. Research one of the first three United States presidents. Where was he born? When did he serve as president? What were his major accomplishments?

 Writing Imagine you are President Thomas Jefferson. Write a speech explaining why you think the United States should purchase the Louisiana Territory. Include at least three reasons in your speech.

Primary Source

Preamble to the United States Constitution

The Preamble is the first part of the United States Constitution. It tells why the Founding Fathers created the United States.

We the people of the United States, in order to form a more perfect union . . .

▶ If you had the opportunity to create a "more perfect" country, what would it be like?

The Nation Grows

CD 3
TR 31

FOCUS QUESTION
How did the United States grow during the early nineteenth century?

1 **Meriwether Lewis**
2 **William Clark**
3 **Sacajawea**
4 **frontier**
5 **prairie**
6 **Mississippi River**

7 **woodlands**
8 **buffalo**
9 **pioneer**
10 **log cabin**
11 **Trail of Tears**

frontier: the undeveloped area beyond settled land

Saint Louis

New Orleans

Gulf of Mexico

woodlands: land covered with trees

Word Study

Suffixes

The suffix -**less** means "without."

Dry regions such as grasslands and deserts are often **treeless**.

The word **treeless** tells you that these regions are without trees.

1492   1500   1600   1700

pioneer: one of the first people to settle in an undeveloped area

Trail of Tears: the forced movement of Native Americans from their land east of the Mississippi River to the West

Vocabulary in Context CD 3 TR 32

During the nineteenth century, millions of people settled in the American West.

In 1804, President Jefferson sent **Meriwether Lewis** and **William Clark** to explore the Louisiana Territory. With a Native American guide named **Sacajawea**, they crossed the large, treeless **prairie** west of the **Mississippi River**. They met groups of Native Americans who hunted **buffalo** for food and used the skins to make clothing and homes.

During this time, white settlers began moving into the **woodlands** east of the Mississippi River. They settled on the new **frontier**. These **pioneers** cut down trees to clear the land for farms. They used the wood to build **log cabin** homes.

Over time, white settlers pushed Native Americans out of the woodlands. By the 1830s, Native Americans were forced to move to the prairies west of the Mississippi River. In 1838, thousands of Native Americans died on a cruel march later called the **Trail of Tears**.

✅ Check Your Understanding

1. Look at the pictures of the prairie and the buffalo on the prairie. How would you describe the land?
2. Who were Lewis and Clark?
3. Who was Sacajawea?

Critical Thinking Making a Prediction
4. How do you think life changed for the Native Americans who were forced to move from the woodlands to the prairies?

1803	MAY 1804	FEBRUARY 1805	NOVEMBER 1805	SEPTEMBER 1806	1838
The U.S. buys the Louisiana Territory	Lewis and Clark begin their exploration of the American West	Sacajawea joins Lewis and Clark	Lewis and Clark reach the Pacific Ocean	Lewis and Clark return to St. Louis	Native Americans march along the Trail of Tears

1803	1838				
1800		**1900**	**2000**	**2010**	**Present**

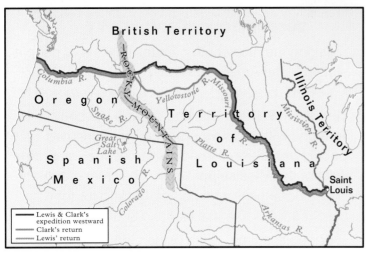

Lewis & Clark's
expedition westward
Clark's return
Lewis' return

The route that Lewis and Clark traveled from Saint Louis to the Pacific Ocean

The Lewis and Clark Expedition 🎧 CD 3 TR 33

President Jefferson wanted Lewis and Clark to explore the Louisiana Territory. He sent them on an **expedition** to find an easy way to the Pacific Ocean.

Lewis and Clark and forty-eight men left St. Louis in May 1804. They sailed up the Missouri River. Then they crossed several **rugged** mountain ranges before the heavy winter snow arrived. Although they reached the Pacific Ocean in November 1805, they did not find an easy route.

Social Studies Skill   Reading a Route Map

A route map shows the path or route taken on a journey. The map above shows the route Lewis and Clark's expedition took from Saint Louis to Oregon. It also shows their return route.

1. What river did Lewis and Clark follow from Saint Louis to the Rocky Mountains?
2. Which rivers did Lewis and Clark follow from the Rocky Mountains to the Pacific Ocean?
3. On his journey back east, which river did Clark follow between the Rocky Mountains and the Missouri River?

Pioneers outside a sod house on the prairie

Frontier Life 🎧 CD 3 TR 34

When white settlers moved to the frontier east of the Mississippi River, they found a vast **wilderness**. Most of the land was woodlands. Pioneers had to cut down trees to plant crops. They used the wood to build log cabins, fences, and **barns**.

Pioneers who settled on the treeless prairie did not have wood to build houses. Sometimes they used soil to build **sod houses**. The prairie was dry, so pioneers often settled near streams.

Native Americans on the Plains CD 3 TR 35

During the 1830s, the United States government began to make Native Americans leave their land. They forced Native Americans from the woodlands toward the **Great Plains**.

At this time, few white people lived on the Great Plains. They usually **passed through** the plains on their way further west. During this time, the government left the Native Americans and buffalo of the plains alone.

Native Americans look at a wagon train crossing the Great Plains.

Academic Vocabulary

Word	Explanation	Sample Sentence	Visual Cue
pass through (phrasal verb)	to go through an area	The cars have to **pass through** the toll plaza to cross the bridge.	

✔ Check Your Understanding

1. When did Lewis and Clark reach the Pacific Ocean?
2. How did the pioneers adapt to life in the wilderness?
3. During the 1830s, how did American settlers affect Native Americans living on the plains?

Critical Thinking Comparing and Contrasting

4. During the 1830s, American pioneers traveled into Native American lands. How were Native Americans of the Eastern Woodlands and Native Americans of the Great Plains affected in the same way? How were they affected differently?

Kids in History

Sacajawea was only about sixteen years old when she joined the Lewis and Clark expedition. She helped guide the expedition and served as translator for them.

▶ Why was it important for Lewis and Clark to have an interpreter?

 Research and Inquiry Use the Internet, the library, or your social studies book to answer these questions.

1. Who was the governor of Florida in 1821 and later became president of the United States?
2. Which country invited Americans to settle in Texas in the 1820s?
3. What was the Monroe Doctrine of 1823?

 Writing If you were traveling with the Lewis and Clark expedition, what would you take with you? Make a list of things you would take and explain your choices.

Expansion and Reform

How did westward expansion and reform efforts affect the nation?

CD 3
TR 36

1 expansion

2 border

3 Missouri Compromise

4 harbor

5 ranch

6 Elizabeth Cady Stanton

7 Lucretia Mott

8 suffrage

1

expansion: the process of becoming greater in size

2

border: the line separating two states, countries, or other territories

3

States formed by Missouri Compromise

Free states and territories closed to slavery

Slave states and territories open to slavery

Missouri Compromise: an agreement that became law in 1820 that tried to balance the number of slave states and free states

Word Study

Loan Words

Many English words come from other languages such as Spanish. The English word **ranch** comes from the Spanish word "rancho." The Spanish used the word "rancho" in the American Southwest.

Ben lives on a **ranch** and rides a horse every day.

4

harbor: a protected body of water deep enough for ships to dock

| 1492 | 1500 | 1600 | 1700 |

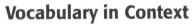

5

6

7

Vocabulary in Context

CD 3
TR 37

Westward **expansion** affected many aspects of life in the United States. First, it caused conflict over slavery. People disagreed about whether slavery should be allowed in new states. This disagreement led to the **Missouri Compromise** of 1820.

Second, expansion led to war. In 1846, a disagreement over a **border** led to a war between Mexico and the United States. The United States won and took control of present-day New Mexico, California, and other land. The United States also gained **harbors** along the Pacific Ocean.

Finally, expansion led to reforms for women's rights. Women who lived in the Western states often owned farms and **ranches**. They also participated more equally in government. The first states to grant **suffrage** to women were in the West. Women's rights leaders from the East such as **Elizabeth Cady Stanton** and **Lucretia Mott**, fought for the same rights given to those women living in the West.

8

suffrage: the right to vote

✔ Check Your Understanding

1. Why did westward expansion cause conflict over slavery?
2. What issue led to the war between Mexico and the United States?
3. Who were Elizabeth Cady Stanton and Lucretia Mott?

Critical Thinking Paraphrasing
4. Describe in your own words how women in the West influenced the women's rights movement.

1820
Missouri Compromise becomes law

1846
War between Mexico and the U.S. begins; The U.S. and Great Britain divide Oregon

1848
War with Mexico ends; Women's rights convention is held in Seneca Falls, New York

1869
Wyoming Territory allows women to vote

1820 | 1869
1800 | 1900 | 2000 | 2010 | Present

📖 Workbook page 145

Senator Henry Clay proposed the Missouri Compromise.

Texans fought for independence from Mexico at the Alamo in 1836.

Mexico and the United States went to war in 1846.

Women voting in the Wyoming Territory

The Missouri Compromise CD 3 TR 38

Most Southerners wanted the West to allow slavery. Most Northerners did not.

In 1819, Missouri wanted to become a state and allow slavery. Northerners and Southerners were **divided** on the issue of slavery in Missouri.

As a result, Senator Henry Clay proposed the Missouri Compromise. The Compromise stated that Missouri could have slavery. But in the future, slavery would only be allowed in the Western **territories** south of Missouri.

Academic Vocabulary

Word	Explanation	Sample Sentence	Visual Cue
divide (verb)	to separate into parts	Dolores **divided** the pie into eight pieces.	

War with Mexico CD 3 TR 39

In the 1840s, President James K. Polk wanted Texas, Oregon, and California to become part of the United States. The president's wishes soon came true. In 1836, Texas had won its independence from Mexico and became an American state in 1845.

In 1846, the United States and Great Britain both occupied land in the Oregon Country. Both nations agreed to divide the land in Oregon, but Mexico refused to sell California.

At the same time, a disagreement about the border between Texas and Mexico led to the Mexican-American War. The United States won and gained present-day New Mexico, California, and other land as part of the westward expansion.

Women's Rights CD 3 TR 40

In 1848, Elizabeth Cady Stanton and Lucretia Mott held a meeting about women's rights in Seneca Falls, New York. Later, they wrote a **Declaration of Sentiments**. This document, which included words from the Declaration of Independence, demanded equal rights for women, including the right to vote. The first steps toward suffrage for women occurred in the West. In 1869, women in the Wyoming Territory gained the right to vote.

Social Studies Skill — Reading a Map Key

This map shows women's voting rights before passage of the 19th Amendment, which gave full voting rights to all women. Use the map key to answer the questions.

1. Did women generally have more voting rights in Western states or Eastern states before passage of the 19th Amendment?

2. Name three states where women did not have full voting rights until the passage of the 19th Amendment. Look at the maps on page 150 for help with state names.

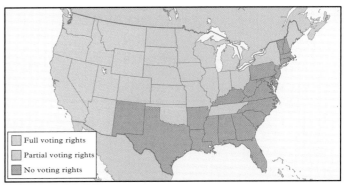

Full voting rights
Partial voting rights
No voting rights

Women's voting rights before the 19th Amendment

✔ Check Your Understanding

1. Who did not want slavery in new states: Southerners or Northerners?

2. What land did the United States gain after the Mexican-American War?

3. What document demanded equal rights for women?

Critical Thinking Comparing and Contrasting

4. What did President Polk think should happen to Oregon and California? How did Polk make those things happen?

 Research and Inquiry Use the Internet, the library, or your social studies book to answer these questions.

1. President Andrew Jackson wanted Texas to become part of the United States. What was the main reason Jackson was unable to make this happen when he was president?

2. In 1846, where did Mexico say its border with Texas was located? Where did the United States say it was located?

3. Was Elizabeth Cady Stanton or Lucretia Mott alive when the 19th Amendment became law?

 Writing Imagine you are living in the early 1800s. Do you think westward expansion is a good idea or a bad idea? Write a letter to the president telling him what you think and why.

Primary Source

Seneca Falls Declaration

In 1848, Elizabeth Cady Stanton read from the *Declaration of Sentiments* at Seneca Falls, New York:

"We hold these truths to be self-evident: that all men and women are created equal."

▶ Compare this opening line with the similar line in the Declaration of Independence on page 141. What difference do you see?

FOCUS QUESTION

How did settlement change the frontier?

CD 3
TR 41

1 **gold rush**

2 **trail**

3 **wagon train**

4 **transcontinental railroad**

5 **Sierra Nevada Mountains**

6 **Rocky Mountains**

7 **Great Plains**

8 **cattle**

9 **reservation**

gold rush: a sudden movement of people into a newly discovered gold mining area

Word Study

Multiple-Meaning Words

The word **reservation** has different meanings.

One meaning refers to the land the United States government set aside for Native Americans.

Some Native Americans live on a **reservation**.

Another meaning refers to the saving of a place in advance.

Amanda and Cristina made a **reservation** at an Italian restaurant.

A third meaning refers to a concern or worry about something.

Carlos had **reservations** about sharing his homework with Letty.

transcontinental railroad: a railroad that goes across a continent

1492 1500   1600   1700

reservation: land in North America the United States government set aside for Native Americans to live on

Vocabulary in Context CD 3 TR 42

In 1848, gold was discovered in California. A year later, 100,000 people moved there, hoping to find gold and get rich. This was called the California **Gold Rush**.

To get to California, settlers traveled in **wagon trains** across the **Great Plains**, the **Rocky Mountains**, and the **Sierra Nevada Mountains**. The **trails** were often rough, making the trip slow and difficult.

Settlers wanted a quicker and easier way to travel between the East and California. In 1863, construction began on the **transcontinental railroad**. Travelers would now have a faster route to California. Construction finished in 1869.

Not everyone decided to move to California. Some people decided to settle on the Great Plains. Native Americans and buffalo both lived on the Great Plains. As the settlers moved into this area, they killed the buffalo. The buffalo ate the grass their **cattle** needed. Soon there were no buffalo left. The Native Americans could no longer follow their old way of life and were forced to live on **reservations**.

✔ Check Your Understanding

1. Look at the pictures. Describe the natural vegetation of the West.
2. Why did so many people move to California in 1849?
3. Look at the map. Which mountain range is located in the far West?

Critical Thinking Comparing and Contrasting
4. How did settlers and Native Americans both depend on the grasslands of the Great Plains? How did they differ about the use of the grasslands?

1841	**1848**	**1849**	**1863**	**1869**	**1876**
First large wagon trains travel across North America	Gold is discovered in California	The gold rush begins	Construction begins on the transcontinental railroad	Transcontinental railroad is finished	Battle of Little Bighorn is fought

1841   1876

1800   **1900**   **2000 Present**

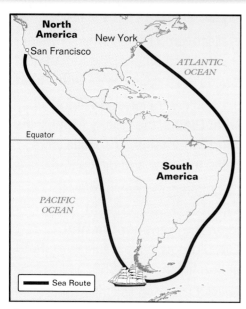

The sea route from New York to San Francisco, California

The Central Pacific and the Union Pacific railroads met in Utah in 1869.

Crossing the Continent CD 3 TR 43

Getting to California was difficult. Wagons were small, so settlers could take only tools and a few items they needed. Wagon trains had to cross the mountains before the winter snows fell. It was often difficult to find fresh water in the deserts between the Rocky Mountains and the Sierra Nevada Mountains.

Going by sea was also difficult. Sailing from New York to San Francisco required going around South America.

The Transcontinental Railroad 🎧 CD 3 TR 44

California's population grew quickly as a result of the gold rush. Trade grew, too. Many people wanted a better form of transportation to travel across the country.

The Union Pacific started building a railroad in Omaha, Nebraska. Irish **immigrants** did much of the work there. The Central Pacific started building a railroad in Sacramento, California. Chinese immigrants did much of that work. The railroads met in Utah in 1869, forming the country's first transcontinental railroad.

Social Studies Skill Comparing and Contrasting Visual Images

These pictures *below* show two ways to travel across North America in the nineteenth century.

1. How are these types of travel alike?
2. Which type of transportation would be quicker?
3. Which type of transportation can carry more people and goods?

A railroad train and a wagon train

Transforming the Great Plains 🎧 CD 3 TR 45

Beginning in the 1840s, many settlers traveled to California. They crossed the Great Plains, but did not settle there. However, in the 1860s, railroad builders, ranchers, **miners**, and **homesteaders** began settling on the Great Plains. Settlement brought towns, fences, crops, sheep, and cattle, **transforming** the land.

Not all Native Americans living on the Great Plains allowed the settlers to transform their land and way of life. Some Native Americans fought for their land at battles such as the one fought near the Little Big Horn River in Montana. By 1890, the Great Plains were settled and the frontier days were over.

Native Americans defeated the United States Army at the Battle of Little Big Horn.

Academic Vocabulary

Word	Explanation	Sample Sentence	Visual Cue
transform (verb)	to change from one shape or appearance to another	Adriana's new haircut **transformed** her appearance.	

✔ Check Your Understanding

1. How did settlement change the frontier?
2. What two immigrant groups helped build the transcontinental railroad?
3. In addition to ranching and homesteading, what other economic activity brought settlers to the Great Plains?

Critical Thinking Making Inferences
4. Why did Native Americans die from the diseases settlers brought with them?

 Research and Inquiry Use the Internet, the library, or your social studies book to answer these questions.

1. How were the Chinese workers treated during the California Gold Rush?
2. Los Angeles was connected to the transcontinental railroad system in the 1870s. What effect did the railroad have on the population of Los Angeles?
3. Why is the Battle of Little Big Horn also known as "Custer's Last Stand"?

 Writing What would you look for in a ghost town to find evidence of how people once lived there? Write a paragraph explaining what you would look for and what that evidence would tell you.

Historical Photograph

This photograph shows the once active mining town of Virginia City, Nevada. It is now a ghost town, where no one lives or works. The signs of mining are still visible.

▶ Why do you think towns where no one lives or works are called ghost towns?

A Nation Divided

CD 3
TR 46

1 **abolitionist**

2 **free state**

3 **slave state**

4 **fugitive**

5 **Harriet Tubman**

6 **Frederick Douglass**

7 **Underground Railroad**

8 **civil war**

abolitionist: someone who worked to end slavery

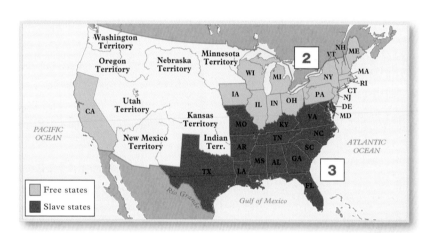

Free states

Slave states

fugitive: a person who is running away or has escaped

Word Study

Multiple-Meaning Words

The word **state** has different meanings.

State can be a noun and mean "a part of a country with distinct borders."

In 1850, California became the thirty-first **state**.

State can be a verb and mean "to say something."

In the story, the abolitionists **state** that slavery is wrong.

| 1492 | 1500 | 1600 | 1700 |

Underground Railroad: a system of secret routes and safe places that helped African American slaves escape from the South

civil war: a war between two or more groups within the same country

Vocabulary in Context CD 3 TR 47

In 1848, fifteen states allowed slavery and fifteen did not. The nation was divided about whether the territory gained after the Mexican-American War should allow slavery.

Abolitionists such as **Frederick Douglass** and **Harriet Tubman** wanted to end slavery. Abolitionists, and others, wanted California to be a **free state**. White Southerners disagreed. They argued that their way of life was being threatened. The economy of **slave states** in the South was mainly agricultural and used slave labor.

A compromise was reached. California was admitted as a free state, but the Fugitive Slave Act of 1850 required Northerners to capture slaves who were **fugitives**. Many slaves who had escaped through the **Underground Railroad** became free in the North. Now, if slaves were caught, the law said that Northerners had to return them to their owners.

The country was divided on the issue of slavery. The nation was heading toward **civil war**.

✔ Check Your Understanding

1. In 1848, how many slave states were there?
2. What is an abolitionist?
3. What did the Fugitive Slave Act of 1850 require?

Critical Thinking Recognizing Cause and Effect
4. How did the Mexican-American War lead to a conflict about slavery?

1850	1857	1859	1860	1861
Congress passes Fugitive Slave Act	Supreme Court rules that African Americans are not citizens	John Brown leads a raid at Harpers Ferry	Abraham Lincoln is elected president	The Confederacy is formed

1850   1861

1800   **1900**   **2000 2010 Present**

Workbook page 153

The Supreme Court said Dred Scott and other African Americans were not citizens.

Slavery and the *Dred Scott* Decision 🎧 CD 3 TR 48

Slaves were considered **property** with few rights. When slaves were sold, family members often were separated and sent to live on different plantations.

A slave named Dred Scott challenged the system of slavery. Scott's owner took him to a free state. Scott argued that this made him free. When he returned to a slave state, Scott **sued** for his freedom. In 1857, the Supreme Court ruled against Scott, saying African Americans were not citizens. The Court added that Congress could not stop slavery from spreading to the Western territories. The decision angered many Northerners.

Academic Vocabulary

Word	Explanation	Sample Sentence	Visual Cue
property (noun)	something that is owned by a person or group of people	Sindhu's backpack is her personal **property**.	

Advertisement announcing the sale of slaves

Social Studies Skill — Interpreting Primary Source Documents

Look at the advertisement announcing the sale of slaves. In the advertisement, the word "Negroes" refers to African Americans. This term is no longer acceptable.

1. When was the advertisement published?

2. Why are the slaves being sold?

The Abolitionists 🎧 CD 3 TR 49

Abolitionists worked to end slavery. Frederick Douglass, who had been a slave, spoke and wrote against slavery. Harriet Tubman, another former slave, helped slaves escape through the Underground Railroad.

John Brown was a white abolitionist who led a **raid** at Harpers Ferry, Virginia. His plan was to steal weapons and give them to slaves, so they could fight for their freedom. However, government soldiers caught Brown and he was brought to trial. He was later put to death.

John Brown was captured at Harpers Ferry, Virginia.

The Election of Abraham Lincoln 🎧 CD 3 TR 50

In November 1860, Abraham Lincoln was the Republican Party's candidate in the presidential election. The **Republican Party** said it would stop slavery from spreading to new territories. Lincoln won the free states, which had more voters, and was elected president. He did not, however, win any slave states.

By the time Lincoln took office in March 1861, seven slave states had **seceded** from the national government. These seven states set up their own government and called it the **Confederacy**. Jefferson Davis became president of the Confederate states.

Thousands of people attended the ceremony at which Lincoln became president.

✅ Check Your Understanding

1. What did the Supreme Court decide in the *Dred Scott* case?
2. What did Harriet Tubman do?
3. How many slave states had seceded by the time Abraham Lincoln took office?

Critical Thinking Comparing and Contrasting
4. How were the abolitionists Frederick Douglass and John Brown alike? How were they different?

 Research and Inquiry Use the Internet, the library, or your social studies book to answer these questions.
1. What did the Kansas-Nebraska Act of 1854 say about slavery?
2. Who was Stephen Douglas?
3. What were the first seven states to secede from the United States?

 Writing Imagine you are a slave who escaped through the Underground Railroad. You are now safe in the North. Write a letter to Harriet Tubman telling her how her work has changed your life.

Primary Source

"The time for compromise has now passed, and the South is determined to maintain her position, and make all who oppose her smell Southern powder and feel Southern steel."

Jefferson Davis, inaugural speech, February 16, 1861

▶ What do you think "Southern powder" and "Southern steel" refer to?

CD 3
TR 51

1 secede

2 Union

3 Confederacy

4 Jefferson Davis

5 Battle of Gettysburg

6 Abraham Lincoln

secede: to withdraw formally from a group, organization, or from a country

Union
Confederate
Land not yet states

Word Study

Irregular Plurals

Life has an irregular plural form. The **-fe** changes to **-ves**. The plural of **life** is **lives**.

More soldiers lost their **lives** in the Battle of Gettysburg than in any other battle during the Civil War.

1492   1500   1600   1700

Vocabulary in Context 🎧 CD 3 TR 52

By mid-1861, eleven Southern slave states had **seceded** from the **Union**. The Southern states formed a new government called the **Confederacy** with **Jefferson Davis** as their president. United States president **Abraham Lincoln** faced the greatest crisis in the nation's history.

The Civil War began when the Confederacy attacked Fort Sumter, South Carolina, on April 12, 1861. At first, each side thought it would win the war. Southerners had more experience with guns and horses. Since most of the fighting took place in the South, Southerners were fighting in familiar surroundings and they had less distance to travel. However, the North had a larger population and army. The North also had more factories, a strong navy, and railroads to transport supplies and people.

The Confederacy grew weaker after the **Battle of Gettysburg** in July 1863. In 1864, the Union army destroyed cities, railroads, and plantations across much of the South. The war ended soon after the main Confederate army surrendered on April 9, 1865.

Battle of Gettysburg: an important battle fought July 1–3, 1863, that resulted in the most deaths during the Civil War

✅ Check Your Understanding

1. What was the new government in the South called?
2. Where did the first battle occur?
3. How many years did the Civil War last?

Critical Thinking Comparing and Contrasting
4. What strengths did each side have in fighting the war?

1861	1863	1864	1865
The Civil War begins	The Battle of Gettysburg is fought	Lincoln is reelected president	Lincoln is assassinated; The Civil War ends

1861		1865			
1800		1900		2000	2010 Present

 Workbook page 157

Many soldiers died because of harsh living conditions during the Civil War.

A Long and Difficult War

CD 3 TR 53

More Americans died in the Civil War than in all other wars involving the United States. In addition to dying from **wounds**, many soldiers died because of the harsh living conditions and from disease. Soldiers often did not have medicine, clean water, or fresh food.

The South had difficulty getting food, medicine, and weapons because the Union **blockaded** Southern **ports**. The blockade also affected the economy of the South. It **prevented** Southerners from selling cotton, a major source of income, **overseas**.

Academic Vocabulary

Word	Explanation	Sample Sentence	Visual Cue
prevent (verb)	to stop something from happening	The barrier **prevented** us from driving on the road.	ROAD CLOSED

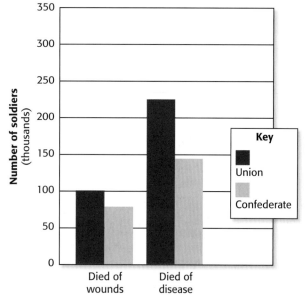

Civil War military deaths

Number of soldiers (thousands)

Key
Union
Confederate

Died of wounds
Died of disease

Social Studies Skill — Reading Double Bar Graphs

This double bar graph shows the number of soldiers who died during the Civil War.

1. Which side had more deaths due to wounds?
2. Did more soldiers die of wounds or disease?
3. Overall, which side suffered more deaths?

General Lee (seated on left) surrendered to General Grant (seated on right) in 1865.

The South Surrenders

CD 3 TR 54

Ulysses S. Grant, a Union soldier, had been a strong leader in several battles. In 1864, Lincoln made Grant commander of the Union forces.

On April 2, 1865, Grant's soldiers took control of Richmond, Virginia, an important economic center and capital of the Confederacy. A week later, the main Confederate army led by **Robert E. Lee** surrendered at Appomattox Court House, Virginia.

After four years of fighting and the loss of more than 630,000 lives, the Civil War was finally over.

The Assassination of President Lincoln CD 3 TR 55

After General Lee surrendered, there was hope that the divided nation would **reunite**. However, days later, President Lincoln was **assassinated**.

John Wilkes Booth, a Confederate supporter, shot Lincoln while he was watching a play in a theater. Lincoln died the next morning. Booth escaped, but he was caught and killed two weeks later.

Vice President Andrew Johnson became president. He now had to rebuild the nation.

President Lincoln was assassinated while watching a play at Ford's Theater in Washington, D.C.

✓ Check Your Understanding

1. Who did President Lincoln make commander of the Union forces in 1864?
2. What happened at Appomattox Court House, Virginia, in 1865?
3. What happened to President Lincoln just a few days after General Lee surrendered?

Critical Thinking Recognizing Cause and Effect
4. How did the Union's blockade make the South weaker?

 Research and Inquiry Use the Internet, the library, or your social studies book to answer these questions.

1. Who was the commanding general of the Confederate army?
2. Who was Clara Barton?
3. What was the Gettysburg Address?

Writing Imagine you are a soldier in the Union or the Confederate army at the beginning of the Civil War. Write a letter to a family member explaining why you think your side will win the war.

Kids in History

By some estimates, as many as a half a million boys under the age of 18 fought in the Civil War. Some were as young as ten years old.

Edward Francis Jemison was just seventeen years old when he was killed fighting as a Confederate soldier.

▶ Why do you think so many boys fought in the Civil War?

Reconstruction and the New South

CD 3
TR 56

1 **Andrew Johnson**

2 **Emancipation Proclamation**

3 **13th Amendment**

4 **sharecropper**

5 **Freedmen's Bureau**

6 **Ku Klux Klan**

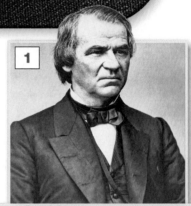

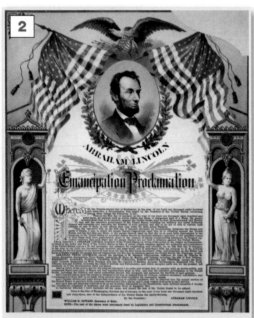

Emancipation Proclamation: President Lincoln's order that freed the slaves

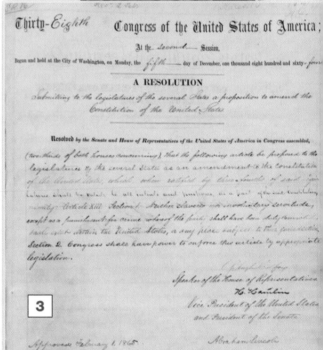

13th Amendment: a change made to the United States Constitution in 1865 that ended slavery

Word Study

Suffixes

Adding the suffix *–ize* to a noun changes it to a verb.

terror + ize = terrorize

The Ku Klux Klan **terrorized** people by setting fires around their homes.

sharecropper: a person who does farm work and receives a small part of the crops or money in exchange

| 1492 | 1500 | 1600 | 1700 |

5

6

Ku Klux Klan: a hate group made up of white Southerners who terrorized black Americans

Vocabulary in Context CD 3 TR 57

After the North won the Civil War, President **Andrew Johnson** was faced with the problem of how to rebuild the nation. This time after the Civil War is called Reconstruction.

The **Emancipation Proclamation** freed some slaves, but not all slaves became free until after the war. In 1865, the **13th Amendment** abolished slavery in the United States. Congress created the **Freedmen's Bureau** to provide education, medical care, food, and clothing to former slaves.

Although some things were better for African Americans after the Civil War, life was still difficult. Most former slaves became **sharecroppers**.

A system of unfair practices developed to keep black Americans separate from white Americans. Schools and hospitals for African Americans were not as good as those for whites. Most African Americans were not able to vote, and members of the **Ku Klux Klan** often terrorized them.

✅ Check Your Understanding

1. What is the time after the Civil War called?
2. What did the 13th Amendment do?
3. What was the Freedmen's Bureau?

Critical Thinking Making Inferences

4. Why do you think the Freedmen's Bureau was created?

1863	**1865**	**1866**	**1872**	**1896**
Emancipation Proclamation is issued	13th Amendment is added to the U.S. Constitution; Freedmen's Bureau is created	Ku Klux Klan is formed	Freedmen's Bureau closes	Supreme Court hears *Plessy v. Ferguson* case

1863 | 1896

1800	1900	2000 2010 Present

📖 Workbook page 161

After the Civil War, most African Americans in the South continued to work on farms.

The South after the War CD 3 TR 58

President Johnson's plan for Reconstruction required Southern states to abolish slavery before they could become part of the United States again.

The end of the Civil War meant a new way of life in the South. Even though some plantation owners hired their former slaves as sharecroppers, most African Americans remained very poor. However, for a short time African Americans were able to vote in much of the South. Some African Americans were even elected to Southern state legislatures and to Congress.

A Freedmen's Bureau school

The Freedmen's Bureau CD 3 TR 59

Freedmen were slaves who were freed during or after the Civil War. Congress created the Freedmen's Bureau to help former slaves. The bureau distributed food and clothing and helped in **emergencies**. The bureau also built schools and health **clinics**.

Academic Vocabulary

Word	Explanation	Sample Sentence	Visual Cue
emergency (noun)	a crisis or dangerous situation	People call 911 when there is an **emergency**.	

During Reconstruction, African Americans such as Joseph Rainey were elected to Congress.

Black Codes and Jim Crow CD 3 TR 60

Even though slavery ended after the Civil War, Southern **legislatures** passed laws limiting the rights of African Americans. These unfair laws became known as **Black Codes**.

A system of **segregation** known as "Jim Crow" also began to develop in the United States. In 1896, the Supreme Court heard the case of ***Plessy v. Ferguson***. The Court ruled that segregating whites and blacks was acceptable as long as the **facilities** were "**separate but equal**." This policy remained in effect until the mid-1900s.

Social Studies Skill Interpreting a Photograph

Look at the photograph of the two men. In the sign "For Colored Only," the word "colored" refers to African Americans. That term is no longer acceptable.

1. What are the men doing?
2. What does the sign mean?
3. What do you think the sign says on the other side of the water fountain?

Black Americans and white Americans were segregated in the South.

✓ Check Your Understanding

1. Where did most former slaves work after they became free?
2. What was a freedman?
3. What were the Black Codes?

Critical Thinking Summarizing

4. What was the Supreme Court's ruling in the 1896 case of *Plessy v. Ferguson*?

Research and Inquiry Use the Internet, the library, or your social studies book to answer these questions.

1. What was Lincoln's Ten Percent Plan for Reconstruction?
2. What was the 14th Amendment?
3. Who was elected president of the United States in 1868?

Writing Imagine you are living in the South after the Civil War. Write a letter to the president explaining why separating black Americans and white Americans is wrong.

Primary Source

Emancipation Proclamation

". . . all persons held as slaves within any state . . . in rebellion against the United States, shall be . . . forever free."

Abraham Lincoln, Emancipation Proclamation, 1863

▶ What do the words "emancipation" and "proclamation" mean?

The Industrial Revolution in the United States

FOCUS QUESTION

What was the Industrial Revolution and how did it affect people's lives?

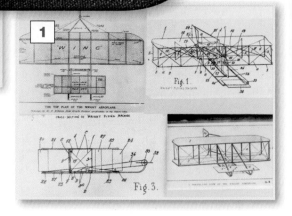

 CD 3 TR 61

1 invention
2 transportation
3 factory
4 industry
5 assembly line

6 union
7 strike
8 urban
9 immigrants

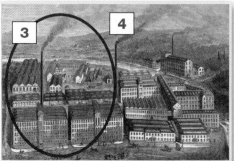

industry: the production of goods, especially those made in factories

Word Study

Prefixes

A prefix is a letter or group of letters added to the beginning of a word. A prefix changes a word's meaning.

The prefix **trans-** means "move across" or "change."

Before the invention of cars, horses were a main form of **transportation.**

The industrial revolution **transformed** people's lives.

union: an organization of workers created to protect workers' rights

1492	1500		1600		1700

strike: to stop work until an employer meets workers' demands

urban: related to, or located in, a city

Vocabulary in Context
CD 3 TR 62

The Industrial Revolution was a time of great change in America. New **inventions** transformed **industry**, agriculture, and **transportation**. **Factories** spread and large businesses grew quickly. **Assembly lines** allowed products to be made faster and more economically.

Workers were not always treated well. Many organized themselves into **unions** to get fair pay and safe working conditions. Sometimes workers went on **strike**, refusing to work until their working conditions improved.

The way people lived and worked changed, too. Many people moved to cities to find work. **Urban** areas grew. Millions of **immigrants** from all over the world came to the United States in search of a new life. The increasing population of cities created both opportunities and challenges.

✔ Check Your Understanding

1. Look at the photo of the urban scene. Describe what you see.
2. Why did workers sometimes go on strike?
3. Why did workers organize themselves into unions?

Critical Thinking Making Inferences

4. How do you think assembly lines made it possible to create products faster?

ca. 1869	ca. 1879	1892	1899	1913
First labor unions form	Electric lights first used for street lighting	Immigrants begin arriving at Ellis Island	The Bronx Zoo opens in New York City	The moving assembly line transforms manufacturing

1869 · · · · · · · · 1913

1800	1900	2000 Present

 Workbook page 165

John D. Rockefeller, the owner of Standard Oil Company

The Rise of Big Business CD 3 TR 63

Big **corporations** grew after the Civil War. Many of these corporations controlled whole industries. Some were so large and powerful that they put competitors out of business. Such powerful **businesses** that have no competition are called **monopolies**. Without **competition**, the big corporations could set high **prices**. Owners of these businesses, such as Andrew Carnegie in steel, John D. Rockefeller in oil, and Cornelius Vanderbilt in railroads, became rich.

City street lit by gas lamps

Urban Areas Grow CD 3 TR 64

By the late 1800s, fewer people were needed on farms because of the invention of new farm machinery. As more factories opened in urban areas, people moved from the countryside to urban areas. People from all over the world came to cities like New York, Boston, Chicago, and Detroit.

Cultural centers such as museums and libraries opened, as well as many public, open places, such as zoos and parks. For the first time, **consumers** could shop at department stores that sold many types of goods in one place.

Gas and electrical power became more freely available. This brought safer forms of heating and light during the night.

America Becomes Urbanized

Population (in millions) / Year

Urban
Rural

Social Studies Skill — Interpreting Bar Graphs

A bar graph uses bars of different lengths to show things such as changes over time. This bar graph shows how the number of people in rural and urban areas in America changed between 1860 and 1930.

1. What does the horizontal part of the graph refer to?
2. What does the vertical part of the graph refer to?
3. About how many people lived in rural areas in 1910?
4. In which year did more people live in urban areas than in rural areas in the United States for the first time?

Academic Vocabulary

Word	Explanation	Sample Sentence	Visual Cue
consumer (noun)	a person who buys products or services for his or her own use	Discount sales often encourage **consumers** to buy more.	

Problems with City Life  CD 3 TR 65

Many workers lived in crowded apartments called **tenements**. It was not unusual for a family of eight to live in an apartment with just one or two bedrooms. Many tenements had no indoor plumbing, heat, or **sanitation** services. Garbage often rotted in the streets. As a result, disease was common.

Immigrant family in a New York City tenement apartment

✔ Check Your Understanding

1. What is a monopoly?
2. What public places could people go to in the cities?
3. What were some of the problems with the tenement buildings?

Critical Thinking Making Inferences
4. How do you think having lighting at night changed the way people lived?

 Research and Inquiry Use the Internet, the library, or your social studies book to answer these questions.

1. How did businessmen such as Carnegie or Rockefeller contribute to charities?
2. Which industries had the most child laborers?
3. Investigate the Chicago Fire of 1871. How many people were killed? What positive changes in safety resulted?

 Writing Imagine what your life would be like if you did not have electric lighting at night. Write a paragraph about it.

Kids in History

Child labor was a big problem during the Industrial Revolution. Children as young as four years old worked in dangerous conditions. Sometimes, instead of going to school, children worked in places such as factories, mines, or farms.

▶ In what kind of industry do you think these children are working?

The Spanish-American War and the United States as a World Power

FOCUS QUESTION
How did the United States become a world power in the late 1800s?

CD 3
TR 66

1 *U.S.S. Maine*

2 Cuba

3 Caribbean

4 Puerto Rico

5 Philippines

6 Buffalo Soldiers

7 Rough Riders

8 Panama Canal

1

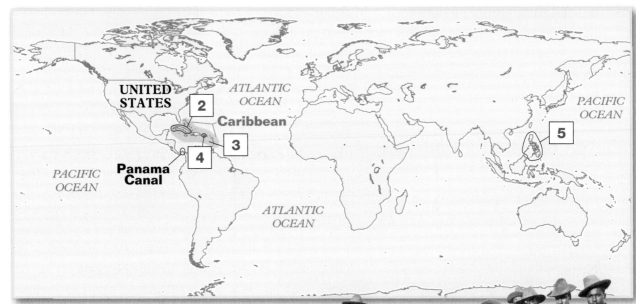

UNITED STATES

2

ATLANTIC OCEAN

Caribbean

3

4

Panama Canal

PACIFIC OCEAN

PACIFIC OCEAN

5

ATLANTIC OCEAN

Word Study

Multiple-Meaning Words

The word **rule** can mean "to govern."

The king **ruled** the country for many years.

Rule can also be a statement about what should or should not be done.

A school **rule** is that we must arrive by 8:00 A.M.

6

Buffalo Soldiers: experienced, African American soldiers who fought in the Spanish-American War

1492   1500   1600   1700

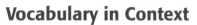

Vocabulary in Context

CD 3
TR 67

The first Spanish explorers arrived in **Cuba** in 1492. Soon after, Spain began ruling Cuba and other countries in the **Caribbean** and Pacific. By the 1800s, Cubans wanted their independence. Many Americans supported Cuba's struggle for independence.

In February 1898, an American ship, the ***U.S.S. Maine***, exploded in a harbor in Cuba, killing 266 people. The United States declared war on Spain because it believed Spain caused the explosion.

In December 1898, the United States and Cuba signed a peace treaty with Spain. Cuban soldiers had fought alongside American soldiers such as the **Rough Riders** and **Buffalo Soldiers**. As a result, Cuba became an independent country. Spain lost its control of the **Philippines** in the Pacific. Spain also lost control of the Caribbean island of **Puerto Rico**. As part of the peace treaty, the United States now had land in the Pacific and the Caribbean.

With land in the Caribbean, the United States could build the **Panama Canal**. This canal created a shorter route between the Atlantic and Pacific Oceans. The United States was on its way to becoming a world power.

7

Rough Riders: a group of American volunteer soldiers who fought in the Spanish-American War

8

✓ Check Your Understanding

1. Look at the map. Which two oceans does the Panama Canal connect?

2. What happened in February 1898 that caused the United States to declare war on Spain?

3. Who were the Rough Riders and the Buffalo Soldiers?

Critical Thinking Hypothesizing

4. Why would a shorter route between the Atlantic and Pacific Oceans help the United States become a world power?

1895	FEBRUARY 1898	APRIL 1898	DECEMBER 1898	1904
Cuban War for Independence begins	*U.S.S. Maine* explodes in Cuba	U.S. declares war on Spain	Spain, U.S., and Cuba sign peace treaty	U.S. begins building Panama Canal

1895 | 1904 |

| 1800 | 1900 | 2000 2010 Present |

People accused newspapers such as the *New York Journal* of "yellow journalism."

Yellow Journalism CD 3 TR 68

Americans read about Cuba's struggle for independence from Spain in newspapers such as the *New York World* and the *New York Journal*. To get more readers, these two newspapers sometimes **exaggerated** the cruel treatment of Cubans by the Spanish. While some stories of Spanish cruelty were true, many people called the reporting **yellow journalism**. This is a writing style that exaggerates events. The newspaper articles made Americans angry with Spain.

Rough Riders, Buffalo Soldiers, and Yellow Fever CD 3 TR 69

With the help of the Rough Riders and the Buffalo Soldiers, Cubans gained their independence from Spain. Their victory meant Cuba was now an independent country.

About 4,000 people died during the Spanish-American War from the fighting or from **yellow fever**. A Cuban doctor discovered that a mosquito carried the disease and spread it to humans.

The Rough Riders loading their guns in Cuba

The Panama Canal CD 3 TR 70

After the Spanish-American War, the United States owned new land in the Caribbean. The United States also began building a canal across **Central America** to **connect** the Pacific and Atlantic Oceans. Work on the canal started in 1904. This shorter route would make transportation easier and faster for American businesses and the United States Navy.

Thousands of people worked to build the canal. Most of these workers came from the Caribbean and many of them were **descendants** of African slaves.

Workers digging the Panama Canal

Academic Vocabulary

Word	Explanation	Sample Sentence	Visual Cue
connect (verb)	to join together	The bridge **connects** the island to the mainland.	

Social Studies Skill   Analyzing Historical Photographs

This photograph was taken during the Spanish-American War. It shows United States Army doctors taking care of hurt soldiers.

1. What do you think the man who is standing is holding?

2. What problems do you think doctors had in treating hurt soldiers?

A historical photograph

✔ Check Your Understanding

1. What is "yellow journalism"?

2. How was yellow journalism connected to the Spanish-American War?

3. What insect spread yellow fever during the Spanish-American War?

Critical Thinking Summarizing

4. What are some of the changes in the Caribbean after the Spanish-American War?

Research and Inquiry Use the Internet, the library, or your social studies book to answer these questions.

1. Who were Dr. Carlos Finlay and Dr. Walter Reed? What medical contributions did they make during the Spanish-American War?

2. Which member of the Rough Riders became president of the United States?

3. How many miles was the trip by sea from New York City to San Francisco, California, before the Panama Canal was built? How many miles was the trip after the Panama Canal was built?

Writing Think of an event that happened in your community. Write a paragraph in the style of yellow journalism. Create a headline for the story.

Primary Source

Remember the *Maine* Pin

Before and during the Spanish-American War, Americans said, "Remember the *Maine*." This encouraged Americans to support the war.

▶ Why do you think this pin would encourage Americans to support the war?

FOCUS QUESTION

How did the Industrial Revolution change American society?

CD 3
TR 71

1 **light bulb**

2 **camera**

3 **telephone**

4 **sweatshop**

5 **Jane Addams**

6 **Ellis Island**

7 **Theodore Roosevelt**

8 **muckraker**

sweatshop: a factory where workers are paid low wages and work long hours, often in crowded or unsafe conditions

Word Study

Compound Words

Compound words are made of two words put together.

A **sweatshop** is a cramped factory where many people work.

sweat (perspiration) + shop (factory) = sweatshop

Muckrakers are writers who call attention to dishonesty in business and government.

muck (mud or filth) + raker (someone who gathers something with a rake) = muckraker

| 1492 | 1500 | 1600 | 1700 |

7

Vocabulary in Context CD 3 TR 72

Many new and exciting inventions were introduced during the Industrial Revolution. The **light bulb** allowed people to do more at night. The **telephone** made it possible for people to speak with each other over great distances. New types of **cameras** allowed more people to take photographs.

During this time period, millions of people immigrated to the United States looking for jobs and freedom. Many immigrants came from southern and eastern Europe. They entered the United States through **Ellis Island** in New York and created new neighborhoods.

While the Industrial Revolution created new opportunities, it also created new problems. **Sweatshops** were introduced to the working public. Workers were paid low wages and worked long hours.

Reformers such as **Jane Addams** tried to improve conditions for sweatshop workers and others. Addams helped the poor and needy. **Muckrakers** called attention to dishonesty in business and government. **Theodore Roosevelt** worked to protect consumers from unsafe food and medicine.

8

muckraker: someone who calls attention to dishonesty in business and government

✔ Check Your Understanding

1. Look at the pictures. What inventions changed American society?

2. What new problems did the Industrial Revolution create for workers?

3. How did reformers of this time try to improve life for Americans?

Critical Thinking Hypothesizing

4. Look at the photograph of the workers in the sweatshop. Why do you think such a place was called a "sweatshop"?

1876	1889	1892	1903	1911
Bell invents the telephone	Addams opens Hull House	Ellis Island opens	Wright Brothers fly first airplane	Fire breaks out at the Triangle Shirtwaist Factory

| 1876 | 1911 |

| 1800 | 1900 | 2000 | 2010 | Present |

Workbook page 173

The Wright brothers and their airplane

Inventors and Inventions of the Industrial Revolution CD 3 TR 73

Many new inventions saved people time and work, and also made their lives more enjoyable. Alexander Graham Bell invented the telephone. People could now talk to each other across long distances. Thomas Edison invented the light bulb, movie camera, and **phonograph**.

The **mass production** of automobiles at the beginning of the 1900s allowed more people to buy cars. Henry Ford's Model T was the most popular early car.

The airplane was another new form of transportation. Two brothers, Wilbur and Orville Wright, flew the first airplane on December 17, 1903.

Reformers CD 3 TR 74

The **public** learned about the terrible working conditions in some factories after a fire at the Triangle Shirtwaist Factory in New York City. This event, which killed 146 people, led to reforms. **Labor unions** became more organized. Reformers worked to make factories safer and fire departments got better **equipment**.

Muckrakers wrote about **corruption** in business and government. They called attention to issues such as **unsanitary** conditions in meat-packing factories. Muckraking helped convince Congress to pass the Pure Food and Drug Act.

Firefighters trying to put out the fire at the Triangle Shirtwaist Factory in 1911

Academic Vocabulary

Word	Explanation	Sample Sentence	Visual Cue
equipment (noun)	items such as tools and machines that are used for a specific purpose	Firefighters use special **equipment** to put out fires.	

The New Americans CD 3 TR 75

New immigrants from southern and eastern Europe moved to American cities. They often lived in crowded neighborhoods. The languages, customs, and religions of these immigrants were new to many Americans. Reformers like Jane Addams said immigrants could learn to live in America and keep their customs. Many immigrants faced **discrimination**, but over time their cultural traditions became part of American society.

The new immigrants lived in neighborhoods such as Little Italy in New York.

Social Studies Skill — Studying Primary and Secondary Sources

Primary and secondary sources provide information about important time periods in American history.

Primary sources are records of the past that were created by people who witnessed or experienced the events themselves. **Secondary sources** are accounts of the past that were created by people writing about the events after they actually happened.

1. Which of the descriptions of Ellis Island are primary sources?
2. Which are secondary sources?

Ellis Island in New York Harbor welcomed millions of immigrants between 1892 and 1954. Read the quotations about Ellis Island and then answer the questions.

1. "At Ellis Island, men were separated from women and children at once. They were lined up separately for medical inspection."

   Barry Moreno, Librarian and Historian, National Park Service, 1997

2. "We were herded there to be examined. My father referred to Ellis Island as the Palace of Tears because everyone was so fearful."

   Euterpe Dukakis, Immigrant, Ellis Island, 1913

3. "There was a doctor there that examined you. Examined mostly your hair, your head, your eyes. There were people who did not pass. At Ellis Island, they were put aside and had to go back."

   Esther Gidiwicz, Immigrant, Ellis Island, 1905

✅ Check Your Understanding

1. What two important forms of transportation were invented during the Industrial Revolution?
2. Where did most of the new immigrants to America come from?
3. What law did muckrakers convince Congress to pass?

Critical Thinking Recognizing Cause and Effect

4. What positive changes did the Triangle Shirtwaist Factory fire lead to?

 Research and Inquiry Use the Internet, the library, or your social studies book to answer these questions.

1. Research five to ten inventions introduced during the Industrial Revolution. How did each of these inventions affect the lives of ordinary Americans?
2. Research the conditions that led to the Triangle Shirtwaist Factory fire. How could the fire have been prevented?
3. Many of the new immigrants settled in American cities. What were some of these cities?

 Writing Imagine you are a new immigrant who has just arrived in the United States. Would you rather live in a neighborhood filled with people from your home country, or a neighborhood with people who have been living in the United States for a long time? Explain your answer.

Primary Source

Statue of Liberty

At the base of the Statue of Liberty is a poem. It expressed America's feelings toward immigrants.

"Give me your tired, your poor, your huddled masses yearning to breathe free. . . ."

From "The New Colossus" by Emma Lazarus, 1883

▶ In your own words, what does this line from the poem mean?

The United States in World War I

CD 4
TR 1

1 **Woodrow Wilson**

2 **invasion**

3 **neutral**

4 *Lusitania*

5 **army**

6 **propaganda**

7 **peace**

invasion: an attack, usually of a country or region

neutral: not on either side in a disagreement

Word Study

Syllabification

Syllabification means "breaking a word into its syllables." You can use syllabification to make long words such as **propaganda** easier to read and say.

propaganda = prop · a · **gan** · da

Posters were an imortant type of **propaganda** during World War I.

1492   1500   1600   1700

5

army: an organized group of soldiers

6

COME AND DO YOUR BIT

JOIN NOW

propaganda: information used to persuade people that something is true and should be supported

7

peace: harmony and cooperation

Vocabulary in Context CD 4 TR 2

World War I started in Europe in 1914. Germany attacked France. Together France and Great Britain fought to stop the German **invasion**.

President **Woodrow Wilson** reacted by saying the United States would remain **neutral**. In 1915, a German submarine sank the ***Lusitania*** and killed 128 Americans. Germany's action angered many Americans, but most wanted the United States to stay out of the war.

In 1917, the number of German submarine attacks greatly increased and President Wilson asked Congress to declare war. The size of the United States **army** was increased and two million American soldiers went to fight in France. Not all Americans supported the president's decision to enter the war. To change people's opinion about the war, **propaganda** movements were started. These movements encouraged people to support the war.

World War I was the bloodiest war ever. Wilson was determined that there be no wars like it. He presented a plan called the Fourteen Points to end the war and bring **peace** to the world.

✓ Check Your Understanding

1. What did the United States do when World War I first started in Europe?
2. Why did the *Lusitania* sink?
3. What was the Fourteen Points plan?

Critical Thinking Analyzing Information

4. Look at the propaganda poster. What is the poster asking people to do?

| **1914** World War I begins | **1915** A German submarine sinks the *Lusitania* | **1916** Woodrow Wilson is reelected president | **1917** U.S. declares war on Germany | **1918** President Wilson presents his Fourteen Points; World War I ends |

1914 | 1918

| 1800 | 1900 | 2000 2010 Present |

Workbook page 177

1856	Thomas Woodrow Wilson is born in Virginia
1910	Wilson is elected governor of New Jersey
1912	Wilson is elected president of the U.S.
1916	Wilson is re-elected president of the U.S.
1920	Wilson receives the Nobel Peace Prize
1924	Wilson dies

A timeline of Woodrow Wilson's life

A cartoon showing an American soldier being welcomed in France

President Wilson presented his Fourteen Points to the United States Congress.

The United States Remains Neutral 🎧 CD 4 TR 3

In 1914, most Americans believed wars in Europe did not affect them, but that soon changed. First, German submarines attacked American ships. Second, the war helped America's economy because the United States sold war supplies to Great Britain and France.

By the 1916 presidential election, Americans were divided on whether to fight Germany. President Wilson wanted to remain neutral and that policy helped to get him elected to a second **term** as president. His **slogan** during the **campaign** was "He kept us out of war."

Social Studies Skill Interpreting a Timeline

Look at the timeline of Woodrow Wilson's life, noting when each event happened.

1. When was Wilson born? Where was he born?
2. Wilson was governor of which state before he was president?
3. What prize did Wilson receive in 1920?

The United States in World War I 🎧 CD 4 TR 4

By 1917, President Wilson decided it was time for the United States to enter the war. He was reacting to Germany sinking any ship going to Great Britain.

In France, American goods, soldiers, and money supported the war against Germany. The American and British **navies** joined together to defeat the German submarines.

Wilson and the Fourteen Points 🎧 CD 4 TR 5

On January 8, 1918, President Wilson delivered a speech to Congress. He presented fourteen ideas that he believed would bring peace to the world. Not all countries agreed with Wilson's Fourteen Points plan. Wilson had to **compromise** to make sure that his most important **point**, the creation of the **League of Nations**, was approved.

Many Americans opposed the League of Nations. Without enough support from Congress or the American public, the United States never joined the League.

Academic Vocabulary

Word	Explanation	Sample Sentence	Visual Cue
point (noun)	an item of information	Angela agreed with only one of the three **points** on the page.	

✔ Check Your Understanding

1. When World War I started in Europe, what did most Americans believe about wars in Europe?

2. In 1917, what made President Wilson decide to go to war with Germany?

3. According to President Wilson, which of his Fourteen Points was most important?

Critical Thinking Summarizing

4. In a few words, what was President Wilson's policy toward World War I in each of the following years: 1914, 1916, 1917, 1918?

 Research and Inquiry Use the Internet, the library, or your social studies book to answer these questions.

1. What is an "armistice"? On what date and at what time did the armistice of 1918 take place?

2. Isolationists were against the United States joining the League of Nations. What is an "isolationist"?

3. What happened to President Wilson in Pueblo, Colorado, in 1919?

 Writing Think about creating a propaganda poster today. What would you want to persuade people to do? Who is the audience for your poster? Write a paragraph answering these questions.

Primary Source

Army Identity Document for Major Truman

Millions of Americans joined the military during World War I. The government gave each soldier an identity card. This is the identity card for Harry Truman. He became president of the United States in 1945.

▶ Do you have an identity document? If so, who issued it?

The 1920s

CD 4
TR 6

1 prosperity

2 radio

3 Model T

4 19th Amendment

5 jazz

6 stock market

7 Herbert Hoover

prosperity: a time when the economy is good

19th Amendment: the amendment added to the United States Constitution in 1920 that gave women the right to vote

Word Study

Homonyms

The words **by** and **buy** are homonyms. They are pronounced the same way, but they are spelled differently and have different meanings.

By means "next to" or "near."

On her way to the high school, Jennifer walks **by** the middle school.

Buy is a verb that means "to purchase."

Tommy wants to **buy** a new computer.

September 11, 1920

Leslie's

Illustrate ...paper

...ice—15 Cents
...tion Price $7.00 a year

VOTING BOOTH NO 1

jazz: a form of American popular music

stock market: a place where people can buy and sell shares (or stock) in a company

Vocabulary in Context CD 4 TR 7

The 1920s were a time of **prosperity** in the United States. Goods made on assembly lines allowed Americans to buy more products at lower prices than in the past. Most Americans also had more money to spend. Millions of consumers bought goods such as **radios** and **Model T** Ford cars.

The 1920s were also a time of social change. The **19th Amendment** gave women the right to vote. African Americans developed a new musical style called **jazz**.

Many Americans hoped to get rich by investing their money in the **stock market**. They bought shares, or stock, in companies. At first, the prices for stock rose very quickly. In 1929, however, the prices for stock suddenly dropped and the stock market crashed. Many people lost all their money almost overnight. Although President **Herbert Hoover** said the economy was still strong, the prosperous Roaring Twenties had ended.

✔ Check Your Understanding

1. What was a Model T?
2. Which amendment gave women the right to vote?
3. What is jazz?

Critical Thinking Paraphrasing

4. Why did many people lose all their money in 1929?

1920	1923	1928	1929
19th Amendment is passed; First commercial radio broadcast to the public	Duke Ellington first plays jazz in Harlem	Herbert Hoover is elected president	Stock market crashes

		1920	1929		
1800		**1900**			**2000 Present**

Workbook page 181

A 1920s car advertisement

In the 1920s, women who did not follow traditional ways of behaving were called flappers.

People gathered outside the stock market in New York City after the crash in 1929.

A Time of Business CD 4 TR 8

Assembly lines now produced goods at a faster rate than in the past. Americans also had more money and looked to spend it on new products. **Advertisements** showed radios, the Model T, and other types of cars that people could buy. Banks offered loans to help Americans purchase these and other new consumer goods. However, these loans created big debts for many Americans.

Academic Vocabulary

Word	Explanation	Sample Sentence	Visual Cue
advertisement (noun)	a notice of a product or service that tries to get people to buy that product or service	After Lourdes saw the **advertisement** for the bicycles, she wanted to buy one.	

Changes in Society CD 4 TR 9

In the 1920s, women gained greater control over their lives. Women had more freedom to go to public places, such as theaters, without a male **chaperone**. Many women took jobs outside the home and earned their own money.

In cities outside the South, African Americans also gained more control over their lives. Artists, writers, and musicians gathered in the Harlem area of New York City, where they created the **Harlem Renaissance**. Harlem became famous for clubs where musicians, such as Duke Ellington, played jazz.

The Stock Market Crash CD 4 TR 10

On October 29, 1929, a **panic** started at the stock market in New York City. Prices of stocks had risen to more than what the stocks were really worth. Everyone wanted to sell their shares of stock, but there were no buyers. October 29, 1929 became known as Black Tuesday.

Stock prices crashed. President Hoover said the economy was still strong and asked companies to keep making goods. However, few people had money to buy goods anymore. Companies stopped production and fired workers. Some of these workers could not pay their debts and some of them became **homeless**.

Social Studies Skill Reading a Graph

This graph shows how stock prices rose and fell over time on the stock market.

1. What was the stock worth in December 1925?
2. What was the stock worth on October 29, 1929, the day known as Black Tuesday?
3. What was the stock worth at the end of 1929?

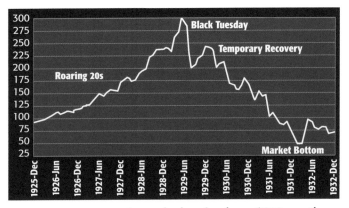

A graph showing how $100 worth of stock rose and fell over a period of time

✓ Check Your Understanding

1. How did Americans buy goods they did not have money for?
2. What place became famous for its jazz clubs?
3. What happened on October 29, 1929?

Critical Thinking Recognizing Evidence
4. What evidence suggests President Hoover was wrong when he said that prosperity would continue after the stock market crash?

Research and Inquiry Use the Internet, the library, or your social studies book to answer these questions.

1. What was the Florida land boom of the 1920s?
2. When the Ku Klux Klan reappeared in the 1920s, it targeted African Americans and what other groups?
3. How did the law passed by Congress cut immigration from Europe in the 1920s?

Writing Name something you have seen that you wanted because you saw an advertisement for it. What in the advertisement made you like it? Write a paragraph telling how the advertisement persuaded you to purchase the product or service.

Primary Source

Historical Photograph

The prosperity of the 1920s meant more people could go away for vacations. Atlantic City, New Jersey, was a popular place for family vacations in the 1920s.

▶ What tells you that this photograph was taken many years ago?

The Great Depression and the New Deal

CD 4
TR 11

FOCUS QUESTION

What was the New Deal and how did it change the United States?

1 economic depression

2 unemployment

3 Great Depression

4 Dust Bowl

5 Franklin D. Roosevelt

6 New Deal

7 Social Security

economic depression: a long period of time when many people are unemployed and businesses are not making very much money

unemployment: being without a job

Great Depression: a time during the 1930s with the worst unemployment and business conditions in modern history

Word Study

Antonyms

Temporary and **permanent** are antonyms, words with opposite meanings.

Temporary means "for a short time."

Permanent means "for a long time."

The Work in Progress Administration was only a **temporary** New Deal program, but Social Security was a **permanent** one.

Dust Bowl: an area of the Great Plains where soil was blown away during the drought of the 1930s

New Deal: the programs and policies President Franklin D. Roosevelt introduced in the 1930s to improve the country's economy

Social Security: a government program that provides monthly payments to retired American workers and other citizens who cannot work

Vocabulary in Context CD 4 TR 12

The stock market crash of 1929 led to an **economic depression**. **Unemployment** became a huge problem. Unemployed workers in cities could not afford to buy or stay in their homes. Many people became homeless. President Herbert Hoover created some programs to help the economy. However, his programs did not solve the country's problems, and the economy got worse. This period of time became known as the **Great Depression**.

On the Great Plains, farm workers lost their jobs, too. Drought dried the soil and the wind blew it away. The drought created the **Dust Bowl** in which crops and animals died. People were forced to move and many went to California to search for work.

In 1932, **Franklin D. Roosevelt** was elected president. He promised strong actions to fix the economy. His **New Deal** programs gave people temporary work building bridges, libraries, and parks. Some workers planted trees to protect soil on the Great Plains. Other New Deal programs introduced permanent reforms, such as **Social Security**.

✅ Check Your Understanding

1. Look at the picture of the Dust Bowl. Describe what you see.
2. Why did workers plant trees on the Great Plains?
3. In 1932, what did Franklin D. Roosevelt promise the American people?

Critical Thinking Comparing and Contrasting
4. How did the Great Depression affect people in cities and the Great Plains in the same way? How did it affect them differently?

| **1929** The stock market crashes | **1931** Severe drought begins on the Great Plains | **1932** Franklin D. Roosevelt is elected president of the U.S. | **1933** President Roosevelt introduces the New Deal | **1935** Congress passes the Social Security Act | **1936** Roosevelt is re-elected |

1800   1900   2000 Present

Many people began living in towns crowded with shacks.

A mother and her children at their home in Elm Grove, Oklahoma, 1936

The Great Depression CD 4 TR 13

By 1932, one in four workers was unemployed. Many people lost their life savings when banks closed down. People became angry that President Hoover was not doing enough to end the economic depression. Many Americans lost their homes and had to live in shacks. Thousands of **migrants** moved from the Dust Bowl to California to find jobs.

Franklin D. Roosevelt promised Americans he would do more to end the Depression. He easily defeated Hoover in the 1932 presidential election.

Social Studies Skill   Interpreting Historical Photographs

This photo shows a mother and her children during the Great Depression. They are standing in front of their home.

1. What is their home made of?
2. How would you describe their clothes?
3. Do you think their home has running water?

New Deal Programs CD 4 TR 14

Franklin Roosevelt became president on March 4, 1933. He acted quickly to solve the country's economic problems. He made sure that the money in banks was safe and started **public works** programs to reduce unemployment.

Roosevelt explained his new programs to the American people in "fireside chats" on the radio. The president's wife, Eleanor Roosevelt, traveled around the country to see how New Deal programs were doing.

President Roosevelt delivering a fireside chat on the radio

A family listening to President Roosevelt on the radio

Effects of the New Deal

CD 4
TR 15

Temporary New Deal programs such as the Works Progress Administration did not completely end unemployment. However, these temporary programs gave many people jobs and hope.

The New Deal also brought permanent changes. In the South, the Tennessee Valley Authority built **dams** to stop floods and **generate** electricity. The New Deal also created the **Social Security** system as a way to support all Americans in their old age.

Academic Vocabulary

Word	Explanation	Sample Sentence	Visual Cue
generate (verb)	to produce or create	By cycling hard, Anna **generated** enough power to finish the bike race.	

A Works Progress Administration (WPA) poster

✔ Check Your Understanding

1. Where did thousands of migrants from the Dust Bowl go?
2. What was a fireside chat?
3. In what region of the United States was the Tennessee Valley Authority?

Critical Thinking Summarizing
4. What were the effects of the New Deal?

Research and Inquiry Use the Internet, the library, or your social studies book to answer these questions.

1. What disease did Franklin Roosevelt get in 1921? How did this disease affect him?
2. Did former president Hoover support the New Deal? Why or why not?
3. Who was the first woman member of a president's cabinet in United States history? What office did she hold? Who appointed her to this position?

Writing Imagine it is 1936. Write a letter to the newspaper explaining why you support the re-election of President Roosevelt.

Kids in History

Inexpensive forms of entertainment were popular during the Great Depression. For ten cents, a person could spend an entire afternoon at the movies. During this time, people played newly invented board games such as Monopoly® and Scrabble®.

▶ What kinds of games that do not cost very much do you enjoy playing?

The United States in World War II

1

CD 4
TR 16

FOCUS QUESTION
Why was the United States involved in World War II?

1 Pearl Harbor

2 D-Day

3 internment camp

4 Dwight D. Eisenhower

5 atomic bomb

6 Harry Truman

7 Hiroshima

8 Nagasaki

2

D-Day: June 6, 1944, the day the Allies invaded Europe from the sea

3

4

Word Study
Nouns Used as Verbs

The word **bomb** can be a noun or a verb.

In the following sentence, **bomb** is a noun.

The **bomb** destroyed the building.

In the following sentence, **bomb** is a verb.

The air force **bombs** enemy targets during wartime.

| 1492 | 1500 | 1600 | 1700 |

5

6

JAPAN

7

8

Hiroshima

Nagasaki

Vocabulary in Context CD 4 TR 17

World War II began in 1939. The United States did not enter the war until December 7, 1941, when Japan attacked **Pearl Harbor**, Hawaii. After this attack, the United States joined the Allies in the war.

The war created many changes in American life. Millions of Americans joined the military. Women took over the jobs men had been doing. The government was afraid that Japanese Americans might help Japan in the war. Even though most were American citizens, the government sent many Japanese Americans, especially those living on the West Coast, to **internment camps**.

To win the war, the Allies had to conquer large areas controlled by Germany and Japan. On **D-Day**, June 6, 1944, American general **Dwight D. Eisenhower** led his army across the English Channel to invade Europe.

The United States was not only involved in the war in Europe, but also in Japan. The war against Japan ended in 1945 after President **Harry Truman** used **atomic bombs** on **Hiroshima** and **Nagasaki**.

✔ Check Your Understanding

1. When did the United States enter World War II?
2. Which group of Americans was sent to internment camps after the attack on Pearl Harbor?
3. What was D-Day?

Critical Thinking Analyzing Information
4. How did geography make it hard for the Allies to end the war? Explain your answer.

1939	1941	1942	JUNE 6, 1944	1945
World War II begins	U.S. Congress passes Lend-Lease law; Japan attacks the U.S. at Pearl Harbor	U.S. government forces Japanese Americans into internment camps	Allies invade Europe on D-Day	U.S. drops the atomic bomb on Japan; World War II ends

		1939	1945		
1800		**1900**		**2000**	**2010** **Present**

Workbook page 189

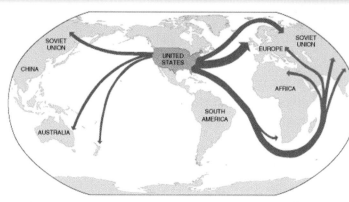
Lend-Lease supply routes

The Road to Pearl Harbor 🎧 CD 4 TR 18

The United States tried to stay out of the war. However, President Franklin D. Roosevelt said that Americans should help the Allies who were fighting Germany and Japan. In March 1941, Congress passed the **Lend-Lease** law, which provided military supplies to Great Britain. In **response**, German submarines attacked American ships.

Then, on December 7, 1941, Japan attacked Pearl Harbor. Much of the United States Navy was sunk and thousands of Americans were killed. This attack united Americans and made them want to fight Japan and its ally, Germany.

Academic Vocabulary

Word	Explanation	Sample Sentence	Visual Cue
response (noun)	a reaction to something	In **response** to the gift, Rafael smiled.	

Women factory workers in Long Beach, California, 1944

The War at Home 🎧 CD 4 TR 19

In 1942, many Japanese Americans were forced into internment camps. At the same time, many other Americans moved to new places to take wartime jobs. War industries were not allowed to **discriminate** against African Americans, but the military remained **segregated**.

America's economy grew quickly. Americans made more **armaments** than any other country involved in the war. Goods such as gasoline and beef were **rationed** and taxes went up. However, most people were better off than they were before the war.

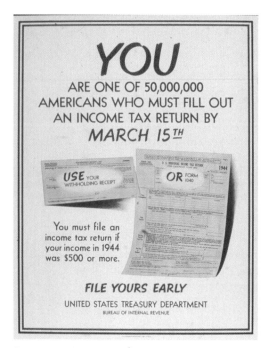

YOU
ARE ONE OF 50,000,000
AMERICANS WHO MUST FILL OUT
AN INCOME TAX RETURN BY
MARCH 15TH

USE YOUR WITHHOLDING RECEIPT   OR FORM 1040   1944

You must file an income tax return if your income in 1944 was $500 or more.

FILE YOURS EARLY

UNITED STATES TREASURY DEPARTMENT
BUREAU OF INTERNAL REVENUE

A government war-time poster

Social Studies Skill   Analyzing Primary Sources

During the war, the government needed money for ships, airplanes, tanks, and other things necessary to fight. As a result, the United States government increased people's taxes.

1. How many Americans had to file an income tax return for 1944?

2. What government department produced this poster?

Defeat of Germany and Japan CD 4 TR 20

The American military fought across much of the world. After D-Day, Eisenhower's army and the Soviet army invaded Germany from two directions. Just before Germany surrendered, President Roosevelt died. His vice president, Harry Truman, became president.

Japan continued fighting. Thousands of Americans died trying to conquer small Pacific islands held by the Japanese such as **Iwo Jima**. President Truman ordered the dropping of two atomic bombs on Japan in 1945. Soon after, Japan surrendered.

Marines raising the American flag on Iwo Jima

✅ Check Your Understanding

1. How did Germany respond to the Lend-Lease law?
2. What were two goods rationed in the United States during World War II?
3. How did Eisenhower's army and the Soviet army defeat Germany?

Critical Thinking Comparing and Contrasting

4. How did World War II affect American women, African Americans, and Japanese Americans? Compare and contrast how the war affected these groups.

 Research and Inquiry Use the Internet, the library, or your social studies book to answer these questions.

1. Four main countries made up the Allied powers after the attack on Pearl Harbor. What were these countries?
2. Which international organization was formed by the Allies at a meeting held in San Francisco in April 1945?
3. Who ruled Japan after it surrendered in 1945?

 Writing What do you think was the most interesting change in the United States during World War II? Write a paragraph telling why that change is of most interest to you.

World War II Propaganda Poster

Wartime propaganda tried to influence women to work in war industries. This propaganda suggested that women could do jobs they had once been considered too weak to do. This poster of "Rosie the Riveter" is one of the best-known posters from World War II.

▶ Why do you think this poster was effective in getting women to work in the war industries?

Suburbanization and the Cold War

CD 4
TR 21

FOCUS QUESTION
How did the United States change after World War II?

1 college

2 suburb

3 highway

4 drive-in movie theater

5 shopping mall

6 Korean War

7 Nikita Khrushchev

8 John F. Kennedy

9 nuclear missile

10 Fidel Castro

suburb: a small town outside of a large city with more houses than businesses

Word Study

Word Families

Prosperous means "successful in business."

Prosper means "to grow in wealth."

Many Americans **prospered** after World War II.

Prosperity means "a good economic period."

After the war ended, Americans enjoyed a time of **prosperity.**

1492	1500	1600	1700

Korean War: a military conflict fought in Korea from 1950 to 1953

Vocabulary in Context CD 4 TR 22

The United States experienced a time of prosperity after World War II. More people could afford to go to **college** and buy a house in the **suburbs**. New **highways** made it easier for people to get from one place to another. People drove to **drive-in movie theaters** and new **shopping malls**.

However, during this time of prosperity, Americans also were concerned that communism was spreading. In 1950, the United States joined the **Korean War** in an effort to stop the spread of communism.

The United States also competed with the Soviet Union to develop **nuclear missiles**. In 1962, **Fidel Castro**, the communist leader of Cuba, allowed the Soviet Union to place nuclear missiles on the island of Cuba, only ninety miles from the United States. President **John F. Kennedy** demanded that the leader of the Soviet Union, **Nikita Khrushchev**, remove the missiles.

✔ Check Your Understanding

1. Look at the pictures. Name two places Americans drove to in their cars.
2. In what year did the United States start fighting in the Korean War?
3. What was one way the United States competed with the Soviet Union?

Critical Thinking Making Inferences

4. Why do you think Americans needed more highways after World War II?

1950	1953	1959	1961	1962
Korean War starts	Dwight D. Eisenhower becomes president of the U.S.	Fidel Castro becomes leader of Cuba	John F. Kennedy becomes president of the U.S.	Cuban Missile Crisis occurs

1950 | 1962

1800 **1900** **2000 2010 Present**

Workbook page 193

Teenagers at a fast food restaurant in 1967

Prosperity and Suburban Living CD 4 TR 23

After World War II, the middle class grew. The American government introduced the **G.I. Bill** to help **veterans** attend college and get better jobs. The G.I. Bill also helped veterans buy homes.

As more people moved to the suburbs, they needed cars and highways to go to shopping malls, **fast food** restaurants, and other places. Cars were useful, but they created traffic **congestion** and **smog**.

Academic Vocabulary

Word	Explanation	Sample Sentence	Visual Cue
congestion (noun)	overcrowding in a small area	Traffic **congestion** became a problem after World War II because so many people bought cars.	

Housing for soldiers and their families on a United States military base in 1957

The Cold War CD 4 TR 24

After World War II, Americans were worried about the spread of communism. By the 1950s, tensions between communist countries and democratic countries led to the **Cold War**. In the Korean War, the United States fought alongside South Korea to stop a communist invasion from happening there.

Because of concern about the spread of communism, America's **armed forces** expanded. President Dwight D. Eisenhower was concerned that the **military** could become too powerful and **interfere** with Americans' freedoms.

American and Soviet military ships near Cuba

The Cuban Missile Crisis CD 4 TR 25

The Soviet Union supported Fidel Castro after he took control of Cuba. Beginning in 1962, Americans faced a new challenge: the Cuban Missile Crisis. Americans learned that the Soviet Union had put nuclear missiles pointed at the United States in Cuba. President John F. Kennedy sent warships to stop Soviet ships from bringing more missiles to Cuba. The crisis ended when the Soviets agreed to remove the missiles and Americans agreed not to **invade** Cuba.

Social Studies Skill — Analyzing a Primary Source

This map appeared in a newspaper during the Cuban Missile Crisis. It shows the distances that missiles would travel from Cuba to various cities in North America.

1. According to the map, which American city is closest to Cuba?

2. Why might this map cause alarm in the United States?

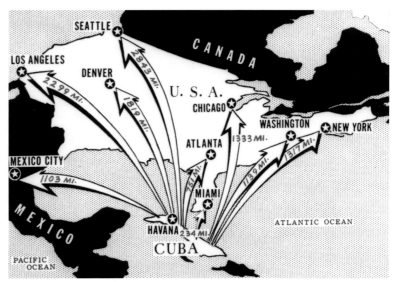

Distances of major North American cities from Cuba

✔ Check Your Understanding

1. What was the G.I. Bill?

2. What did President Eisenhower say about the military in the United States?

3. How did the United States stop more Soviet missiles from getting to Cuba?

Critical Thinking Summarizing

4. Summarize the effects of suburban expansion after World War II.

 Research and Inquiry Use the Internet, the library, or your social studies book to answer these questions.

1. Who was Joseph McCarthy and what did he do?

2. When Castro came to power, many Cubans moved to the United States. In which American city did most Cubans settle?

3. What happened in Dallas, Texas, on November 22, 1963?

 Writing How does living in a suburb compare to living in a city? What is the best and worst thing about each area? Write a paragraph explaining your answer.

Primary Source

Historical Photograph

During the Cold War, some Americans built bomb shelters in their back yards in case of a nuclear attack. This photograph shows the inside of an underground shelter on Long Island, New York, in 1955.

▶ What are some of the items that the family has placed inside the shelter?

The Civil Rights Era

FOCUS QUESTION

How did American society change during the Civil Rights era?

CD 4
TR 26

1 discrimination

2 civil rights

3 segregation

4 Rosa Parks

5 Dr. Martin Luther King, Jr.

6 sit-in

7 march

8 César Chávez

9 Betty Friedan

discrimination: unfair treatment, especially because of ethnicity, sex, age, or religion

segregation: separating or setting apart from others

civil rights: the freedoms that all Americans have, including freedom of speech, the right to vote, and the right to hold meetings

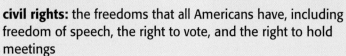

Word Study

Antonyms

Antonyms are words with opposite meanings.

Integration means "the mixing of different groups of people."

Segregation means "the separation of different groups of people."

| 1492 | 1500 | 1600 | 1700 |

sit-in: a protest in which people refuse to leave a place in order to bring attention to a problem

Vocabulary in Context CD 4 TR 27

Throughout American history, many different groups of people have faced **discrimination. Segregation** and unfair voting laws hurt African Americans, especially in the South. In the 1950s, people began demanding **civil rights** for all Americans. Leaders such as **Dr. Martin Luther King, Jr.,** and **Rosa Parks** began organizing **marches** and **sit-ins** to get equal rights for African Americans.

Other groups of Americans also fought for equal rights. For example, **César Chávez** helped organize a labor union to improve conditions for farm workers. Leaders of the American Indian Movement worked to get fair treatment for Native Americans.

Women also faced discrimination. **Betty Friedan** and others started the National Organization for Women to make sure women were treated equally in the workplace, schools, and the military.

✔ Check Your Understanding

1. In the United States, what does "civil rights" refer to?
2. What group worked for the fair treatment of Native Americans?
3. What did César Chávez do?

Critical Thinking Hypothesizing
4. Look at the photos of the sit-in and march. How do you think these actions made other people aware of discrimination against African Americans?

1954	**1960**	**1962**	**1964**	**1966**
Supreme Court rules segregation in schools is illegal	First sit-in protesting segregation is held	César Chávez organizes labor union for farm workers	Civil Rights Act becomes law	The National Organization for Women is created

1954 | 1966

1800 **1900** **2000 2010 Present**

Civil rights leaders such as Rosa Parks were arrested.

A 1963 sit-in in Mississippi

Federal troops were sent to keep the peace when schools were ordered to integrate.

African Americans and Civil Rights 🎧 CD 4 TR 28

Beginning in the 1800s, segregation kept African Americans and other people of color separate from whites. Schools, movie theaters, public pools, and other places were segregated.

Starting in the 1950s, African Americans began using **nonviolent protests** to try to end discrimination. For example, Rosa Parks refused to give her bus seat to a white person. Dr. Martin Luther King, Jr., organized marches. Many civil rights workers were **arrested** for their actions.

Social Studies Skill Analyzing Historical Photographs

Look at the photograph of the 1963 sit-in.

1. Where do you think the photograph was taken?
2. What are the people who are standing doing to the people who are sitting?
3. How is this sit-in a form of nonviolent protest?

The Law Is Challenged 🎧 CD 4 TR 29

Civil rights leaders began **challenging** unfair laws in court. In 1954, the Supreme Court said racial segregation in public schools was **unconstitutional**. Public schools throughout the country had to integrate. Ten years later, the government passed the landmark Civil Rights Act of 1964. This law **guaranteed** equal rights for all citizens.

Academic Vocabulary

Word	Explanation	Sample Sentence	Visual Cue
guarantee (verb)	to promise that something will happen	President Johnson signed the Civil Rights Act of 1964, which **guaranteed** equal rights for all citizens.	

Other Groups Struggle for Rights

In 1966, César Chávez helped form the United Farm Workers. This labor union helped protect the rights of **migrant** farm workers. Many of these **Latino** workers traveled throughout the United States picking crops. The United Farm Workers organized boycotts and protests, and filed **law suits** to protect migrant workers.

The American Indian Movement protested the unfair treatment of Native Americans. Leaders, like Russell Means, led protests so that Native Americans could have equal access to things such as housing and education.

Women won the right to vote in 1920, but they did not have the same rights as men. In 1963, Congress passed the Equal Pay Act. This law said employers could not pay women less than men for the same job.

Farm workers working in the fields

✔ Check Your Understanding

1. Who refused to give up her bus seat to a white person?
2. What did the Supreme Court rule in 1954?
3. What labor union did César Chávez help form in 1966?

Critical Thinking Relating to Your Own Experiences
4. Have you ever seen or experienced discrimination? What happened?

 Research and Inquiry Use the Internet, the library, or your social studies book to answer these questions.

1. What role did Dolores Huerta play in the United Farm Workers?
2. Who was Gloria Steinem?
3. What is "Title IX"?

 Writing If you lived during the Civil Rights era, would you have participated in marches and other nonviolent protests? Why or why not?

Primary Source

Letter from Birmingham Jail

In 1963, Dr. Martin Luther King, Jr., was put in jail for being involved in a nonviolent protest against discrimination. While in jail, he wrote a letter that was later published. The letter stated:

"Injustice anywhere is a threat to justice everywhere."

▶ In your own words, what was Dr. King saying?

The Vietnam War

FOCUS QUESTION

Why was the United States involved in the Vietnam War?

CD 4
TR 31

1 Ho Chi Minh   5 advisor

2 domino theory   6 containment

3 North Vietnam   7 Lyndon B. Johnson

4 South Vietnam

domino theory: the idea that if one country becomes communist, other nearby countries would also become communist

Word Study

Prefixes

The prefix **un-** means "not."

The Vietnam War became very **un**popular in the United States.

When the war took longer than expected, it became **un**clear that the United States would win.

advisor: a person who gives advice and makes recommendations on what to do

1492   1500   1600   1700

6

North Korea

Sea of Japan

Yellow Sea

South Korea

containment: the act of holding something in and stopping it from spreading

7

Vocabulary in Context CD 4 TR 32

Vietnam had been a French colony for many years. In 1954, the communist leader **Ho Chi Minh** and his forces defeated the French army. Vietnam was divided into two countries. **North Vietnam** became communist. **South Vietnam** opposed communism. The two countries soon began to fight one another over that issue.

The United States government believed that if one country became communist, others in the area would also become communist. This idea became known as the **domino theory**.

To stop communism in Southeast Asia, the United States sent **advisors** to support the South Vietnamese government. As the United States had done in Korea, Americans believed a policy of **containment** would stop the spread of communism. In 1964, Congress said President **Lyndon B. Johnson** could use military force in Southeast Asia. In 1965, the first American troops arrived in South Vietnam.

The United States never formally declared war. But the conflict became known as the Vietnam War and quickly became unpopular with the American public.

✔ Check Your Understanding

1. Vietnam was divided into which two countries?
2. What did America's policy of "containment" try to do?
3. Who did Congress allow to use military force in Southeast Asia?

Critical Thinking Paraphrasing
4. In your own words, what is the domino theory?

1954	1961	1964	1965	1975	1976
Vietnam is divided into North and South	U.S. sends advisors to South Vietnam	Congress approves military force in Southeast Asia	First U.S. troops sent to South Vietnam	South Vietnam surrenders to North Vietnam	North and South Vietnam are united under communist rule

1954 | 1976

1800   1900   2000   2010   Present

 Workbook page 201

An example of a Viet Cong soldier hiding place in the jungle

A Long and Different Kind of War
🎧 CD 4 TR 33

American soldiers fought in the Vietnam War from 1965 to 1973. The way this war was fought was different from ways Americans had fought wars in the past.

The North Vietnamese government supported the **Viet Cong**, a communist **guerrilla** army in South Vietnam. The Viet Cong hid in the jungles and attacked by surprise.

American forces sprayed chemicals that killed vegetation to destroy the Viet Cong's hiding places. They also used **napalm**, a highly controversial chemical that destroyed vegetation and burned people badly. Some Americans opposed the use of napalm because it burned people badly.

Vietnam War protestors

Protests Against the War
🎧 CD 4 TR 34

In 1965, the United States felt confident it would win the war quickly. However, the war took longer than expected and it became unclear that the United States would win. The war became increasingly unpopular with Americans.

Many Americans showed their dislike for the war by organizing protests against the war and the **draft**. They organized marches and sit-ins, and some even burned their draft cards.

Academic Vocabulary

Word	Explanation	Sample Sentence	Visual Cue
draft (noun)	a system that requires people to serve in the military	Some Americans protested the **draft** by burning their draft cards.	

A political cartoon showing an American soldier walking up a foggy staircase

Social Studies Skill Interpreting a Political Cartoon

This cartoon was drawn in 1965. Look at the cartoon and answer the questions.

1. Who is the figure in the cartoon?
2. What was going on in the United States in 1965, the year of the cartoon was drawn?
3. Why do you think the artist drew the soldier walking up into a fog?

The War Comes to an End

The United States had begun to withdraw troops from Vietnam in the early 1970s. By April 29, 1975, the North Vietnamese army and the Viet Cong were close to capturing Saigon, the capital of South Vietnam. The United States realized that the war was coming to an end and that Vietnam would soon become a communist country. The United States began **evacuating** American civilians and Vietnamese **refugees** by helicopter.

On April 30, 1975, the North Vietnamese captured Saigon and renamed it Ho Chi Minh City. North Vietnam and South Vietnam were united as one country under communist rule. Many Vietnamese refugees went to Australia, Canada, France, and the United States to live.

Americans and Vietnamese refugees being evacuated from Vietnam

✔ Check Your Understanding

1. Who were the Viet Cong?
2. How did some Americans protest the Vietnam War?
3. What was Saigon named after North Vietnam captured it in 1975?

Critical Thinking Analyzing Information
4. What are some of the reasons that the Vietnam War was unpopular with many Americans?

 Research and Inquiry Use the Internet, the library, or your social studies book to answer these questions.

1. Which country did most Vietnamese refugees settle in after the war?
2. What was the Tet Offensive?
3. What was Agent Orange?

 Writing Imagine you lived in the United States during the Vietnam War. Write a letter to President Johnson explaining why you support or oppose the war.

Primary Source

Vietnam Veterans Memorial

In 1982, the United States built the Vietnam Veterans Memorial in Washington, D.C. Maya Lin, a 21-year-old student, designed this memorial. The names of American soldiers who died in the war are etched into the marble surface.

▶ Why do you think public memorials like this one are important to people?

The United States in the Twenty-First Century

FOCUS QUESTION
What global issues does the United States face today?

CD 4
TR 36

1 global
2 imports
3 exports
4 terrorism

5 natural resource
6 fossil fuels
7 renewable energy

global: related to the entire world

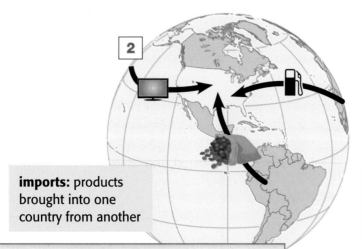

imports: products brought into one country from another

exports: products sent from one country to another

Word Study

Nouns Used as Verbs

The words **export** and **import** can be nouns or verbs.

In the following sentence, **export** is a noun.

An **export** is a product that one country sends to another country.

In the following sentence, **export** is a verb.

The company **exports** televisions to other countries.

In the following sentence, **import** is a noun.

An **import** is a product that one country brings in from another country.

In the following sentence, **import** is a verb.

Bananas are **imported** to the United States.

terrorism: the use of violence by a person or an organized group to frighten societies or governments, often for political reasons or to promote their own beliefs

| 1492 | 1500 | 1600 | 1700 |

5

natural resource: material in nature that people value, such as wood, fresh water, petroleum, and minerals

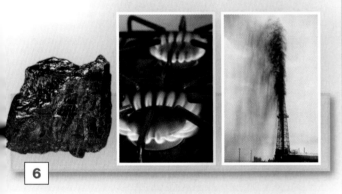

6

7

Vocabulary in Context CD 4 TR 37

By the beginning of the twenty-first century, the United States had become more connected to other countries through the **global** economy. A big change occurred in which the American economy began **importing** more than it **exported**.

The American population was also changing. Americans were living longer, and immigrants continued to come to the United States from all over the world.

However, the United States also faced new challenges. Fear of **terrorism** grew after the United States was attacked on September 11, 2001. Soon after that event, American troops were sent to the Middle East to fight in America's "War on Terror."

Another challenge for Americans was the cost of **natural resources. Fossil fuels** such as natural gas, petroleum, and coal became harder to get and more expensive. As a result, the United States explored **renewable energy** from the sun, wind, and water.

✓ Check Your Understanding

1. How was the American population changing in the twenty-first century?
2. What happened on September 11, 2001?
3. Name one kind of fossil fuel and one kind of renewable energy.

Critical Thinking Comparing and Contrasting
4. How are imports and exports the same as and different from each other?

1976	1977	2001	2008
The U.S begins importing more goods than it exports	U.S. Department of Energy is created	Terrorists attack New York City and Washington, D.C.	Barack Obama is elected 44th president of the U.S.

1976 | 2008 |

| 1800 | 1900 | 2000 | 2010 | Present |

Workbook page 205

A Changing Population 🎧 CD 4 TR 38

By the beginning of the twenty-first century, the average American was expected to live to the age of 78. Just 100 years ago, the average life expectancy was 49. Americans were living longer because of advances in medicine. Vaccines and antibiotics for serious diseases helped people stay healthy.

The number of people in the United States who were born in other countries continued to grow. The United States was home to more cultures and religions than in the past. This diversity made America a more **multicultural** nation.

The changing population in the United States

Academic Vocabulary

Word	Explanation	Sample Sentence	Visual Cue
multicultural (adjective)	representative of many peoples' cultures, nationalities, or ethnic groups	We have a **multicultural** classroom.	

The Graying of America: 65+ Population 1950–2030

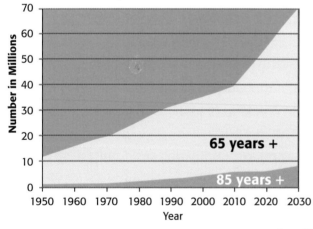

People sixty-five and older in the United States, 1950–2030

Social Studies Skill Analyzing Line Graphs

The number of older Americans has been steadily increasing. The line graph shows the number of Americans who lived to be over sixty-five years old in 1950 and how many are expected to live to that age by 2030.

1. How many people lived to be sixty-five or older in 1950?

2. How many people age of sixty-five or older are estimated to be living in 2030?

Challenges Facing the United States 🎧 CD 4 TR 39

As the United States entered the twenty-first century, it faced new challenges, including a weakening economy. America had more imports than it had exports. There was also growing concern about jobs moving from the United States to other countries where labor was cheaper.

On September 11, 2001, a terrorist attack killed almost 3,000 people in the United States. **Al Qaeda**, a terrorist group, said they were responsible. Concerns about terrorism grew. The United States soon sent troops to the Middle East.

Breakthroughs in the Twenty-First Century

 CD 4 TR 40

In addition to facing challenges, Americans made many **breakthroughs** at the beginning of the twenty-first century. One such breakthrough was that more **minorities** had been elected to public office. In 2008, Americans elected the first African American president, **Barack Obama**.

Americans also tried to use fewer fossil fuels. They made advances in renewable energy, including wind, water, and solar energy. Car makers developed **hybrid** cars that used either gasoline or electricity.

Some factories in the United States closed when jobs moved to other countries.

Barack Obama was elected president of the United States in 2008.

✔ Check Your Understanding

1. At the beginning of the twenty-first century, the average American was expected to live to what age?

2. Name three challenges the United States faced at the beginning of the twenty-first century.

3. What are three renewable forms of energy?

Critical Thinking Recognizing Cause and Effect

4. Why are people living longer?

 Research and Inquiry Use the Internet, the library, or your social studies book to answer these questions.

1. From what country did most of the immigrants to the United States come from last year?

2. What does "outsourcing" mean?

3. Research one form of renewable energy. Describe how it works.

 Writing Did your family or someone you know come to the United States from another part of the world? Write a few sentences telling what you know about that part of the world.

Origins and Structure of Our Government

FOCUS QUESTION

What ideas about government influenced the founders of the United States?

1 republic

2 citizens

3 Magna Carta

4 Jean-Jacques Rousseau

5 John Locke

6 United States Constitution

7 separation of powers

CD 4
TR 41

republic: a form of government in which citizens choose people to represent them and make laws

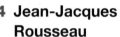

citizens: members of a country, state, or city

Magna Carta: a document the king of England signed into law in 1215 that guaranteed certain rights to people in England

Word Study

Multiple-Meaning Words

The word **right** can be a noun, an adjective, or an adverb.

The noun **right** can mean "something guaranteed by law."

Citizens have the **right** to life, liberty, and property.

The adjective **right** can mean "correct."

The student's answer is **right**.

The adverb **right** can mean "toward the right side."

Turn **right** at the corner to get to the library.

6

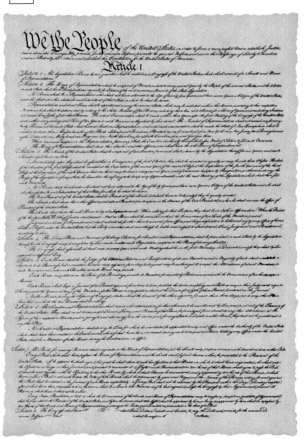

Vocabulary in Context CD 4 TR 42

America's founders were influenced by the ideas of people who lived in earlier times in history. The ancient Romans, the writers of the **Magna Carta**, and the Enlightenment thinkers provided important ideas for America's founders. These ideas were a foundation for the **United States Constitution**.

The idea of a **republic** came from the ancient Romans. In this form of government, **citizens** vote for their representatives.

The idea of basic rights came from documents such as the Magna Carta. It guaranteed some basic rights to the people of England.

America's founders read the ideas of European Enlightenment thinkers such as **John Locke** and **Jean-Jacques Rousseau**. Locke wrote that people have the right to life, liberty, and personal property. Rousseau believed people have the right to choose how they are governed.

The United States government is based on the **separation of powers**. Each part of government is separate and has a special function.

7

separation of powers: when each part of government is separate from the other and has a special function

✔ Check Your Understanding

1. From which ancient civilization did the idea of a republic come?
2. Who was John Locke and what did he believe?
3. What does separation of powers mean?

Critical Thinking Summarizing
4. Name some ideas that influenced America's founders.

📖 Workbook page 209

After winning the American Revolution, the leaders of the new nation wrote the United States Constitution.

Establishing schools is a power reserved to the states.

The Foundations of Government

CD 4
TR 43

When the American colonists declared their independence from Great Britain, they had to create a new government.

Many American leaders had read the works of the Enlightenment thinkers. They agreed that everyone was born with certain rights that could not be taken away by government. The Declaration of Independence states this idea. America's founders agreed that citizens would have basic rights and all people would have to follow the law.

The United States Constitution

CD 4
TR 44

The Constitution is the highest law in the nation. It explains how the national government works.

The national government has certain **expressed powers**. These powers include collecting taxes from citizens, printing money, and declaring war. **Reserved powers** are controlled by the states.

The Constitution can be changed through **amendments**. Amendments are changes that are made to the Constitution. The first 10 amendments are called the **Bill of Rights**.

The Separation of Powers

CD 4
TR 45

The United States government is divided into three **separate** parts or branches. The **legislative** branch makes the laws. The **judicial** branch interprets the laws. The **executive** branch **enforces** the laws.

Having three separate branches of government with different functions is known as the separation of powers. This system provides **checks and balances** in the government. These checks and balances help to make sure that no one branch of government becomes too powerful.

Academic Vocabulary

Word	Explanation	Sample Sentence	Visual Cue
separate (adjective)	apart; not together	In the nineteenth century, boys and girls often sat on **separate** sides of the classroom.	

Legislative Branch	Judicial Branch	Executive Branch
made up of the Senate and House of Representatives	made up of the court system, including the Supreme Court	made up of the president, vice president, and other officials
• makes new laws • changes laws	• interprets the laws	• enforces laws

This table shows each branch of government and what it does.

Social Studies Skill Reading a Table

First, look carefully at the heads of each column in the table. They tell you what information is found in the table. Then, look at the information in the table.

1. Which branch includes the Supreme Court?

2. Which branch includes the president and vice president?

3. Which branch can make or change laws?

✅ Check Your Understanding

1. What Enlightenment idea does the Declaration of Independence reflect?

2. Name one expressed power that the national government has.

3. What does "the separation of powers" in government mean?

Critical Thinking Making Inferences

4. How does a checks and balances system keep one part of government from becoming too powerful?

Research and Inquiry Use the Internet, the library, or your social studies book to answer these questions.

1. What are three freedoms that are guaranteed by the Bill of Rights?

2. How many people make up the Senate and the House of Representatives?

3. Who are the current president and vice president of the United States?

 Writing The United States Constitution was written more than 200 years ago. Why do you think the Constitution has sometimes been changed? Write a paragraph explaining your answer.

Primary Source

Rousseau's *The Social Contract*

"Man is born free, yet everywhere he is found in chains."

Jean-Jacques Rousseau, The Social Contract, 1762

▶ What are some of the "chains," or limitations, on your freedoms?

The Legislative Branch

FOCUS QUESTION
What is the legislative branch of the government?

CD 4
TR 46

1 Congress

2 House of Representatives

3 Senate

4 bill

5 law

6 elect

7 representative

8 committee

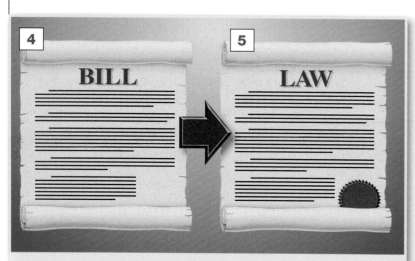

bill: a proposed law
law: a rule made by the government that people must obey

Word Study

Prefixes

The prefixes **con-** and **com-** mean "together" or "with."

A **congress** is a group of people who come together to represent others.

A **committee** is a group of people who work together as a team for a specific purpose.

☐ Gloria Sanchez

☐ Tom Smith

☐ William Lee

Vocabulary in Context CD 4 TR 47

Congress is the legislative branch of government. Members of Congress write **bills** that can become national **laws** in the United States. Congress is made up of two parts, or houses, the **Senate** and the **House of Representatives**. Voters **elect** the members of Congress.

When the United States government was created, leaders debated how many representatives each state should have in Congress. Large states with many people wanted the number of **representatives** to be based on population. Small states with few people argued that each state should have an equal number of representatives.

The leaders reached a compromise. Each state would have representatives based on its population. However, each state would also have two senators, regardless of the state's population.

Once they are elected, senators and representatives serve on Congressional **committees**. These committees work on important issues affecting the entire country as well as individual states.

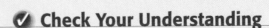

✔ Check Your Understanding

1. What are the two houses of Congress?
2. What did leaders debate when the United States government was created?
3. What are Congressional committees?

Critical Thinking Comparing and Contrasting
4. How are the memberships of the houses of Congress alike and different?

📖 Workbook page 213

The Senate in session

The seal of the United States House of Representatives

The Senate CD 4 TR 48

The Senate has 100 members, two members from each state. Senators are elected for six-year terms. There is no limit on the number of terms they can serve.

The vice president of the United States **presides** over the Senate. If the vice president is absent, the President **Pro Tempore** leads the meeting. The President Pro Tempore is usually the senator with the most years of experience.

The House of Representatives CD 4 TR 49

There are 435 members in the House of Representatives. Every ten years, the number of representatives for each state is **adjusted** based on the state's population. Each state has at least one representative.

Members of the House of Representatives serve two-year terms. There are no limits on the number of terms they can serve.

The Speaker of the House is the leader of the House of Representatives. The speaker is elected by the representatives of the house and presides over house discussions.

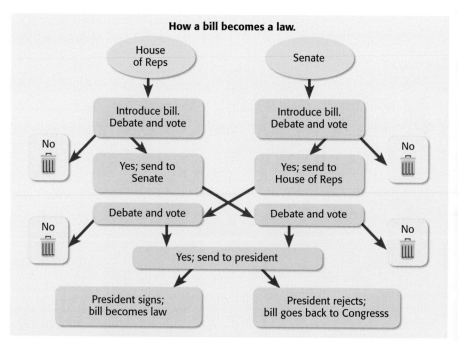

How a bill becomes a law.

Social Studies Skill Reading a Flow Chart

Flow charts show step-by-step how a process works. This flow chart shows how a bill becomes a law.

1. In which house of Congress can a bill be introduced?
2. If the president rejects a bill, what happens to it?

Bills and Congressional Committees

CD 4
TR 50

A bill is a proposal for a new law. If a **majority** in both houses of Congress approves it, the bill goes to the president. The president can sign a bill into law or **veto** it. If the president vetoes it, a two-thirds majority vote is needed to pass the bill into law.

Thousands of bills are presented in Congress every year. Congressional committees study bills and suggest changes to them or **reject** them.

Academic Vocabulary

Word	Explanation	Sample Sentence	Visual Cue
majority (noun)	more than half, but not all	The **majority** of the class voted to take a class trip to Washington, D.C.	

✔ Check Your Understanding

1. How many United States senators are there?
2. What is the leader of the United States House of Representatives called?
3. What is a new proposal for a law called?

Critical Thinking Comparing and Contrasting

4. How are the terms that senators and representatives serve alike and different?

Research and Inquiry Use the Internet, the library, or your social studies book to answer these questions.

1. Who are the United States senators in your state?
2. Who is the representative for your district in Congress?
3. What is the difference between the expressed and implied powers of Congress?

Writing Read the section on *Kids Making a Difference* (*right*) to learn about cyberbullying. Would you support a new law against cyberbullying? Write a letter to your senator or representative expressing the reasons why you support or do not support such a law.

Kids Making a Difference

Speaking to Congress about Cyberbullying

Girl Scout Dominique Napolitano spoke in front of the United States House of Representatives in 2010 about the problem of cyberbullying. Cyberbullying is using the Internet or cell phones to threaten or hurt others. Dominique and other Girl Scouts worked together to create a Web site that provides information about how to use the Internet safely.

▶ If you could speak before Congress about a problem at your school or in your community, what issue would you tell them about?

The Executive Branch

FOCUS QUESTION
What is the executive branch of the government?

1

CD 4
TR 51

1 vice president

2 president

3 cabinet

4 armed forces

5 Washington, D.C.

6 White House

7 ambassador

8 secretary of state

9 veto

cabinet: a group of advisors that the president chooses

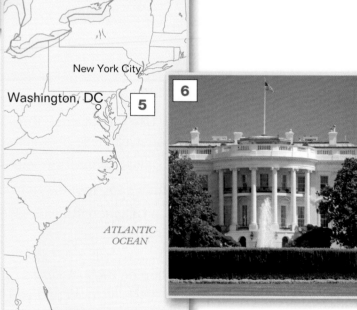

New York City

Washington, DC 5

ATLANTIC OCEAN

Word Study

Multiple-Meaning Words

The word **cabinet** has different meanings.

A **cabinet** can be a cupboard with shelves and doors that is used to store things.

The president's **cabinet** is a group of important government officials who give advice.

ambassador: a government official who represents the president in other countries

secretary of state: the leader of the United States Department of State, which deals with other countries

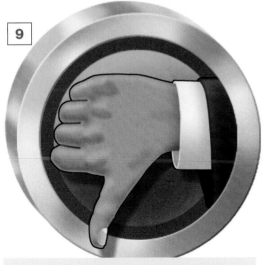

veto: to stop a bill from becoming a law

Vocabulary in Context 🎧 CD 4 TR 52

The executive branch is the part of the United States government that carries out the laws. The executive branch includes the **president**, the **vice president**, and the president's **cabinet**. It also includes the **armed forces** and law enforcement organizations like the Federal Bureau of Investigation (FBI).

The president lives and works in the **White House** in **Washington, D.C.** Leaders from around the world go to the nation's capital to meet with the president. The president represents the United States when visiting other countries. **Ambassadors** serve as the president's representative in other countries, too.

The **secretary of state** and the president work together to develop guidelines to work with other countries. These guidelines are America's foreign policy.

The president has other important responsibilities, such as considering bills that Congress passes. The president can sign a bill into law. If the president disagrees with a bill, the president can **veto** it by refusing to sign it into law. The bill then goes back to Congress.

✔ Check Your Understanding

1. Who is part of the executive branch of the government?
2. Who helps the president develop America's foreign policy?
3. What happens if the president vetoes a bill?

Critical Thinking Hypothesizing

4. Why do you think the president of the United States sends ambassadors to other countries?

📖 Workbook page 217

The office of the president of the United States

Vice President

Speaker of the House

President of the Senate

Secretary of State

Secretary of the Treasury

Secretary of Defense

Attorney General

The first seven officials in the presidential line of succession

President Ronald Reagan's cabinet gave him advice about important issues.

The President and Vice President 🎧 CD 4 TR 53

The president is elected for a four-year **term**. Presidents can serve no more than two terms. The president is the **commander-in-chief** of the **military**. He is also America's main **diplomat** and **negotiates** foreign policy.

If something happens to the president, the vice president is first in line of **succession** to take over the president's duties. The vice president also presides over the Senate.

Congress may **impeach** the president if the members believe the president is guilty of crimes.

Academic Vocabulary

Word	Explanation	Sample Sentence	Visual Cue
succession (noun)	coming after or following another	After President John F. Kennedy was killed, Vice President Lyndon Johnson was next in the line of **succession** to become president.	

Social Studies Skill Interpreting a Diagram

A diagram is a drawing or outline that explains how something works. This diagram shows the order of succession of the first seven government officials to become president should the president resign, become too ill to do the job, or die.

1. Who is first in line to become president should anything happen to the president?
2. Who is the next in line to become president after the secretary of state?

The President's Cabinet 🎧 CD 4 TR 54

The president's cabinet is a group of advisors that the president chooses. Cabinet members give advice related to their departments. The cabinet includes the leaders of the fifteen departments in the government, including the Departments of Education, Transportation, and Energy. The leaders of most cabinet departments are called secretaries. However, the leader of the Department of Justice is called the attorney general.

The President's Rights and Responsibilities CD 4 TR 55

The Constitution lists the president's main responsibilities. For example, the president must report to Congress about the condition of the country. This report is called the State of the Union **address**. The president usually gives this speech at the beginning of each year.

The Constitution also gives the president the right to appoint ambassadors and **Supreme Court** judges and to make **treaties**. The Senate must agree with the president on these decisions.

President Bill Clinton giving his State of the Union address in 1997

✔ Check Your Understanding

1. Who is commander-in-chief of the military?
2. Who is part of the president's cabinet?
3. What is the State of the Union address?

Critical Thinking Making Inferences

4. Why do you think that the president needs advice from the cabinet?

 Research and Inquiry Use the Internet, the library, or your social studies book to answer these questions.

1. Who is the current vice president of the United States?
2. What are the fifteen departments whose leaders are part of the president's cabinet?
3. When and where did President George Washington give the first State of the Union address?

Writing Why do you think someone would want to become president of the United States? Write a paragraph explaining your answer.

Primary Source

The Resolute desk

The Resolute desk has been used by a number of United States presidents. This desk is made from the wood of a British ship, the *HMS Resolute*. The desk was a gift from Queen Victoria of England to President Rutherford Hayes in 1880.

▶ Why do you think the leaders of countries give each other gifts?

The Judicial Branch

FOCUS QUESTION
What is the judicial branch of the government?

CD 4
TR 56

1 **Supreme Court**

2 **federal**

3 **court**

4 **trial**

5 **lawyer**

6 **judge**

7 **appeal**

8 **crime**

1

2

federal: related to the central government of the United States

3

court: a place where a judge and often a jury hear disagreements

Word Study

Multiple-Meaning Words

The word **court** has different meanings.

A **court** of law refers to the place where people argue legal matters before a judge and often a jury.

A **court** is a marked area where people play a sport such as basketball.

4   5   6

trial: a legal process to decide an issue such as guilt or innocence

7

appeal: to ask a higher court to review a lower court's decision

Vocabulary in Context

 CD 4 TR 57

The judicial branch is the part of the United States government that explains and interprets the laws. It includes all the **courts** of the **federal** government. Federal court **judges** hear cases that can affect all the states.

The highest court in the nation is the **Supreme Court.** It is made up of nine judges called justices. The Supreme Court can get rid of or change laws if the justices decide the laws do not agree with the Constitution.

Courts settle disagreements between people, companies, or governments. Some courts also hold **trials** for people accused of **crimes**. In court, **lawyers** represent each side of a case. Lawyers present evidence to support their argument. A judge or jury decides which side is right. If one side disagrees with the court's decision, the lawyers for that side can **appeal** to a higher court.

✔ Check Your Understanding

1. What is the highest court in the nation?
2. What do courts do?
3. Who presents evidence in a court of law?

Critical Thinking Making Observations

4. Look at the picture of the trial. Who do you think is in charge of the courtroom?

8

crime: an action that is against the law

In 1981, Sandra Day O'Connor became the first female justice on the Supreme Court.

Supreme Court:
Mostly reviews appeals; judges, no jury

Courts of Appeal:
Reviews appeals; judges, no jury

District Courts:
New cases; judges and juries

The federal court system

Lawyers present arguments and evidence in court.

The Supreme Court CD 4 TR 58

The Supreme Court explains and interprets the Constitution. Justices are **appointed** by the president and approved by the Senate. The justices serve for life unless they decide to retire. They can be removed from office for wrongdoing. The head judge of the Supreme Court is called the chief justice.

The Supreme Court's decisions are final and cannot be appealed. If the Supreme Court refuses to hear a case from a lower court, then the lower court's decision is final.

The Federal Courts CD 4 TR 59

The district courts and courts of appeal are other examples of federal courts.

District courts are the first level of federal courts. If lawyers appeal a district court case, the court of appeal reviews it.

There are thirteen regional courts of appeal. They are also known as circuit courts.

Social Studies Skill Reading a Diagram

Look at the diagram of the federal court system.
1. In which court do both judges and juries decide cases?
2. Which courts hear appeals?

Court Procedures CD 4 TR 60

When two sides disagree, they can have their case heard before a court. Lawyers present arguments and evidence. Depending on what type of court it is, a jury or judge considers the evidence.

In the Supreme Court, the justices do not always agree. The view of most of the justices is called the majority opinion. The view of the justices who disagree with the majority opinion is called the **dissenting opinion**. If all the justices are in agreement, it is called a **unanimous** decision.

Academic Vocabulary

Word	Explanation	Sample Sentence	Visual Cue
unanimous (adjective)	being in complete agreement	The students were **unanimous** in their decision to take the test before winter break.	

✅ Check Your Understanding

1. What is the head judge of the Supreme Court called?
2. What do we call the lowest courts in the federal court system?
3. What is a dissenting opinion?

Critical Thinking Hypothesizing
4. What are the benefits of having Supreme Court justices serve for life?

 Research and Inquiry Use the Internet, the library, or your social studies book to answer these questions

1. Why is the 1803 case of *Marbury v. Madison* so important for the Supreme Court?
2. Who are the current members of the Supreme Court?
3. Who was the first African American appointed to the Supreme Court? When was he appointed?

 **Writing** What type of person do you think would make a good Supreme Court justice? What kind of education and training do you think the person should have? Write a paragraph explaining your answer.

Quote

"Our Constitution is color-blind … all citizens are equal before the law."

John Marshall Harlan, Supreme Court Justice, 1896

▶ What do you think Justice Harlan meant when he said that the United States Constitution is "color-blind"?

FOCUS QUESTION

What duties, responsibilities, and rights do citizens have?

CD 4
TR 61

1 obey
2 taxes
3 jury
4 vote

5 demonstrate
6 volunteer
7 Bill of Rights

obey: to follow an order or law

taxes: required payments to the government

Word Study

Nouns Used as Verbs

Vote can be a noun or a verb.

In the following sentence, **vote** is a noun:

They counted the **votes** after the election.

In the following sentence, **vote** is a verb:

José **voted** in the class election.

5

demonstrate: to march in protest

6

volunteer: to give or offer a service without being paid

Vocabulary in Context CD 4 TR 62

In the United States, citizens have duties, or things they must do. They must **obey** the law and they must pay their **taxes**. If they are asked to serve on a **jury**, they must appear in court.

Citizens also have responsibilities, or things they should do. For example, it is their responsibility to **vote** in elections. Citizens should stay informed about important issues and speak up if they think that something is unfair. They can write to members of Congress or **demonstrate** to make things better in society. They also should **volunteer** to improve their community by doing such things as helping in hospitals.

In addition to duties and responsibilities, citizens also have civil rights. The **Bill of Rights** contains the first ten amendments, or additions, to the Constitution. These first ten amendments guarantee people important freedoms. These freedoms include the right to speak freely and the right to follow any or no religion.

✔ Check Your Understanding

1. What are two duties of a citizen?
2. What is the Bill of Rights?
3. What are two freedoms guaranteed by the Constitution?

Critical Thinking Hypothesizing

4. How does a community benefit when citizens volunteer their time?

7

Workbook page 225

Citizens are required to obey all laws.

Duties of Citizens CD 4 TR 63

Citizens have certain duties. One of the things they must do is obey city, state, and national laws. Obeying laws protects individuals and property and can prevent problems between people and groups. Those individuals who do not obey the law can be punished.

In addition, citizens may be required to serve in the armed forces during times of war.

Social Studies Skill — Analyzing a Comparison Chart

A comparison chart compares the characteristics of something. This comparison chart compares the duties, responsibilities, and rights of a citizen.

1. Is serving on a jury a duty or a right?
2. Name one of the responsibilities of a citizen.
3. Which of the rights listed do you think is the most important? Why?

Duties	Responsibilities	Rights
obey the law	vote in elections	speak freely
pay taxes	volunteer in community	meet peacefully
serve on a jury	stay informed	follow any or no religion
serve in armed forces, if called	speak up if something is unfair	have a public trial if accused of a crime

A comparison chart of some of the duties, responsibilities, and rights of citizens

Responsibilities of Citizens CD 4 TR 64

Participating in civic life is one of the responsibilities of a citizen. All citizens should stay informed about important issues. One way to stay informed is to participate in the government. Citizens take part in government by voting and expressing their ideas to their representatives. Responsible citizens also volunteer to improve their communities.

American citizens are part of a **global** community. Because of this, they should also stay informed about events in other parts of the world.

Citizens can speak at government meetings to express their ideas.

Rights of Citizens CD 4 TR 65

The Bill of Rights provides people in the United States with basic rights. These rights include freedom of speech, the freedom to meet peacefully, and the freedom to demonstrate peacefully.

All citizens have the right to a trial by jury. Every person **accused** of a crime has the right to a public trial and the right to have a lawyer. If a person cannot afford a lawyer, the court must provide one.

These citizens are demonstrating peacefully.

Academic Vocabulary

Word	Explanation	Sample Sentence	Visual Cue
accuse (verb)	to blame or charge someone with wrongdoing	Jennifer **accused** Paul of starting the argument.	

 ✔ Check Your Understanding

1. How is obeying laws good for society?
2. What is an example of a responsibility that citizens have?
3. What are two basic rights of every person accused of a crime?

Critical Thinking Comparing and Contrasting
4. How is a duty different from a responsibility?

Research and Inquiry Use the Internet, the library, or your social studies book to answer these questions.

1. Is there a sales tax in your state? If so, how much is it?
2. Why is the 1963 Supreme Court case *Gideon v. Wainright* important?
3. Which Supreme Court case ruled that people accused of a crime cannot be questioned until they are informed of their rights?

Writing What issue is so important to you that you would volunteer your time to support it? Why is this issue important to you? Write a paragraph expressing the reasons why you would volunteer to support this issue.

Kids Making a Difference

Ryan's Well Foundation

When he was younger, Ryan Hreljac learned in school that polluted water led to disease and death in many parts of the world. He decided to raise money to help solve the problem. In 1999, his organization, Ryan's Well Foundation, built its first well in an African village. Today, Ryan's organization brings clean water to communities around the world.

▶ If you could start an organization to solve a problem in the world, what would it be? What would you name your organization? What problem would it solve?

Voting and Elections

FOCUS QUESTION
How are government leaders elected in the United States?

CD 4
TD 66

1 election
2 campaign
3 candidate

4 politician
5 Democratic Party
6 Republican Party

election: an organized event at which people vote

campaign: an organized series of actions to win a political position
candidate: a person who is competing to win a public office

Word Study

Multiple-Meaning Words

The word **party** has different meanings.

A **party** can be a political group with a particular set of beliefs.

There are two major political **parties** in the United States.

The word **party** can also be a social event where people drink, eat, and have fun.

We went to a **party** on New Year's Eve.

politician: a person who is competing for, or already holds, public office

5

6

Vocabulary in Context CD 4 TD 67

Citizens of the United States have the right to vote. People are not required to vote, but it is the responsibility of every citizen over the age of eighteen.

During **campaigns, candidates** say what they believe about important issues. During an **election**, citizens vote for candidates to represent them in the government. Citizens can vote **politicians** into or out of government positions.

The two major political parties, or groups, in the United States are the **Democratic Party** and the **Republican Party**. In general, the Democratic Party supports social and economic programs for Americans. Americans must pay for these programs with taxes. The Republican Party generally believes in lower taxes. This sometimes limits the party's support for social and economic programs.

Republicans encourage the growth of business to create more jobs. They want fewer government rules for businesses. Democrats also want a strong economy, but they believe in government rules for businesses.

✓ Check Your Understanding

1. Look at the symbols of the two major political parties. Which animal represents each party?
2. What is a campaign?
3. What happens during an election?

Critical Thinking Summarizing
4. What are some of the main differences between the Democratic and Republican parties?

📖 Workbook page 229

Voters make their choices on a ballot.

Special interest groups try to influence government policy.

Special Interest Group	Concerns
American Association of Retired Persons (AARP)	Issues that affect people aged 50 and over
American Federation of Labor/Congress of Industrial Organizations (AFL/CIO)	Issues affecting workers
American Medical Association (AMA)	Issues affecting medical doctors
League of United Latin American Citizens (LULAC)	Issues affecting Latinos
National Association for the Advancement of Colored People (NAACP)	Issues affecting African Americans
National Association of Manufacturers (NAM)	Issues affecting owners of industries
National Organization for Women (NOW)	Issues affecting women

Some special interest groups and the issues that concern them

Voters and the Voting Process CD 4 TD 68

In order to vote in elections, a person must be a citizen of the United States. Voters also must be at least eighteen years old.

In most states, citizens must **register** to vote before Election Day. After registering, voters receive information telling them where they should go to vote. On Election Day, people go to their **polling station** and select their candidate. Voters who are unable to get to their polling station can vote by **absentee ballot**.

Academic Vocabulary

Word	Explanation	Sample Sentence	Visual Cue
register (verb)	to sign up for something	Students must **register** at school before they can attend.	

Political Parties and Special Interest Groups CD 4 TD 69

Since 1853, the president of the United States has been either a Democrat or a Republican. However, candidates who are members of smaller political parties, such as the Green Party, also run for political office.

In addition to political parties, **special interest groups** try to influence government policy. These groups bring together people who share ideas or interests. Some groups are based on economic interests. Others are formed to represent certain groups of people.

Social Studies Skill Reading a Table

First, look carefully at the heads of each column in the table. They tell what information is found in the table. Then look at the information in each column and answer the questions below.

1. Which organization is concerned with issues that affect people over the age of 50?
2. What does "NOW" stand for?
3. Which organization is concerned with issues affecting medical doctors?

Presidential Election Campaigns 🎧 CD 4 TD 70

In the United States, presidential elections are held every four years. However, candidates begin their campaigns many months before the election.

In an election year, most states have **primary elections** at the beginning of the year to choose the top candidates. During the summer, political parties have **conventions** to select their candidates for president and vice president. The presidential election is held in November and the newly elected president takes office the following January.

Presidential conventions are usually held in the summer.

✔ Check Your Understanding

1. How old must a citizen be to vote in the United States?
2. What are special interest groups?
3. How often are presidential elections held?

Critical Thinking Relating to Your Own Experiences

4. Would you consider running for student government at your school? Why or why not?

 Research and Inquiry Use the Internet, the library, or your social studies book to answer these questions.

1. What amendment made 18 the voting age?
2. Select a special interest group and research its work. What is its main concern? Where is the group's headquarters located?
3. Which state traditionally holds the first primary election in presidential elections?

 Writing What do you think is the most important issue in America today? Would you join a special interest group to try to influence government policy on this issue? Why or why not? Write a paragraph expressing your ideas.

Primary Source

The 22ⁿᵈ Amendment to the United States Constitution

"No person shall be elected to the office of the President more than twice…"

▶ Do you agree that the president should be in office for no more than two terms?

Franklin D. Roosevelt was the only United States president who served more than two terms.

Governments Around the World

What forms of government exist in the world?

CD 4
TR 71

1 government
2 dictatorship
3 monarchy
4 military dictatorship

5 theocracy
6 democracy
7 parliament
8 prime minister

1
government: the political system that rules or controls a country or area

2

dictatorship: a form of government in which one ruler has total power

3

monarchy: a form of government in which a member of a royal family rules or has a symbolic role

4

military dictatorship: a form of government in which a group of military officers rules a country with total power

Word Study

Word Parts

The word **theocracy** comes from the Greek language.

The word part **theo-** means "god."

The word part **-cracy** means "rule."

A **theocracy** is a government ruled by religious leaders.

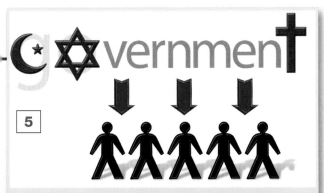

theocracy: a government ruled by religious law

democracy: a government elected by the people

parliament: a legislative body, led by a prime minister, that makes or changes laws in a country or state

prime minister: usually the political leader in a country that has a parliament

Vocabulary in Context CD 4 TR 72

There are many forms of **government** throughout the world.

Some governments have just one person who rules the entire nation. In a **dictatorship**, one person has total control of the government. In a **monarchy**, members of a royal family usually inherit their positions.

Military leaders or religious leaders run the government in some parts of the world. In some countries, a small group of people, such as a **military dictatorship**, rules the country. In other countries, religious leaders control the laws. This kind of government is called a **theocracy**. Religious law is the foundation of the government in a theocracy.

Governments in which the people elect their leaders are called **democracies**. In representative democracies, politicians represent the interests of the people who elected them. Some of these democratic governments have a **parliament** that makes and changes laws. The leader of the parliament is often called the **prime minister**.

✔ Check Your Understanding

1. Name two forms of government in which one person rules the nation.
2. What is a military dictatorship?
3. What form of government has religious law as its foundation?

Critical Thinking Summarizing
4. Describe the main characteristics of each of these forms of government: dictatorship, monarchy, military dictatorship, theocracy, democracy.

📖 Workbook page 233

Dictator Rafael Trujillo used military force to rule the Dominican Republic.

Today, the emperor of Japan is the head of state, but the prime minister has the real governing power.

Indira Gandhi, prime minister of India, walks past Indian soldiers on Republic Day, 1967.

Government by Dictatorship   CD 4 TR 73

In a dictatorship, one person rules the country with total power. Often this person is not elected by the people and usually rules by force. Sometimes a dictator takes control by a **coup d'etat,** a sudden overthrow of the government. Usually dictators do not allow any opposing political parties and do not **hold** elections.

Academic Vocabulary

Word	Explanation	Sample Sentence	Visual Cue
hold (verb)	to cause (an event) to take place	The school **holds** a big dance every spring.	

Government by Many People CD 4 TR 74

In parliamentary governments, the executive branch is made up of **ministers** chosen from the parliament. Great Britain's Parliament includes the House of Commons and the House of Lords. Members of Parliament work together to make and change laws.

Parliamentary systems often have a **figurehead** such as a king, a queen, or an emperor. This figurehead serves as **head of state**, but has no real governing power. For example, in Japan, the emperor is the head of state, but the country is ruled by a prime minister and other government leaders.

Democracy as a Form of Government CD 4 TR 75

In a democracy, the people have a voice in government through voting. In representative democracies, such as the United States, citizens elect people to represent them in government.

Other countries, such as Bangladesh, Mexico, and South Africa, also have representative democracies. Some of these countries are led by a president, others by a prime minister.

Social Studies Skill Reading a Political Map

This map shows countries with a system of democratic elections in 2010. Look at this map and the map of the world on page 243 to answer the questions.

1. In 2010, approximately what percentage of countries in the world had a system of democratic elections?

2. Locate and name three countries in Asia that had a system of democratic elections in 2010.

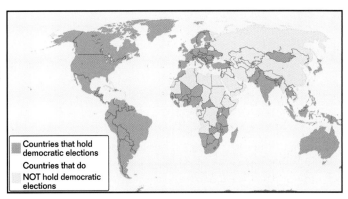

Countries that hold democratic elections

Countries that do NOT hold democratic elections

Countries with a system of democratic elections, 2010

✔ Check Your Understanding

1. What is a coup d'etat?

2. What are the two houses that make up the British Parliament?

3. What is a figurehead?

Critical Thinking Making Inferences

4. Dictators do not allow opposing political parties or democratic elections. Explain why.

Research and Inquiry Use the Internet, the library, or your social studies book to answer these questions.

1. Research the government of another country. How is it similar to the United States? How are the two governments different?

2. Research and describe the British Parliament. How many members are elected to this government body?

3. In the late 1800s and early 1900s, the emperor of Japan had great power. When and why did the emperor become a figurehead?

Writing Which form of government do you think is best? Why? Write a paragraph explaining your choice.

Kids Making a Difference

The Model United Nations

In the Model United Nations, students learn about different countries and the issues they face. Then they get together and role-play a country. This gives students a chance to learn about real-life international relations.

▶ If you could participate in a Model United Nations exercise, which country would you like to represent? Why?

The United States and Canada

Map of the World

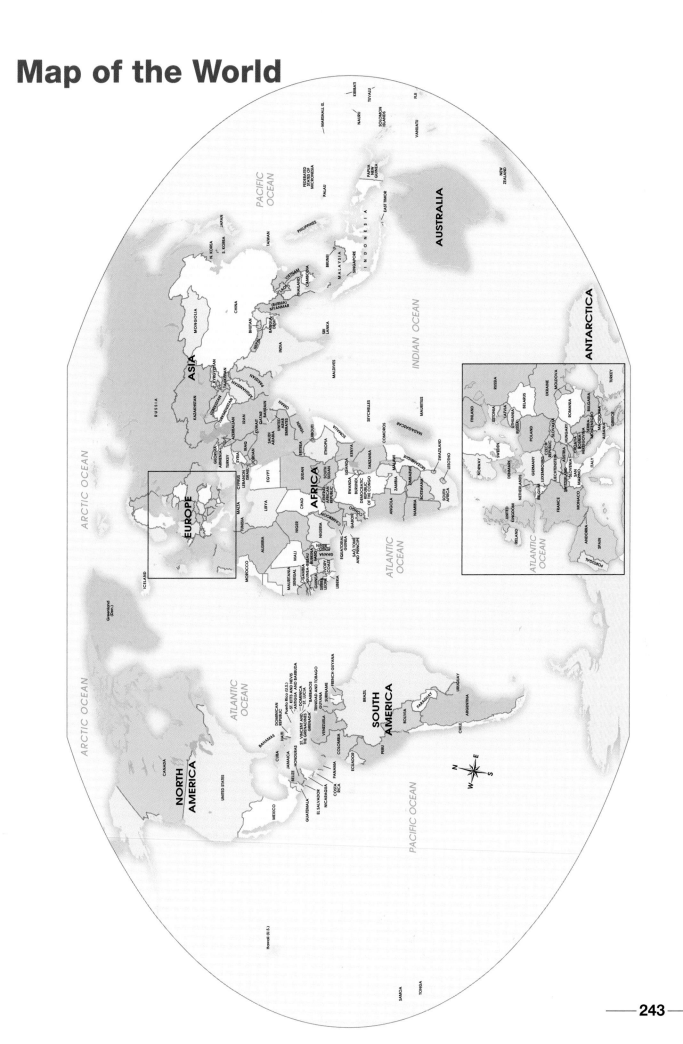

Glossary
with Spanish Translations

Pronunciation Key

a	apple	o	fox
ah	father	oh	know, go
air	where, pear	oo	through, to
ar	hard	yoo	few, music
ay	away, they	or	orange, door
aw	law, off	oi	oil, annoy
e	let, thread	ow	how, about
ee	tree, sea	u	put, book
eer	fear, here	uh	cut, awake
eye	nine, by	er	were, water
i	lips		

19ᵗʰ Amendment /neyen-TEENTH ah-MEND-ment/ *(noun)* The 19th Amendment is the amendment added to the United States Constitution in 1920 that gave women the right to vote. *page 186* [Enmienda 19]

A

abandon /uh-BAN-duhn/ *(verb)* If you abandon a place, thing, or person, you leave permanently or for a long time. *page 76* [abandonar]

abdicate /AB-duh-cate/ *(verb)* If a king or queen abdicates, he or she gives up being king or queen. *page 107* [abdicar]

abolitionist /ab-o-LISH-uh-nist/ *(noun)* An abolitionist is someone who campaigns for the abolition of a particular system or practice. Before emancipation in the United States, abolitionists worked to end the practice of slavery. *page 158* [abolicionista]

Aborigine /a-bor-RIJ-nee/ *(noun)* Aborigines are members of the tribes that were living in Australia when Europeans arrived there. *page 47* [aborigen]

A.D. /AY DEE/ *(adjective)* A.D. is an abbreviation for the Latin phrase "anno domini," which means "year of our Lord" in English. You use A.D. with years, for example "90 A.D.," to indicate that you are referring to a time after the year in which Jesus Christ is believed to have been born. *(page 7)* [A.D.]

address /ad-DRESS/ *(noun)* An address is a formal speech usually given to an audience. *page 225* [discurso]

adjust /ad-JUHST/ *(verb)* If you adjust something, you change it so that it is more effective or appropriate. *page 220* [ajustar, arreglar]

adobe /ah-DOH-bee/ *(noun)* Adobe is a mix of mud and straw that is dried into bricks in the sun and used for building. *page 128* [adobe]

advisor /ad-VEYE-zor/ (*noun*) An advisor is an expert whose job is to give advice to another person or to a group of people. *page 206* [consejero]

afterlife /AF-ter-leyeph/ (*noun*) The afterlife is a life that some people believe begins when you die. *page 60* [vida después de la muerte]

Al Qaeda /al KEYE-da/ (*noun*) Al Qaeda is a terrorist group who said that they were responsible for the terrorist attacks in the United States on September 11, 2001. *page 213* [Al Qaeda]

Allied Powers /AL-eyed POW-erz/ (*noun*) A group of countries fighting together in World War I and World War II including Great Britain, France, Russia, and the United States. *pages 110, 116* [Aliados]

ally /al-LEYE/ (*noun*) An ally is a country, friend, or organization that supports another one, especially in war. *page 111* [aliado(a)]

alphabet /AL-fa-bet/ (*noun*) An alphabet is a set of symbols, usually presented in a fixed order, used for writing words. *page 54* [alfabeto]

Alps /ALPZ/ (*noun*) The Alps are a large mountain range in Europe. *page 26* [los Alpes]

Amazon River /AM-ah-zon RIV-er/ (*noun*) The Amazon River is the largest river in the world and is located in South America. *page 22* [Río Amazonas]

ambassador /am-BASS-a-dor/ (*noun*) An ambassador is an important official who lives in a foreign country and represents his or her national leader and the interests of his or her own country. *page 223* [embajador(a)]

Americas /uh-MER-i-kuhz/ (*noun*) People sometimes refer to North America, Central America, South America, and the Caribbean collectively as the Americas. *page 126* [Américas]

ancestor /AN-ses-tor/ (*noun*) Your ancestors are the people from whom you are descended. *page 50* [antepasado(a), antecesor]

ancient Greece /AYN-shent GREES/ (*noun*) Ancient Greece was a civilization in the 5th and 4th centuries B.C.E. known for its advanced politics and culture. *page 62* [Grecia Antigua]

Andes Mountains /AN-deez MOWNT-enz/ (*noun*) The Andes Mountains are the longest mountain range in the world, extending 4,500 miles from Venezuela to Chile. *page 22* [los Andes, Cordillera de los Andes]

Antarctic Circle /ant-ARC-tik SER-kuhl/ (*noun*) The Arctic Circle is an imaginary line drawn around the southern part of the world at approximately 66° south. *page 2* [Círculo Antártico]

Anti-Federalist /AN-tee FED-er-al-ist/ (*adjective*) A political party of the early United States that believed that the states should have most of the power in government. *page 144* [anti-federalista]

apartment /uh-PART-ment/ (*noun*) An apartment is a set of rooms for living in, usually on one floor of a large building. *page 101* [apartamento]

appeal /ah-PEEL/ (*verb*) If you appeal a decision to someone in authority, you formally ask them to change it. An appeal to a higher court asks them to reverse a lower court's decision. *page 227* [apelar]

Arab /A-rab/ (*noun*) An Arab is a person who speaks Arabic and who comes from the Middle East or part of North Africa. *pages 30, 120* [árabe]

archaeologist /ark-ee-OL-o-jist/ (*noun*) An archaeologist is someone who studies the past by examining the remains of things such as buildings, tools, and other objects. *page 59* [arqueólogo]

architecture /ARK-i-tekt-chur/ (*noun*) Architecture is the art of planning, designing, and constructing buildings. *page 82* [arquitectura]

Arctic /ARK-tik/ (*noun*) The Arctic is an area of the world around the North Pole. It is extremely cold and there is very little light in winter and very little darkness in summer. *page 128* [Ártico]

Arctic Circle /ARK-tik SER-kuhl/ (*noun*) The Arctic Circle is an imaginary line drawn around the northern part of the world at approximately 66° north. *page 2* [Círculo Ártico]

Arctic Ocean /ARK-tik OH-shuhn/ (*noun*) The Arctic Ocean is the ocean north of the Arctic Circle. *page 18* [Océano Ártico]

arid /A-rid/ (*adjective*) Arid land is very dry. Very few plants can grow on it. *page 32* [árido]

armaments /AR-mah-ments/ (noun) Armaments are weapons and military equipment belonging to an army or country. *page 196* [armamento]

armed forces /AHRMD FOR-ses/ (noun) The armed forces are the military forces of a nation. *pages 200, 222* [fuerzas armadas]

army /AR-mee/ (noun) An army is a large organized group of people who are armed and trained to fight on land in a war. Most armies are organized and controlled by governments. *pages 141, 183* [ejército]

arrest /a-REST/ (verb) If the police arrest you, they take charge of you and take you to a police station because they believe you may have committed a crime. *page 204* [arestar]

arroyo /a-ROI-o/ (noun) An arroyo is a low area in the desert that flows with water when it rains. *(page 13)* [arroyo]

Articles of Confederation /AR-tik-cuhls ov con-fed-er-AY-shuhn/ (noun) The Articles of Confederation was the first governing document of the United States. *page 142* [Artículos de la Confederación]

artifact /AR-ti-fact/ (noun) An artifact is an ornament, tool, or other object that was made by a human being. *page 56* [objeto, artefacto]

assassinate /a-SAS-in-ayt/ (verb) When someone important is assassinated, they are murdered as a political act. *page 165* [asesinar]

assembly line /a-SEM-blee LEYEN/ (noun) An assembly line is an arrangement of workers and machines in a factory, where each worker deals with only one part of the production process. The product passes from one worker to another until it is finished. *page 170* [cadena de montaje, cadena de ensamblaje]

astronaut /AS-truh-nawt/ (noun) An astronaut is a person who is trained for traveling in a spacecraft. *page 120* [astronauta]

astronomer /as-TRON-uh-mer/ (noun) An astronomer studies the science of the stars, planets, and other natural objects in space. *page 76* [astrónomo(a)]

Atlantic Ocean /at-LAN-tik OH-shuhn/ (noun) The Atlantic Ocean is the body of water that separates the Americas from Europe and Africa. *page 18* [Océano Atlántico]

atomic bomb /a-TOM-ic BOM/ (noun) An atomic bomb or atom bomb is a bomb that causes an explosion by a sudden release of energy that results from splitting atoms. *pages 116, 195* [bomba atómica]

Australia /aw-STRAL-ya/ (noun) Australia is a conintent and a country. It is located between the Indian and Pacific oceans. Australia has tropical areas as well as mild climates. *page 47* [Australia]

Aztec /AZ-tek/ (noun) The Aztecs were indigenous people who lived in what is now central Mexico between about 1100 C.E. and 1520 C.E. *page 75* [Azteca]

B

barge /BARJ/ (noun) A barge is a long, narrow boat with a flat bottom, used for carrying heavy loads. *page 100* [barca de transporte]

bark /BARK/ (noun) Bark is the tough material that covers the outside of a tree. *page 128* [corteza de árbol]

barn /BARN/ (noun) A barn is a building on a farm in which animals, animal food, or crops can be kept. *page 148* [granero, establo]

barter /BAR-ter/ (verb) To barter is to exchange goods for other goods, rather than selling them for money. *page 16* [intercambiar]

Battle of Gettysburg /BA-tul UHV GET-eez-berg/ (noun) The Battle of Gettysburg occurred during the Civil War in July 1863 and helped to weaken the Confederacy. *page 163* [Batalla de Gettysburg]

B.C./B.C.E. /BEE CEE EE/ (adjective) Non-Christians often use B.C.E. instead of B.C. in dates to indicate a number of years or centuries before the year in which Jesus Christ is believed to have been born. B.C.E. is an abbreviation for "Before the Common Era." *page 6* [antes de Cristo]

Bedouin /BE-doo-in/ (noun) A Bedouin is a member of a particular Arab tribe. *page 32* [beduino(a)]

bill /BIL/ (noun) In government, a bill is a formal statement of a proposed new law that is discussed and then voted on. *page 218* [proyecto de ley]

Bill of Rights /BIL uhv REYETZ/ *(noun)* The Bill of Rights contains the first ten amendments, or additions, to the Constitution. These first ten amendments guarantee people important freedoms. *page 230* **[Carta de Derechos]**

bishop /BI-shuhp/ *(noun)* A bishop is a high-ranking member of the clergy. *page 68* **[obispo]**

blitzkrieg /BLITZ-kreeg/ *(noun)* A blitzkrieg is a surprise attack from both land and air. *page 116* **[guerra relámpago]**

blockade /blok-AYD/ *(verb)* If a group of people blockade a place, they stop goods or people from reaching that place. If they blockade a road or a port, they stop people from using that road or port. *page 164* **[bloqueo]**

bomb /BOM/ *(noun)* A bomb is a device that explodes and damages or destroys a large area. *page 114* **[bomba]**

border /BOR-der/ *(noun)* The border between two countries or regions is the dividing line between them. The border also refers to the land close to this line. *pages 120, 144, 151* **[borde, frontera]**

boycott /BOI-cot/ *(noun)* A boycott is when a country, group, or person refuses to be involved with a country, organization, or activity in any way. *page 138* **[boicotear, hacer un boicot]**

breakthrough /BRAYK-thru/ *(noun)* A breakthrough is an important development or achievement. *page 213* **[adelanto]**

Buddhism /BUD-izm/ *(noun)* Buddhism is a religion which teaches that the way to end suffering is by overcoming your desires. *page 48* **[Budismo]**

buffalo /BUF-a-loh/ *(noun)* A buffalo is a wild animal like a large cow with horns that curve upwards. *page 146* **[búfalo]**

Buffalo Soldiers /BUF-a-lo SOL-djers/ *(noun)* Buffalo Soldiers were African American soldiers who fought in the Spanish-American War. *page 174* **[Soldados afro-americanos que fajaron en la Guerra entre España y los Estados Unidos]**

built environment /BILT en-VEYE-ruhn-ment/ *(noun)* A built environment is created by humans. It includes all human-made structures such as houses, cities, and monuments. *page 14* **[ambiente hecho, ambiente construido]**

C

cabinet /KAB-i-net/ *(noun)* The cabinet is a group of advisors that the president chooses. *page 222* **[consejo de ministros]**

cadaver /kuh-DA-ver/ *(noun)* A cadaver is a dead body. *page 84* **[cadáver]**

camel /KA-mel/ *(noun)* A camel is a desert animal with one or two humps on its back. *page 30* **[camello]**

camera /KA-me-ra/ *(noun)* A camera is a piece of equipment that is used for taking photographs. *page 179* **[cámara]**

campaign /kam-PAYN/ *(noun)* A campaign is a planned set of activities that people carry out over a period of time in order to achieve social or political change, to win a political position. *pages 184, 234* **[campaña]**

canal /kuh-NAL/ *(noun)* A canal is a long, narrow, human-made stretch of water. *page 100* **[canal]**

candidate /KAN-di-dayt/ *(noun)* A candidate is a person who is competing to win a political position. *page 234* **[candidato(a)]**

canyon /KAN-yun/ *(noun)* A canyon is a long, narrow valley with very steep sides. *page 11* **[cañón]**

Caribbean /kar-i-BEE-en/ *(noun)* The Caribbean includes the islands of the Caribbean Sea. *page 175* **[Caribe]**

cash crop /KASH KROP/ *(noun)* A cash crop is a crop that is grown in order to be sold. *page 136* **[cultivo comercial]**

castle /KA-suhl/ *(noun)* A castle is a large building with thick, high walls built in the past to protect people during wars and battles. *page 66* **[castillo]**

Catholic Church /KATH-oh-lik CHERCH/ *(noun)* The Catholic Church is the branch of the Christian Church that accepts the pope as its leader and is based in the Vatican in Rome. *page 86* **[iglesia católica]**

cattle /KA-tuhl/ *(noun)* Cattle are cows and bulls. *page 154* **[ganado]**

cause /KAWZ/ *(noun)* The cause of an event is the thing that makes it happen. *page 140* **[causa]**

C.E. /see ee/ (adjective) Non-Christians often use C.E. instead of A.D. with years to indicate a time after the year in which Jesus Christ is believed to have been born. C.E. is an abbreviation for "Common Era." *page 6* [era común]

cease-fire /SEES FEYE-er/ (noun) A cease-fire is an arrangement in which countries at war agree to stop fighting for a time. *page 112* [cese al fuego]

cell phone /SEL FOHN/ (noun) A cell phone is a type of telephone that does not need wires to connect it to a telephone system. *page 122* [teléfono celular]

Central America /SEN-tral am-ER-i-cuh/ (noun) Central America includes the countries on the North American continent south of Mexico and north of Colombia in South America. *page 176* [América Central]

Central Powers /SEN-tral POW-erz/ (noun) The Central Powers was a group of countries fighting together in World War I including Germany, Austria-Hungary, Bulgaria, and the Ottoman Empire. *page 110* [Potencias Centrales]

century /SEN-chur-ee/ (noun) A century is any period of a hundred years. *page 6* [siglo]

challenge /CHA-lenj/ (verb) **1.** If you challenge someone, you invite them to fight or compete with you in some way. *page 105* [retar, desafiar]

(noun) **2.** A challenge to someone is an act of questioning their authority. *page 204* [desafío]

chickee /CHIK-ee/ (noun) A chickee is an open-sided structure with palms for a roof. The bottom floor of chickees was raised to protect the house from flooding and from animals. *page 129* [casa de indígenos]

child mortality /CHEYELD mawr-TAL-i-tee/ (noun) Child mortality is the number of children who die each year under the age of 5. *page 37* [mortalidad infantil]

Chinese characters /cheye-NEEZ KAR-ak-terz/ (noun) Chinese characters are the symbols used to write the Chinese language. *page 42* [caracteres chinos]

Christianity /kris-chee-AN-i-tee/ (noun) Christianity is a religion based on the teachings of Jesus Christ. *page 65* [cristianidad]

chronological order /kron-o-LOJ-i-kal OR-der/ (adjective) If things are described or shown in chronological order, they are described or shown in the order in which they happened. *page 6* [orden cronológica]

cinnamon /SIN-a-muhn/ (noun) Cinnamon is a sweet spice used for flavoring food. *page 70* [canela]

citizen /SIT-i-zen/ (noun) A citizen of a particular country is someone who is legally accepted as belonging to that country. *pages 62, 214* [ciudadano(a)]

city /SIT-ee/ (noun) A city is a large town. *page 14* [ciudad]

city-state /SIT-ee stayt/ (noun) Ancient Greeks lived in areas called city-states. A city-state had its own laws and government. *page 64* [ciudad-estado]

civil rights /SIV-il reyets/ (noun) Civil rights are the rights that people have in a society to equal treatment and equal opportunities, whatever their race, sex, or religion. *page 202* [derechos civiles]

civil war /SIV-il wawr/ (noun) A civil war is a war that is fought between different groups of people who live in the same country. *page 159* [guerra civil]

civilization /siv-il-i-ZAY-shuhn/ (noun) A civilization is a human society with its own social organization and culture. *page 54* [civilización]

claim /KLAYM/ (verb) If you claim something, you try to get it because you think you have a right to it. *pages 80, 132* [reclamar]

cliff /KLIF/ (noun) A cliff is a high area of land with a very steep side, especially one next to the sea. *page 11* [acantilado]

climate /KLEYE-mit/ (noun) The climate of a particular country or area is the type of weather that it has over a long period of time. *page 32* [clima]

coal /KOHL/ (noun) Coal is a hard, black substance that is extracted from the ground and burned as fuel. *page 100* [carbón]

coast /KOHST/ (noun) The coast is an area of land that is next to the sea. *page 20* [costa]

coffee /kawf-fee/ (noun) **1.** Coffee is the roasted beans of the coffee plant. **2.** Coffee is a drink made from boiling water and ground or powdered coffee beans. *page 94* [café]

Cold War /KOHLD WOR/ (noun) The Cold War was the period of hostility and tension between the Soviet bloc and the Western powers that followed World War II. *pages 118, 200* [**Guerra Fría**]

college /KOL-ej/ (noun) A college is an institution where students study after they have left secondary school. *page 198* [**universidad**]

colonize /KOL-uh-neyez/ (verb) If people colonize a foreign country, they go to live there and take control of it. *pages 24, 81, 118* [**colonizar**]

colony /KOL-uh-nee/ (noun) A colony is a country that is controlled by a more powerful country. *pages 20, 105, 130* [**colonia**]

column /KOL-uhm/ (noun) A column is a tall, often decorated cylinder of stone that forms part of a building. *page 62* [**columna**]

commander-in-chief /ko-MAN-der in cheef/ (noun) The president of the United States is the commander-in-chief, or leader of the military. *page 224* [**comandante en jefe**]

commerce /KOM-mers/ (noun) Commerce is the activities and procedures involved in buying and selling things. *page 144* [**comercio**]

committee /kuh-MIT-ee/ (noun) A committee is a group of people who meet to make decisions or plans for a larger group or organization that they represent. *page 218* [**comité**]

communicate /ko-MY-ni-kayt/ (verb) If you communicate with someone, you share information, for example by speaking, writing, or sending radio signals. *page 41* [**comunicar**]

communism /KOM-yoo-nizm/ (noun) Communism is the political belief that all people are equal, that there should be no private ownership, and that workers should control the means of producing things. *page 118* [**comunismo**]

compass rose /KOM-pas rohz/ (noun) A compass rose shows the directions north, south, east, and west on a map. *page 4* [**rosa de los vientos**]

compromise /KOM-pro-meyez/ (noun) A compromise is a situation in which people accept something slightly different from what they really want, either because of circumstances, or because they are considering the wishes of other people. *page 184* [**solución intermedia**]

computer /kom-PYOO-ter/ (noun) A computer is an electronic machine that can be used for storing and dealing with large amounts of information and for communicating on the Internet. *page 122* [**computadora**]

concentration camp /kon-sen-TRAY-shuhn camp/ (noun) A concentration camp is a place where captured soldiers or ordinary people thought to be enemies of the state are kept in very upleasant conditions during a war. *page 116* [**campo de concentración**]

concept map /KON-sept map/ (noun) A concept map organizes information so the reader can see how ideas are connected. *page 92* [**mapa de concepto**]

Confederacy /kon-FED-er-ah-see/ (noun) The Confederacy was the government formed by the states that seceded from the United States in 1860 and 1861. *pages 161, 162* [**Confederación**]

conflict /CON-flikt/ (noun) Conflict is an angry disagreement between people and groups. *page 33* [**conflicto**]

congestion /kon-JESH-chin/ (noun) If there is congestion in a place, the place is crowded with traffic or people, so that it is difficult to move. *page 200* [**congestión**]

Congress /KON-gres/ (noun) Congress is the elected group of politicians that is responsible for making the law in the United States. It consists of two parts: the House of Representatives and the Senate. *page 218* [**congreso**]

connect /ka-NEKT/ (verb) If something or someone connects one thing to another, or if one thing connects to another, the two things are joined together. *page 176* [**conectar (cosas), relacionar (gente ó ideas)**]

conquer /KON-ker/ (verb) If one country or group of people conquers another, they take complete control of the people and their land. *pages 80, 104* [**conquistar**]

constitution /kon-sti-TOO-shuhn/ (noun) The constitution of a country is the system of laws which formally states people's rights and duties. *page 142* [constitución]

Constitutional Convention /kon-sti-TOO-shuhn-al kon-VEN-shuhn/ (noun) The Constitutional Convention was a meeting held in 1787 where delegates wrote the United States Constitution. *page 142* [Convención de Filadelfia]

consume /kon-SOOM/ (verb) If you consume something, you eat or drink it. *page 36* [consumir]

containment /kon-TAYN-ment/ (noun) Containment is the action or policy of keeping another country's power or area of control within acceptable limits or boundaries. *page 206* [contención]

continent /KON-ti-nent/ (noun) A continent is a very large area of land, such as Africa or Asia, that usually consists of several countries. *pages 2, 12* [continente]

contract /KON-trakt/ (noun) A contract is a legal agreement, usually between two companies or people. *page 136* [contrato]

contrast /KON-trast/ (noun) A contrast is a clear difference between two or more things. *page 24* [contraste]

control /kuhn-TROHL/ (verb) If someone controls a country or system, they have the power to make all the important decisions about the way that it is run. *page 96* [controlar]

convert /kon-VERT/ (verb) To convert someone means to persuade them to change their religious beliefs. *page 97* [convertir(se)]

convicted /KON-vik-ted/ (verb) If someone is convicted of a crime, they are found guilty of it in a court of law. *page 93* [condenado]

corruption /kor-RUHP-shuhn/ (noun) Corruption is dishonesty and illegal behavior by people in positions of authority or power. *page 180* [corrupción]

cottage /KOT-aj/ (noun) A cottage is a small house, usually in the country. *page 101* [casita (or casa) de campo]

cotton /KAH-ton/ (noun) Cotton is a plant that produces soft fibers used in making cloth. *page 98* [algodón]

coup d'etat /KOO da tah/ (noun) A coup d'etat is a sudden overthrow of the government, often by a dictator. *page 240* [coup d'etat]

court /KORT/ (noun) A court is a place where legal matters and disagreements are heard and decided by a judge, or a judge and a jury. *page 226* [corte]

create /kree-AYT/ (verb) To create something means to cause it to happen or exist. *page 84* [crear]

crime /KREYEM/ (noun) A crime is an illegal action or activity for which a person can be punished by law. *page 226* [crimen]

crop /KROP/ (noun) Crops are plants such as wheat or potatoes that are grown in large quantities for food. *page 94* [cosecha]

crossroads /KROS-rohds/ (noun) A crossroads is an important or central place. *page 48* [encrucijada]

Crusades /kru-SAYDS/ (noun) The Crusades were religious wars between European Christians and Muslims in the eastern Mediterranean in the 11th, 12th, and 13th centuries. *page 72* [cruzada]

Cuba /KYOO-ba/ (noun) Cuba is an island in the Caribbean which was once controlled by Spain. *page 174* [Cuba]

culture /KUL-chur/ (noun) 1. The ideas, activities, and ways of behaving that are special to a country, people, or region. *page 14;* 2. A culture is a particular society or civilization, especially considered in relation to its beliefs, way of life, or art. *page 16* [cultura]

cuneiform /KYOO-ni-form/ (adjective) Cuneiform was one of the first systems of writing. It was written on clay tablets. *page 56* [cuneiforme]

currency /KER-en-see/ (noun) The money used in a particular country is referred to as its currency. *page 26* [moneda]

cycle /SEYE-kuhl/ (noun) A cycle is a series of events or processes that is repeated again and again, always in the same order. *page 81* [ciclo]

D-Day /DEE DAY/ (noun) D-Day was June 6, 1944, and was the day the Allies invaded Europe from the sea during World War II. *page 194* [**Día D**]

Dead Sea /DED SEE/ (noun) The Dead Sea is a body of water in the Middle East. It has the lowest point on the surface of the earth. It is called the Dead Sea because it is too salty for animal life. *page 30* [**Mar Muerto**]

debate /de-BAYT/ (verb) If people debate a topic, they discuss it formally, putting forward different views. You can also say that one person debates a topic with another person. *page 142* [**discutir**]

debt /DET/ (noun) A debt is a sum of money that you owe someone. *page 113* [**deuda**]

decade /dek-AYD/ (noun) A decade is a period of ten years, especially one that begins with a year ending in 0, for example, 1980 to 1989. *page 6* [**década**]

Declaration of Independence /dek-la-RAY-shuhn ov in-de-PEN-dans/ (noun) The Declaration of Independence is the official document of July 4, 1776, that stated that thirteen American colonies were no longer ruled by Great Britain. *page 138* [**Declaración de Independencia**]

Declaration of Sentiments /dek-la-RAY-shuhn ov SENT-i-ments/ (noun) The Declaration of Sentiments demanded equal rights for women, including the right to vote. *page 152* [**Declaración de los Sentimientos**]

decline /de-KLEYEN/ (noun) If there is a decline in something, it becomes less in quantity, importance, or strength. *page 72* [**disminución**]

defeat /de-FEET/ (verb) If you defeat someone, you win against them in a battle. *pages 80, 102, 116* [**derrotar**]

delegate /DEL-i-git/ (noun) A delegate is a person who is chosen to vote or make decisions on behalf of a group of other people, especially at a conference or meeting. *page 142* [**delegado(a)**]

democracy /de-MAHK-rah-see/ (noun) Democracy is a system of government in which people choose their leaders by voting for them in elections. *pages 16, 25, 62, 108, 238* [**democracia**]

Democratic Party /dem-i-CRAT-ik PAHRT-ee/ (noun) In general, the Democratic Party supports social and economic programs for Americans. *page 234* [**partido democrático**]

demonstrate /DEM-uhn-strayt/ (verb) When people demonstrate, they come together in public to protest about something or show their support for something. *page 230* [**manifestarse**]

depression /di-PRESH-uhn/ (noun) A depression is a time when there is very little economic activity, which causes a lot of unemployment and poverty. *page 113* [**depresión**]

descendant /di-SEN-dantz/ (noun) Someone's descendants are the people in earlier generations who are related to them. *page 176* [**descendiente**]

desert /DEZ-ert/ (noun) A desert is a large area of land, usually in a hot region, where there is almost no water, rain, trees, or plants. *pages 10, 30* [**desierto**]

develop /di-VEL-uhp/ (verb) When something develops, it grows or changes over a period of time and usually becomes more advanced or complete. *page 20* [**desarrollar**]

diary /DEYE-a-ree/ (noun) A diary is a book which has a separate space for each day of the year. You use a diary to write down things you plan to do, or to record what happens in your life day by day. *page 8* [**diario**]

dictator /DIK-tay-tor/ (noun) A dictator is a ruler who has complete power in a country, especially power which was obtained by force and is used unfairly or cruelly. *page 114* [**dictador(a)**]

dictatorship /dik-TAY-tor-ship/ (noun) A dictatorship is a form of government in which one ruler has total power. *page 238* [**dictadura**]

diplomat /DIP-lo-mat/ (noun) A diplomat is a senior official who discusses affairs with a another country on behalf of his or her own country, usually working as a member of an embassy. *page 224* [**diplomático(a)**]

disabled /dis-AY-buhld/ (adjective) Someone who is disabled has an illness, injury, or condition that tends to restrict the way that they can live their life, especially by making it difficult for them to move about. *page 116* [**inválido, incapacitado**]

discriminate /dis-KRIM-in-ayt/ *(verb)* To discriminate against a group of people means to unfairly treat them worse than other groups. *page 196* [**discriminar**]

discrimination /dis-krim-in-AY-shuhn/ *(noun)* Discrimination is the practice of treating one person or group less fairly or less well than other people or groups. *pages 180, 202* [**discriminación**]

disease /dis-EEZ/ *(noun)* A disease is an illness that affects people, animals, or plants. *page 78* [**enfermedad**]

dissect /deye-SEKT/ *(verb)* If someone dissects a dead body, they cut it up in order to examine it scientifically. *page 84* [**diseccionar, hacer la disección de**]

diverse /di-VERS/ *(adjective)* If a group of things is diverse, it is made up of things that are very different from each other. *page 24* [**diverso**]

divide /di-VEYED/ *(verb)* When people or things are divided or divide into smaller groups or parts, they become separated into smaller groups or parts. *page 152* [**dividir**]

divorce /di-VORS/ *(noun)* A divorce is a formal ending of a marriage by law. *page 89* [**divorcio**]

document /DOK-yoo-ment/ *(noun)* A document is one or more official pieces of paper with writing on them. *page 8* [**documento**]

domesticated /doh-MES-ti-kayt-ed/ *(adjective)* A domesticated animal is an animal that has been bred or learned to live closely with humans. *page 53* [**domesticado**]

domino theory /DOM-i-no THEE-ah-ree/ *(noun)* The belief that if one country becomes communist, others in the area will also become communist. *page 206* [**teoría del dominó**]

draft /DRAFT/ *(noun)* The draft is the practice of ordering people to serve in the armed forces, usually for a limited period of time. *page 208* [**servicio militar obligatorio**]

drive-in movie theater /DREYE-vin MOO-vee THEE-er-ter/ *(noun)* A drive-in movie theater is an outdoor movie theater that people drive to and sit and watch movies from their cars. *page 198* [**autocine**]

drought /DROWT/ *(noun)* A drought is a long period of time during which little rain falls. *page 34* [**sequía**]

dust bowl /DUHST BOHL/ *(noun)* A dust bowl is an area of land, especially in the southern or central United States, that is dry and arid because soil has been eroded by the wind. A dust bowl was created in the Great Plains during the drought of the 1930s. *page 190* [**terreno semidesértico**]

dynasty /DEYE-nas-tee/ *(noun)* A dynasty is a series of rulers of a country who all belong to the same family. *page 58* [**dinastía**]

E

earthquake /ERTH-kwayk/ *(noun)* An earthquake is a shaking of the ground caused by movement in the Earth's crust. *page 36* [**terremoto; temblor de tierra; sismo**]

east /EEST/ *(noun)* The east is the direction where the sun rises. *page 4* [**este**]

East Asia /EEST AY-zhah/ *(noun)* East Asia is made up of the countries in the eastern part of the continent of Asia. It includes China and Mongolia, and the countries east of them. *page 42* [**Asia del Este**]

economic /ek-oh-NOM-ik/ *(adjective)* Economic means concerned with the organization of the money, industry, and trade of a country, region, or society. *page 96* [**económico**]

economic depression /ek-oh-NOM-ik di-PRESH-uhn/ *(noun)* An economic depression is a long period of time when many people are unemployed and businesses are not making very much money. *page 190* [**la depresión económica**]

economics /ek-oh-NOM-ik/ *(noun)* Economics is the study of the way in which money, industry, and commerce are organized in a society. *page 14* [**economía**]

effect /e-FEKT/ *(noun)* An effect is the result of something. *page 140* [**efecto**]

elect /e-LEKT/ *(verb)* When people elect someone, they choose that person to represent them by voting for them. *pages 144, 218* [**elegir**]

election /e-LEK-shuhn/ *(noun)* An election is a process in which people vote to choose a person or group of people to hold an official position. *page 234* [elección]

elevation /el-e-VAY-shuhn/ *(noun)* The elevation of a place is its height above sea level. *page 12* [elevación, altura sobre nivel del mar]

Ellis Island /EL-is EYE-land/ *(noun)* Ellis Island is an island in New York harbor where immigrants from Europe entered the United States. *page 178* [Isla de Ellis]

e-mail /EE MAYL/ *(noun)* E-mail is a system of sending electronic messages from one computer to another. *page 122* [correo electrónico]

empire /EM-peye-yer/ *(noun)* An empire is a number of individual nations that are all controlled by the government or ruler of one particular country. *pages 24, 74* [imperio]

emperor /EM-per-or/ *(noun)* An emperor is a man who rules an empire, or who is the head of state in an empire. *page 42* [emperador]

enemy /EN-e-mee/ *(noun)* An enemy is someone or something that is against you and might try to harm you. *page 112* [enemigo(a)]

Enlightenment, The /THEE en-LEYET-en-ment/ *(noun)* The Enlightenment was a time of great advances in science and philosophy. *pages 28, 90* [Siglo de las Luces, la Ilustración]

enslave /en-SLAYV/ *(verb)* To enslave a person or society means to trap them in a situation from which they cannot escape. *page 81* [esclavizar]

equal /EE-kwal/ *(adjective)* If two things are equal or if one thing is equal to another, they are the same in size, number, or value. *page 92* [igual]

equality /ee-KWAL-i-tee/ *(noun)* Equality is a state in which all members of a society or group have the same status, rights, and responsibilities. *page 106* [igualdad]

equator /e-KWAYT-er/ *(noun)* The equator is an imaginary line around the middle of the earth at an equal distance from the North Pole and the South Pole. *page 2* [ecuador]

equipment /ee-KWIP-ment/ *(noun)* Equipment consists of the things that are used for a particular purpose, for example a hobby or job. *page 180* [equipo]

eruption /e-RUP-shuhn/ *(noun)* When a volcanic eruption occurs, lava, stone, and ash are sent into the atmosphere. *page 36* [erupción]

ethnic group /ETH-nik GROOP/ *(noun)* Ethnic groups are made up of people with similar backgrounds, lifestyles, and beliefs. Some ethnic groups have their own languages and customs. *pages 28, 36* [grupos étnicos]

Eurasia /yu-RAY-zhah/ *(noun)* Eurasia is the area of land that includes Europe and Asia. *page 26* [Eurasia, Euroasia]

euro /YU-roh/ *(noun)* The euro is a unit of currency that is used by some member countries of the European Union. *page 26* [euro]

Europe /yu-RUHP/ *(noun)* The continent of Europe is a large peninsula stretching from western Asia to the Atlantic Ocean. *page 26* [europa]

European Union /yu-ruh-PEE-an YOON-yuhn/ *(noun)* The European Union is an organization of European countries that have the same policies on matters such as trade, agriculture, and finance. *page 26* [Unión Europea]

evacuate /ee-VAK-yoo-wayt/ *(verb)* To evacuate someone means to send them to a place of safety, away from a dangerous building, town, or area. *page 209* [evacuar]

exaggerate /ig-ZAJ-e-rayt/ *(verb)* If you exaggerate, you suggest that something is, for example, worse or more important than it really is. *page 176* [exagerar]

exchange /ex-CHAYNJ/ *(verb)* If you exchange something, you replace it with something different. *page 16* [cambiar]

excommunicate /ek-ske-MYOO-ni-kayt/ *(noun)* To excommunicate someone means to prohibit that person from receiving the holy blessings, especially in the Catholic Church. *page 88* [excomulgar]

execute /EK-se-kyoot/ *(verb)* To execute someone means to kill them as a punishment. *page 93* [ejecutar]

expand /ek-SPAND/ (verb) If something expands or is expanded, it becomes larger. page 144 [expandir(se), aumentar]

expansion /ek-SPAN-shuhn/ (noun) Expansion is the process of becoming greater in size, number, or amount. page 150 [expansión]

expedition /ek-spe-DISH-uhn/ (noun) An expedition is an organized trip made for a particular purpose such as exploration. page 148 [expedición]

expensive /ek-SPEN-siv/ (adjective) If something is expensive, it costs a lot of money. page 100 [caro(a)]

export /ek-SPORT/ (verb) To export products or raw materials means to sell them to another country. page 210 [exportar]

explorer /ek-SPLOR-er/ (noun) An explorer is a person who travels around a place to find out about it. page 78 [explorador(a)]

F

factory /FAK-te-ree/ (noun) A factory is a large building where machines are used to make large quantities of goods. pages 98, 170 [fábrica]

farmland /FAHRM-land/ (noun) Farmland is land that is farmed, or that is suitable for farming. page 21 [tierras cultivable]

fascism /FASH-iz-em/ (noun) Fascism is a system of government in which there is strong control by the state and a powerful role for the armed forces. page 114 [fascismo]

fast food /FAST FOOD/ (noun) Fast food is food that is prepared quickly and inexpensively in a standardized way. page 200 [comida rápida]

federal /FED-e-ral/ (adjective) Federal means related to the central government of the United States, rather than one of the states within it. page 226 [federal]

Federalist /FED-e-ral-ist/ (noun) A political party of the early United States that believed in a strong central government. page 144 [federalista]

Fertile Crescent /FERT-uhl KRES-ent/ (noun) The Fertile Crescent is a region of land in southwest Asia and northeast Africa with very rich soil. page 54 [fértil]

feudalism /FYOOD-uhl-iz-em/ (noun) Feudalism was a system in which people were given land and protection by people of higher rank, and worked and fought for them in return. page 66 [feudalismo]

figurehead /FIG-yur-hed/ (noun) If someone is a figurehead of an organization or country, they are recognized as being its leader, although they have little real power. page 240 [testaferro]

fire /FEYE-er/ (noun) Fire is the hot, bright flames produced by things that are burning. page 50 [fuego]

forest /FOR-est/ (noun) A forest is a large area where trees grow close together. page 10 [bosque]

fossil fuel /FOS-il FYUL/ (noun) Fossil fuel is fuel such as coal or oil that is formed from the decaying remains of plants or animals. page 210 [combustibles fósiles]

Founding Fathers /FOWN-ding FATH-erz/ (noun) The men who created the new government in the United States were referred to as the Founding Fathers. page 144 [Padres Fundadores]

free state /FREE STAYT/ (noun) A free state was a state in the United States in which there were no slaves. page 158 [estado libre]

freshwater /FRESH-WAH-ter/ (adjective) Freshwater is water that is not salty, usually in contrast to the sea. page 12 [agua dulce]

freshwater lake /FRESH-WAH-ter LAYK/ (adjective) A freshwater lake contains water that is not salty. page 36 [lago de agua dulce]

frontier /fruhn-TEER/ (noun) The frontier was the area of undeveloped land beyond settled land. page 146 [frontera]

fugitive /FYOO-ji-tiv/ (noun) A fugitive is someone who is running away or hiding, usually in order to avoid being caught by the police. page 158 [fugitivo]

fur /FER/ (noun) Fur is the thick and usually soft hair that grows on the bodies of many mammals. page 134 [pelaje]

G

Ganges /gahn-JEEZ/ (noun) The Ganges is a river that serves as an important source of water in South Asia. *page 38* **[Ganges]**

gatherer /GATH-er-erz/ (noun) A gatherer is someone who collects or gathers a particular thing. *page 52* **[recolector]**

gay /GAY/ (noun) If someone is gay, they are attracted to someone of the same sex. *page 116* **[gay, homosexual]**

general /JEN-e-ral/ (noun) A general is a high-ranking officer in the armed forces, usually in the army. *page 141* **[general]**

generation /jen er ay shuhn/ (noun) A generation is all the people in a group or country who are of a similar age, especially when they are considered as having the same experiences or attitudes. *pages 16, 52* **[generación]**

geography /jee-AH-gra-fee/ (noun) The geography of a place is the way that features such as rivers, mountains, towns, or streets are arranged within it. *page 10* **[geografía]**

German Empire /JER-man EM-pai-yer/ (noun) The German Empire was created in 1871 when all of the German states except Austria united with Prussia. *page 102* **[Imperio Alemán]**

G.I. Bill /JEE-EYE BILL/ (noun) The G.I. Bill was introduced in America after World War II. It helped veterans attend college and get better jobs. *page 200* **[Ley en beneficio a los soldados que combatieron en la Segunda Guerra Mundial]**

glacier /GLAY-sher/ (noun) A glacier is an extremely large mass of ice that moves very slowly, often down a mountain valley. *page 12* **[glaciar]**

global /GLOH-bal/ (adjective) You can use global to describe something that happens in, or affects, all parts of the world. *page 210* **[global]**

globalization /GLOH-bal-i-zay-shuhn/ (noun) Globalization is the process by which economic, political, and cultural systems become connected across the world as a result of better communications and the influence of international companies. *page 122* **[globalización]**

globe /GLOHB/ (noun) A globe is a ball-shaped object that represents Earth. *page 2* **[globo]**

gold /GOHLD/ (noun) Gold is a valuable, yellow-colored metal that is used for making jewelry and ornaments. *pages 74, 132* **[oro]**

gold rush /GOHLD RUHSH/ (noun) A gold rush is a situation where a lot of people suddenly go to a place where gold has been discovered in the ground, because they want to become rich. The California Gold Rush began around 1849. *page 154* **[fiebre del oro]**

goods /GUDZ/ (noun) Goods are things that are made in order to be sold. *pages 16, 81* **[productos]**

government /GUHV-ern-ment/ (noun) A government is the political system that rules or controls a country or area. *pages 14, 238* **[gobierno]**

grassland /GRAS-land/ (noun) Grassland is land covered with wild grass. *page 12* **[pradera]**

Great Barrier Reef /GRAYT BAR-ee-er REEF/ (noun) The Great Barrier Reef is a coral reef along the northeast coast of Australia. *page 49* **[Gran Barrera de Coral]**

Great Depression /GRAYT di-PRESH-uhn/ (noun) The Great Depression was a time during the 1930s with the worst unemployment and business conditions in modern history. *page 190* **[Gran Depresión]**

Great Plains /GRAYT PLAYNZ/ (noun) The Great Plains is a large area of grassland located west of the Mississippi River and east of the Rocky Mountains. *pages 128, 149, 154* **[Grandes Llanuras]**

Great Wall /GRAYT WAWL/ (noun) Chinese emperors built a 4,000-mile-long wall called the Great Wall. The Great Wall kept the nomads from attacking China. *page 42* **[Gran Muralla]**

grid /GRID/ (noun) A grid is a pattern of straight lines that cross over each other, forming squares. On maps, you use them to help you find a particular thing or place. *page 57* **[cuadrícula]**

guarantee /gar-an-TEE/ (verb) If one thing guarantees another, the first is certain to cause the second thing to happen. *page 204* **[garantizar]**

guerrilla /guh-RIL-uh/ *(noun)* A guerrilla is someone who fights as part of an unofficial army, usually against an official army or police force. *page 208* [**guerrilla**]

gunpowder /GUN-pow-der/ *(noun)* Gunpowder is an explosive substance that is used to make fireworks or to cause explosions. *page 72* [**pólvora**]

H

harbor /HAHR-bor/ *(noun)* A harbor is an area of water that is partly enclosed by land or strong walls, so that boats can be left there safely. *pages 140, 150* [**puerto**]

harvest /HAHR-vist/ *(verb)* 1. When you harvest a crop, you gather it in. *page 81* [**cosechar**]

(noun) 2. The harvest is the crop that is gathered in. *page 133* [**cosecha**]

head of state /HED UHV STAYT/ *(noun)* A head of state is the leader of a country, for example a president, prime minister, figurehead, or queen. *page 240* [**jefe de estado, jefa de estado**]

herder /HERD-er/ *(noun)* A herder is someone who takes care of a group of animals such as cows, goats, or sheep. *page 42* [**vaquero(a)**]

hierarchy /HEYE-e-rar-kee/ *(noun)* A hierarchy is a system of organizing people into different ranks or levels of importance. *page 68* [**jerarquía**]

hieroglyphs /HEYE-roh-glifs/ *(noun)* Hieroglyphs are symbols in the form of pictures that are used in some writing systems, for example those of ancient Egypt. *page 58* [**jeroglífico**]

highway /HEYE-way/ *(noun)* A highway is a main road, especially one that connects towns or cities. *page 198* [**carretera**]

Himalaya Mountains /him-a-LAY-a MOWNT-enz/ *(noun)* The Himalayas are a huge mountain range that separates South Asia from the rest of Asia. *page 38* [**Montañas de Himilaya**]

Hindu /HIN-doo/ *(noun)* A Hindu is a person who believes in Hinduism. *page 38* [**Hindú**]

Hindu temples /HIN-doo TEM-puhlz/ *(noun)* Hindu temples are places Hindus go to pray. *page 38* [**templos hindúes**]

Hiroshima /heer-oh-SHEE-ma/ *(noun)* Hiroshima is a city in Japan where the first atomic bomb was dropped by the United States in 1945. *page 194* [**Hiroshima**]

hold /HOLD/ *(verb)* To cause an event to take place. *page 240* [**tener**]

Holocaust /HOL-oh-cawst/ *(noun)* The Holocaust is used to refer to the killing by the Nazis of millions of Jews and some other groups during World War II. *page 114* [**holocausto**]

hominid /HOM-in-id/ *(noun)* A hominid is a member of a group of animals that includes human beings and early ancestors of human beings. *page 50* [**homínido**]

horizontal timeline /haw-ri-ZON-tal TEYEM LEYEN/ *(adjective)* A horizontal timeline generally has the earliest or first event on the left of the timeline and more recent events on the right. *page 6* [**cronológica horizontal**]

hostility /ho-STIL-i-tee/ *(noun)* Hostility is unfriendly or aggressive behavior toward people or ideas. *page 102* [**hostilidad**]

House of Representatives /HOWS UHV rep-REE-zen-ta-tivs/ *(noun)* The House of Representatives is one of two houses of Congress. There are 435 members in the House of Representatives. Every ten years, the number of representatives for each state is adjusted based on the state's population. Each state has at least one representative. *page 218* [**Cámara de Representantes**]

human /HYU-men/ *(adjective)* Human means relating to or concerning people. *page 14* [**humano**]

human rights /HYU-man REYETZ/ *(noun)* Human rights are basic rights which many societies believe that all people should have. *page 122* [**derechos humanos**]

hunter /HUHN-ter/ *(noun)* A hunter is a person who hunts wild animals for food or as sport. *page 52* [**cazador(a)**]

hunting /HUHN-ting/ *(noun)* Hunting is when people or animals chase and kill wild animals for food or as sport. *page 126* [**caza, cacería**]

hybrid /HEYE-brid/ *(noun)* You can use hybrid to refer to anything that is a mixture of two, or sometimes more than two, things. *page 213* [**híbrido**]

ice /EYES/ (noun) Ice is frozen water. *page 12* [hielo]

igloo /IG-loo/ (noun) An igloo is dome-shaped house built from blocks of snow. *page 128* [iglú]

immigrants /IM-i-grants/ (noun) An immigrant is a person who has come to live in a country from another country. *page 170* [inmigrante]

impeach /im-PEECH/ (verb) If a court or a group in authority impeaches a president or other senior official, it charges them with committing a crime that makes them unfit for office. *page 224* [Acusar a un alto cargo de delitos]

imperialism /im-PIR-ee-a-liz-em/ (noun) Imperialism is a system in which a rich and powerful country controls other countries. *page 94* [imperialismo]

import /im-PORT/ (verb) To import products or raw materials means to buy them from another country for use in your own country. *page 210* [importar]

improvement /im-PROOV-ment/ (noun) An improvement in something makes it better. *page 100* [mejoría]

Inca /EEN-ka/ (noun) The Inca were an indigenous people who lived in South America, from what is now northern Ecuador to central Chile, between about 1200 C.E., and 1533 C.E. *page 74* [Inca]

independence /in-de-PEN-dentz/ (noun) If a country has or gains independence, it has its own government and is not ruled by any other country. *pages 25, 118, 176* [independencia]

indigenous people /in-DIJ-e-nuhs PEE-puhl/ (adjective) Indigenous people are the original people of an area. *page 18* [indígenos]

industry /IN-duhs-tree/ (noun) Industry is the work and processes involved in making things, especially in factories. *pages 98, 170* [industria]

Indus Valley /IN-duhs va-lee/ (noun) The Indus Valley is the valley in South Asia through which the Indus River runs, north of the Arabian Sea. *page 54* [Valle Indus]

interfere /int-er-FEER/ (verb) Something that interferes with a situation, activity, or process has a damaging effect on it. *page 200* [interferir]

international trade /in-ter-NASH-uhn-al TRAYD/ (noun) The exchange of goods and services among countries around the world. *page 122* [comercio internacional]

Internet /in-ter-NET/ (noun) The Internet is the network that allows computer users to connect with computers all over the world, and that carries e-mail. *page 122* [Internet]

internment camp /in-TERN-ment CAMP/ (noun) Internment camps were created during World War II. The United States sent people of Japanese descent to live in internment camps for fear of Japanese spies. *page 194* [campo de internación]

invade /in-VAYD/ (verb) To invade a country means to enter it by force with an army. *pages 40, 200* [invadir]

invader /in-VAYD-er/ (noun) An invader is someone who forcefully enters another country and takes control of it. *page 61* [invasor]

invasion /in-VAY-zhun/ (noun) If there is an invasion of a country, a foreign army enters it by force. *page 182* [invasion]

invention /in-VEN-shuhn/ (noun) An invention is a machine, device, or system that has been thought of and created by someone. *page 170* [invención]

iron /EYER uhn/ (noun) Iron is an element that usually takes the form of a hard, dark gray metal. *page 100* [hierro]

Iron Curtain /EYER-uhn KER-ten/ (noun) The Iron Curtain was referred to as the border that separated communist countries from non-communist countries after World War II. *page 120* [Cortina de Hierro or Telón de Acero]

island /EYE-land/ (noun) An island is a piece of land that is completely surrounded by water. *page 12* [isla]

isolated /EYE-so-layt-ed/ (adjective) The state of being alone, meaning you are completely separate from others. *page 49* [aislado]

isthmus /IS-muhs/ (noun) An isthmus is a narrow piece of land connecting two large areas of land. *page 18* [istmo]

Iwo Jima /ee-woh JEE-ma/ *(noun)* Iwo Jima was a small island held by the Japanese that many Americans died trying to conquer during World War II. *page 197* [Iwo Jima]

J

jade /JAYD/ *(noun)* Jade is a hard green stone used for making jewelry and ornaments. *page 70* [jade]

Jamestown /JAYM-stown/ *(noun)* Jamestown was the first permanent English colony in North America. *page 130* [Jamestown]

jazz /JAZ/ *(noun)* Jazz is a style of music that was invented by African American musicians in the early part of the twentieth century. *page 186* [jazz]

Jew /JOO/ *(noun)* A Jew is a person who believes in and practices the religion of Judaism. *page 116* [judío(a)]

Jewish /JOO-ish/ *(adjective)* Jewish means belonging or relating to the religion of Judaism, or to Jews as an ethnic group. *page 120* [judío]

Judaism /JOOD-a-iz-em/ *(noun)* Judaism is the religion of the Jewish people. It is based on the Old Testament of the Bible and the Talmud. *page 65* [judaísmo]

judge /JUHJ/ *(noun)* In a court of law, a judge is the person whose job is to make decisions, for example, on how a criminal should be punished. *page 226* [juez]

jury /JUR-ee/ *(noun)* In a court of law, the jury is the group of people who have been chosen from the general public to listen to the facts about a crime and to decide whether the accused person is guilty or not. *page 230* [jurado]

K

kangaroo /kan-ga-ROO/ *(noun)* A kangaroo is a large Australian animal. Female kangaroos carry their babies in a pocket on their stomach. *page 46* [canguro]

key /KEE/ *(noun)* The key on a map is a list of the symbols or abbreviations used and their meanings. *page 4* [clave]

kidnap /KID-nap/ *(verb)* To kidnap someone is to take them away illegally and by force. *page 136* [raptar]

king /keeng/ *(noun)* A king is a man who is a member of the royal family of his country and who is the head of state in that country. *page 66* [rey]

kingdom /KEENG-duhm/ *(noun)* A kingdom is a country or region that is ruled by a king or queen. *page 76* [reino]

knight /NEYET/ *(noun)* In medieval times, a knight was a man of noble birth who served his king or lord in battle. *page 66* [caballero de orden]

Korean War /koh-REE-an WAWR/ *(noun)* The Korean War was a war that the United States joined in 1950 in an effort to stop the spread of communism on the Korean Peninsula in Asia. *page 198* [Guerra de Corea]

L

labor union /LAY-bor YOON-yuhn/ *(noun)* A labor union is an organization that represents the rights and interests of workers, for example in order to improve working conditions or wages. *page 180* [sindicato obrero]

lake /LAYK/ *(noun)* A lake is a large area of fresh water surrounded by land. *page 10* [lago]

land bridge /LAND BRIJ/ *(noun)* A land bridge is a strip of land between two continents that connect them, enabling travel from one continent to the other. *page 126* [Puente de Beringia]

landlocked /LAND-lokt/ *(adjective)* A landlocked country is surrounded by other countries and does not have its own seaports. *page 26* [rodeado de tierra, sin salida al mar]

landscape /land-SKAYP/ *(noun)* The landscape is everything you can see when you look across an area of land, including hills, rivers, buildings, trees, and plants. *page 100* [paisaje, vista]

language /LAN-gwij/ *(noun)* A language is a system of communication that consists of a set of sounds and usually written symbols that is used by people of a particular country or region for talking or writing. *pages 14, 52* [lenguaje, lengua, idioma]

Latin America /LA-tin a-MER-i-ka/ *(noun)* Latin America is the name given to the countries in the Americas south of the United States where Spanish and Portugese, and sometimes French, are officially spoken. *page 97* **[latinoamerica]**

Latino /la-TEE-noh/ *(noun)* A Latino is a citizen or resident of the United States who originally came from Latin America, or whose family originally came from Latin America. *page 205* **[Latino]**

latitude line /LAT-i-tood LEYEN/ *(noun)* Latitude lines show the distance north or south of the equator. *page 4* **[línea de latitud]**

law /LAW/ *(noun)* A law is a rule made by the government that people must obey. *page 218* **[ley]**

lawsuit /law-SOOT/ *(noun)* A lawsuit is a case in a court of law that concerns a dispute between two or more people or organizations. *page 205* **[pleito]**

lawyer /LOY-er/ *(noun)* A lawyer is a person who is qualified to advise people about the law and to represent them in court. *page 226* **[abogado(a)]**

League of Nations /LEEG UHV NAY-shuhnz/ *(noun)* The League of Nations was an international organization formed in 1919 that wanted world peace after World War I. *pages 110, 184* **[Liga de las Naciones]**

legal record /LEE-guhl REK-ord/ *(noun)* A legal record is a primary source document that provides information about public matters. *page 8* **[registro, archivo legal]**

Lend-Lease /LEND LEES/ *(noun)* Lend-Lease was a United States law during World War II that provided military supplies to countries fighting Germany and Japan. *page 196*

letter /LET-er/ *(noun)* A letter is a primary source document that usually tells about personal lives. *page 8* **[carta]**

light bulb /LEYET BUHLB/ *(noun)* A light bulb or bulb is the round glass part of an electric light or lamp from which light shines. *page 178* **[bombilla]**

literacy /LIT-e-ra-see/ *(noun)* Literacy is the ability to read and write. *page 28* **[alfabetización]**

literature /LIT-e-ra-chur/ *(noun)* Novels, plays, and poetry are referred to as literature. *page 82* **[literatura]**

livestock /LEYEV-stok/ *(noun)* Animals such as cattle and sheep that are kept on a farm or ranch are referred to as livestock. *page 72* **[ganado]**

location /loh-CAY-shuhn/ *(noun)* On a map or on Earth, a location is the place where something is situated. *page 4* **[posición]**

locomotive /loh-coh-MOHT-iv/ *(noun)* A locomotive is a large vehicle that pulls a train. *page 98* **[locomotora]**

log cabin /LOG KAB-in/ A log cabin is a house made out of logs. *page 146* **[cabina de troncos]**

longitude lines /lawn-ji-TOOD LEYENZ/ *(noun)* Longitude lines show distance east or west of an imaginary line that runs from the North Pole to the South Pole. *page 4* **[línea de longitud]**

lord /LORD/ *(noun)* A lord is a noble who generally controlled an area of land. *page 68* **[noble]**

lower class /LOH-er KLAS/ *(noun)* The lower class is the division of society that is considered to have the lowest social status. *page 101* **[clase baja]**

lowlands /LOH-landz/ *(noun)* Lowlands are an area of low, flat land. *page 36* **[tierra baja]**

Lusitania /loo-si-TAY-nee-ya/ *(noun)* The *Lusitania* was an American ship that was sunk by a German submarine in 1915. *page 182* **[Lusitania]**

M

machine gun /ma-SHEEN GUHN/ *(noun)* A machine gun is a gun that fires a lot of bullets one after the other very quickly. *page 110* **[ametralladora]**

Magna Carta /MAG-nah KART-ah/ *(noun)* The Magna Carta was a document the king of England signed into law in 1215 that guaranteed certain rights to people in England. *page 214* **[Magna Carta]**

majority /mah-JOR-i-tee/ *(noun)* The majority of people or things in a group is more than half of them. *page 221* **[mayoría]**

malnutrition /mal-noo-TRISH-uhn/ *(noun)* If someone is suffering from malnutrition, they are physically weak and extremely thin because they have not eaten enough food. *page 37* **[malnutrición]**

mammal /MAM-al/ (noun) A mammal is a warm-blooded animal. It drinks milk that is produced by its mother. *page 128* **[mamífero(a)]**

manor /MAN-or/ (noun) A manor is the house on a large estate. *page 68* **[feudo, solariega]**

manufacturing /man-yoo-FAK-chur-ing/ (verb) Manufacturing is the part of industry that makes things. *page 21* **[fabricación]**

march /MARCH/ (noun) **1.** A march is a walk by a group people in order to call attention to something. *page 108* **[marcha]**

2. (verb) When a large group of people march for a cause, they walk somewhere together in order to express their ideas or to protest about something. *page 203* **[marcher]**

marine /ma-REEN/ (adjective) Marine is used to describe things relating to the sea. *page 128* **[marino]**

market /MAR-ket/ (noun) A market is a place where goods are bought and sold, often outdoors. *page 70* **[mercado]**

mass production /MASS pro-DUHK-shuhn/ (noun) Mass production is the process by which something is produced in large quantities, especially by machines. *page 180* **[producción en masa]**

massacre /MAS-i-ker/ (noun) A massacre is an occasion when a large number of people are killed at the same time in a violent and cruel way. *page 140* **[masacre]**

mathematician /math-e-ma-TISH-an/ (noun) A mathematician is a person who is trained in the study of mathematics. *page 76* **[matemático(a)]**

Maya /MEYE-ya/ (noun) The Maya were an indigenous people who lived in what is now Mexico, Guatemala, and Belize between about 250 C.E. and 900 C.E. *page 74* **[Maya]**

Mayflower /MAY-flow-er/ (noun) The *Mayflower* was the name of the ship the Pilgrims used to sail from England to North America. *page 130* **[Mayflower]**

medicine /MED-i-sin/ (noun) Medicine is the study and practice of restoring or preserving health. *page 70* **[medicina]**

merchant /MER-chant/ (noun) A merchant is a person who buys or sells goods in large quantities. *page 60* **[comerciante]**

microscope /MEYE-kroh-skohp/ (noun) A microscope is a scientific instrument that makes very small objects look bigger. *page 82* **[microscopio]**

middle class /MID-uhl KLAS/ (noun) The middle class are the people in a society who are not lower class or upper class. *pages 93, 101* **[clase media]**

Middle Colonies /MID-uhl KOL-uh-neez/ (noun) The Middle Colonies were part of the original 13 colonies. The Middle Colonies included New York, New Jersey, Pennsylvania, and Delaware. *page 134* **[Colonias del Medio]**

Middle East /MID-uhl EEST/ (noun) The Middle East is made up of the southwestern countries of Asia and Egypt. *page 30* **[Medio Oriente, Oriente Medio]**

migrant /MEYE-grant/ (noun) A migrant is a person who moves from one place to another, especially in order to find work. *page 205* **[migrante]**

migration /meye-GRAY-shuhn/ (noun) Migration is movement of a group of people from one region to another. *page 50* **[migración]**

milestone /MEYEL-stohn/ (noun) A milestone is an important event in the history or development of something or someone. *page 52* **[hito, hecho clave]**

military /MIL-i-tahr-ee/ (noun) The military is the armed forces of a country. *pages 116, 200, 224* **[fuerzas armadas]**

military dictatorship /MIL-i-tahr-ee DIK-tay-tor-ship/ (noun) A military dictatorship is a form of government in which a group of military officers with total power rules a country. *page 238* **[dictadura military]**

mine /MEYEN/ (noun) A mine is a system of underground holes and tunnels where minerals such as coal, diamonds, or gold are found. *page 100* **[mina]**

mineral /MIN-er-al/ (noun) A mineral is a substance such as tin, salt, or sulfur that is formed naturally in rocks and in the earth. *page 21* **[mineral]**

minister /MIN-i-stir/ *(noun)* In some countries outside of the United States, a minister is a person who is in charge of a particular government department. *page 240* [ministro]

minority /MEYE-nor-i-tee/ *(noun)* A minority is a group of people of the same race, culture, or religion who live in a place where most of the people around them are of a different race, culture, or religion. *page 213* [minoría]

Minuteman /MIN-et-man/ *(noun)* In the American Revolution, a Minuteman was a soldier who promised to be ready to fight in one minute if he was needed. *page 138* [Minuteman]

mission /MISH-uhn/ *(noun)* A mission is a building or group of buildings in which missionary work is carried out. *page 94* [misión]

missionary /MISH-uhn-ahr-ee/ *(noun)* A missionary is a Christian who has been sent to a foreign country to teach people about Christianity. *page 94* [misionero(a)]

Mississippi River /mis-i-SIP-ee RIV-er/ *(noun)* The Mississippi River is the longest river in the United States. It starts in the northern part of the United States (Minnesota) and empties into the Gulf of Mexico. *page 146* [Río Mississippi]

Missouri Compromise /mi-ZOR-ee KOM-pre-meyez/ *(noun)* The Missouri Compromise was an agreement that became law in 1820 that tried to balance the number of slave states and free states. *pages 150, 151* [Compromiso de Misuri]

Model T /MOD-el TEE/ *(noun)* The Model T was an affordable car produced by the Ford Motor Company in the first three decades of the twenty-first century. *page 186* [automóvil Modelo T]

modern /MOD-ern/ *(adjective)* Modern means relating to the present time, for example the present decade or present century. *pages 41, 84* [moderno(a)]

molasses /muh-LAS-iz/ *(noun)* Molasses is a thick, dark brown syrup that is produced when sugar is processed. It is used in cooking. *page 136* [melaza]

monarch /MON-ark/ *(noun)* The monarch of a country is the king, queen, emperor, or empress. *page 108* [monarca]

monarchy /MON-ar-kee/ *(noun)* A monarchy is a form of government in which a member of a royal family rules or has a symbolic role. *pages 90, 238* [monarquía]

monk /MUHNK/ *(noun)* A monk is a member of a male religious community. *page 86* [monje]

monsoon /mon-SOON/ *(noun)* The monsoon is the season in southern Asia when there is a lot of very heavy rain. *page 38* [monzón]

monument /MON-yoo-ment/ *(noun)* A monument is a large structure usually made of stone, which is built to remind people of an event in history or of a famous person. *page 14* [monumento]

mound /MOWND/ *(noun)* A mound is a small hill that may be either natural or created by people. *page 126* [montón, terraplén]

mountain /MOWNT-en/ *(noun)* A mountain is a very high area of land with steep sides. *page 10* [montaña]

mosque /MOSK/ *(noun)* A mosque is a building where Muslims go to worship. *page 38* [mezquita]

muckraker /MUK-rayk-er/ *(noun)* A muckraker is someone who calls attention to dishonesty in business and government. *page 178* [persona que llama atención a la falta de honradez en negocio y gobierno]

multicultural /muhl-TEE-kulche-ral/ *(adjective)* Multicultural means consisting of or relating to people of many different nationalities and cultures. *page 212* [multicultural]

mutinational corporation /muhl-TEE-nash-an-al kor-pa-RAY-shuhn/ *(noun)* A multinational corporation has branches or owns companies in many different countries. *page 122* [corporación multinacional]

mummification /muhm-if-i-KAY-shuhn/ *(noun)* Mummification is the process of preserving a dead body using special oils and wrapping it in long pieces of cloth. *page 60* [momificación]

mummy /MUHM-ee/ *(noun)* A mummy is a dead body which was preserved long ago by being rubbed with special oils and wrapped in cloth. *page 58* [momia]

Muslim /MUHZ-lim/ *(noun)* A Muslim is someone who believes in Islam and lives according to its rules. *page 38* [musulmán]

N

Nagasaki /nag-a-SAK-ee/ *(noun)* Nagasaki is a city in Japan where the second atomic bomb was dropped by the United States in 1945. *page 194* [Nagasaki]

napalm /NAY-pahlm/ *(noun)* Napalm is a substance containing gasoline that is used to make bombs. *page 208* [napalm]

nationalism /NASH-uhn-al-iz-em/ *(noun)* Nationalism is a person's great love for their nation. It is often associated with the belief that a particular nation is better than any other nation. *page 102* [nacionalismo]

Native American /NAY-tiv a-MER-i-kan/ *(noun)* A Native American is a member of one of the many groups who were already living in North America before Europeans arrived. *page 126* [Americano nativo]

natural resource /NACH-uh-ral REE-sors/ *(noun)* Natural resources are all the land, forests, energy sources, and minerals existing naturally in a place and which can be used by people. *pages 20, 210* [recursos naturales]

navy /NAYV-ee/ *(noun)* A country's navy consists of the people it employs to fight at sea, and the ships they use. *pages 105,184* [marina de guerra]

Nazi /NAHT-zee/ *(noun)* A Nazi was a member of the National Socialist German Workers' Party, the political party headed by Adolf Hitler that ruled Germany from 1933 to 1945. *page 114* [Nazi]

negotiate /ni-GO-she-ayt/ *(verb)* If people negotiate with each other, they talk about a problem or a situation in order to solve it. *page 224* [negociar]

neutral /NOO-tral/ *(adjective)* A neutral person or country does not support anyone in a disagreement, war, or contest. *page 182* [neutral]

New England Colonies /NOO IN-gland KOL-uh-neez/ *(noun)* The New England colonies were part of the original 13 colonies. The New England colonies were New Hampshire, Massachusetts, Rhode Island, and Connecticut. *page 134* [Colonias de Nueva Inglaterra]

newspaper article /NOOZ-pay-per ART-i-kuhl/ *(noun)* A newspaper article is a primary source document that provides information about public matters. *page 8* [artículo de periódico]

New Deal /NOO DEEL/ *(noun)* The New Deal was the programs and policies President Franklin D. Roosevelt introduced in the 1930s to improve the country's economy. *page 190* [Nuevo Acuerdo]

New World /NOO WERLD/ *(noun)* The New World was used to refer to the continents of North and South America. *page 78* [Nuevo Mundo]

Nile River /NEYEL RIV-er/ *(noun)* The Nile River is the longest river in the world and flows from central Africa to the Middle East. *page 30* [Río Nilo]

nobility /noh-BIL-i-tee/ *(noun)* The nobility of a society are all the people who have titles and who belong to a high social class. *page 92* [nobleza]

noble /NOHB-uhl/ *(adjective)* Noble means belonging to a high social class and having a title. *page 66* [noble]

nomads /NOH-madz/ *(noun)* A nomad is a member of a group of people who travel from place to place rather than living in one place all the time. *page 42* [nómada]

nonviolent protest /non-VEYE-oh-lent PRO-test/ *(noun)* A nonviolent protest is a protest that tries to bring about change without hurting people or causing damage. *page 204* [protesta no violenta]

north /NORTH/ *(noun)* The north is the direction which is on your left when you are looking toward the direction where the sun rises. *page 4* [norte]

North Africa /NORTH AF-ri-ka/ *(noun)* North Africa is a region that consists of Morocco, Algeria, Tunisia, and Libya. *page 30* [África del Norte]

North America /NORTH a-MER-i-ka/ *(noun)* North America is the continent located between the North Atlantic Ocean and the North Pacific Ocean. *page 18* [América del Norte]

North Vietnam /NORTH VEE-et-nahm/ (*noun*) North Vietnam was the part of Vietnam that became communist. *page 206* [**Vietnam del Norte**]

North Pole /NORTH POHL/ (*noun*) The North Pole is the tip of land that is farthest toward the north on Earth. *page 2* [**Polo Norte**]

northeast /NOR-theest/ (*adjective*) The northeast is the direction that is between north and east. *page 129* [**noreste, nordeste**]

Northern Hemisphere /NOR-thern HEM-i-sfeer/ (*noun*) The Northern Hemisphere is the area of land and bodies of water that is north of the equator. *page 2* [**Hemisferio Norte**]

nuclear missile /NOO-klee-ar MIS-el/ (*noun*) A nuclear missile is a weapon that explodes by using the energy released when the nuclei of atoms are split or combined. *page 198* [**misil nuclear**]

O

obey /oh-BAY/ (*verb*) If you obey a person, a command, or an instruction, you do what you are told to do. *page 230* [**obedecer**]

object /OB-jekt/ (*noun*) An object is an example of a primary source. An object is also anything that has a fixed shape or form, and that is not alive. *page 8* [**objeto**]

ocean /OH-shuhn/ (*noun*) An ocean is one of the wide areas of salty water that cover much of the Earth's surface. *page 10* [**océano**]

official /uh-FISH-uhl/ (*noun*) An official is a person who holds a position of authority in an organization. *page 60* [**oficial**]

Olympic Games /uh-LIM-pik GAYMZ/ (*noun*) The Olympic Games are a set of international sports competitions that take place every four years, each time in a different city. *page 62* [**juegos olímpicos**]

oppose /uh-POHZ/ (*verb*) If you oppose someone, or if you oppose their plans or ideas, you disagree with what they want to do, and you try to prevent them from doing it. *page 88* [**oponer(se)**]

original 13 colonies /uh-RIJ-i-nal thir-TEEN KOL-uh-neez/ (*noun*) The original 13 colonies were founded along the east coast of what is present-day United States. These colonies included Connecticut, Delaware, Georgia, Maryland, Massachusetts, New Hampshire, New Jersey, New York, North Carolina, South Carolina, Pennsylvania, Rhode Island, and Virginia. *page 134* [**trece colonias originales**]

Outback /owt-BAK/ (*noun*) The parts of Australia that are far away from the coast are referred to as the Outback. Not many people live there. *page 46* [**el interior despoblado de Australia**]

overseas /oh-ver-SEEZ/ (*adjective*) You use overseas to describe things that relate to or exist in foreign countries, usually across a sea or ocean. *page 164* [**ultramar**]

P

Pacific Northwest /pa-SIF-ik NORTH-west/ (*noun*) The Pacific Northwest is a region of the United States which is west of the Rocky Mountains and centered on the Columbia River. *page 128* [**Noroeste Pacífico**]

Pacific Ocean /pa-SIF-ik OH-shuhn/ (*noun*) The Pacific Ocean is a very large area of water that separates North and South America from Asia and Australia. *page 18* [**Océano Pacífico**]

painting /PAYNT-ing/ (*noun*) A painting is a picture that someone has painted. *page 82* [**pintura**]

Palestine /PAL-e-steyen/ (*noun*) Palestine is an area of southwest Asia whose people are Arabs. There is conflict about the border between Palestine and Israel. *pages 33, 72* [**Palestina**]

Panama Canal /PAN-a-ma kuh-NAL/ (*noun*) The Panama Canal is a canal that the United Sates built across the Isthmus of Panama to create a shorter route between the Atlantic and Pacific Oceans. *page 174* [**el canal de Panamá**]

paper money /PAY-per MUHN-ee/ (*noun*) Paper money is money that is made of paper. Paper money is usually worth more than coins. *page 72* [**dinero de papel**]

papyrus /pa-PEYE-ruhs/ (noun) Papyrus is a type of paper made from papyrus stems. It was used in ancient Egypt, Rome, and Greece. *page 60* [**papiro**]

parliament /PAHR-li-ment/ (noun) Parliament is a legislative body, led by a prime minister, that makes or changes laws in a country of state. *page 238* [**parlamento**]

Parthenon /PAR-thi-non/ (noun) The Parthenon is an ancient monument or temple in Greece. *page 62* [**Partenón**]

participate /par-TIS-i-payt/ (verb) If you participate in an activity, you take part in it. *page 64* [**participar**]

pass through /PAS THROO/ (verb) If you pass through a place, you travel through it on your way to another place. *page 149* [**pasar por**]

peace /PEES/ (noun) Peace is harmony and cooperation. If countries or groups involved in a war or violent conflict are discussing peace, they are talking to each other in order to try to end the conflict. *pages 120, 182* [**paz**]

Pearl Harbor /PURL HAR-bor/ (noun) Pearl Harbor is a harbor in Hawaii that was attacked by Japan during World War II. This caused the United States to join the Allies in World War II. *page 194* [**Puerta Perla**]

peasant /PEHZ-ent/ (noun) People refer to small farmers or farm workers in poor countries as peasants. *page 93* [**campesino**]

peninsula /pe-NIN-soo-la/ (noun) A peninsula is a long narrow piece of land that extends from the mainland and is almost completely surrounded by water. *page 26* [**península**]

pepper /PEP-er/ (noun) Pepper is a hot-tasting spice used to flavor food. *page 70* [**pimienta**]

percent /per-SENT/ (noun) You use percent to talk about amounts as parts of a hundred. One hundred percent (100%) is all of something, and 50 percent (50%) is half. *page 12* [**por ciento**]

petroglyph /PE-troh-glif/ (noun) A petroglyph was a drawing or engraving that was carved into rocks by early humans. *page 126* [**petroglifo**]

pharaoh /FEYER-oh/ (noun) A pharaoh was a king of ancient Egypt. *page 58* [**faraón**]

Philippines /fil-i-PEENZ/ (noun) The Philippines is a country in the Pacific Ocean that was once controlled by Spain. *page 174* [**Filipinas**]

philosophy /fi-LAHS-oh-fee/ (noun) Philosophy is the study or creation of theories about basic things such as knowledge, truth, and life. *page 62* [**filosofía**]

phonograph /FOH-na-graf/ (noun) A phonograph is a record player. *page 180* [**fonógrafo**]

photograph /FOH-toh-graf/ (noun) A photograph is a picture that is made using a camera. A photograph can be a primary source. *page 8* [**fotografía**]

physical map /FIZ-i-kal map/ (noun) A physical map shows Earth's natural features. *page 4* [**mapa físico**]

Pilgrim /PIL-grim/ (noun) Pilgrims were a group of people who left England because they wanted to worship freely. They started a colony in Plymouth, Massachusetts. *page 130* [**peregrino**]

pioneer /peye-i-NEER/ (noun) A pioneer is someone who is the first to settle in an undeveloped area. *page 146* [**pionero**]

plague /PLAYG/ (noun) A plague is an infectious disease that spreads quickly and kills large numbers of people. *page 72* [**plaga**]

plantation /plan-TAY-shuhn/ (noun) A plantation is a large piece of land where crops such as cotton, rubber, tea, or sugar are grown. *page 94* [**plantación**]

playwright /PLAY-reyet/ (noun) A playwright is a person who writes plays. *page 84* [**dramaturgo(a)**]

Plymouth /PLIM-uhth/ (noun) Plymouth is the site where the Pilgrims landed in North America in 1620 and started a colony. *page 130* [**Plymouth**]

poet /POH-et/ (noun) A poet is a person who writes poems. *page 141* [**poeta**]

point /POYNT/ (noun) A point is an opinion, idea, or fact expressed by someone. *page 184* [**punto**]

poison /POYZ-ohn/ *(noun)* Poison is a substance that harms or kills people or animals if they swallow it or absorb it. *page 112* [veneno]

polar climate /POH-lar KLEYE-mit/ *(noun)* A polar climate is a climate that is very cold. *page 20* [clima polar]

political /poh-LIT-i-kal/ *(adjective)* Political means relating to the way power is achieved and used in a country or society. *page 96* [político]

political map / poh-LIT-i-kal MAP/ *(noun)* A political map shows place names and borders. It also shows state names and capital cities. *page 4* [mapa político]

political prisoner / poh-LIT-i-kal PRIZ-on-er/ *(noun)* A political prisoner is someone who has been imprisoned for criticizing or disagreeing with their own government. *page 93* [prisionero político]

politician /po-li-TISH-uhn/ *(noun)* A politician is a person whose job is in politics, and who is competing for or already holds elected office. *page 234* [político(a)]

polluted /poh-LOOT-ed/ *(adjective)* If a place is polluted, its water, air, or land is dirty and dangerous to live in or use. *page 100* [contaminado]

Pope /POHP/ *(noun)* The Pope is the head of the Roman Catholic Church. *pages 68, 86* [El Papa]

port /PORT/ *(noun)* A port is a town by the sea or river, which has a harbor where large ships can stop. *page 164* [puerto]

Portuguese /por-choo-GEEZ/ *(noun)* Portuguese is the official language of Portugal, Brazil, Angola, and Mozambique. *page 22* [portugués]

pottery /POT-e-ree/ *(noun)* Pottery is pots, dishes, and other objects made from clay. *page 126* [ceramic, artesanía de barro]

prairie /PRAIR-ee/ *(noun)* A prairie is a large area of flat, grassy land in North America where very few trees grow. *page 146* [pradera, llanura, pampa]

prehistoric /pree-his-TOR-ik/ *(adjective)* Prehistoric people and things existed at a time before history was written down. *page 50* [prehistórico]

preserve /pre-ZERV/ *(verb)* If you preserve something, you save it or protect it. *page 60* [preservar]

preside /pre-ZEYED/ *(verb)* If you preside over a meeting, event, or a group, you are in charge. *page 220* [presidir]

president /PREZ-id-ent/ *(noun)* The president is the head of the country. The president is the commander-in-chief of the military. He is also America's main diplomat and negotiates foreign policy. *page 222* [presidente]

prevent /pre-VENT/ *(verb)* To prevent something means to ensure that it does not happen. *page 164* [evitar]

priest /PREEST/ *(noun)* A priest is a member of the Christian clergy in the Catholic, Anglican, or Orthodox church. *page 60* [cura, sacerdote]

primary sources /PREYE-mar-ee SOR-ses/ *(noun)* Primary sources are records of the past that were created by people who witnessed or experienced the events themselves. *page 181* [fuentes primarias]

prime minister /PREYEM MIN-i-stir/ *(noun)* A prime minister is the leader of a country, usually one that has a parliament. *page 238* [primer ministro]

printing press /PRINT-ing PRES/ *(noun)* A printing press is a machine used for printing, especially one that can print books, newspapers, or documents in large numbers. *page 82* [imprenta, prensa de imprenta]

Pro Tempore /proh TEM-pe-ray/ *(noun)* The President Pro Tempore leads meetings in the Senate if the vice president is absent. *page 220* [Pro Tempore]

propaganda /prop-ah-GAN-da/ *(noun)* Propaganda is information that a political organization publishes or broadcasts in order to influence or deceive people. *page 182* [propaganda]

property /PROP-er-tee/ *(noun)* Someone's property is all the things that belong to them or something that belongs to them. *page 160* [propiedades]

prosperity /pra-SPER-i-tee/ (*noun*) Prosperity is a situation in which a person or community is succeeding financially. *page 186* [**prosperidad**]

prosperous /PROS-pe-ruhs/ (*adjective*) Prosperous people, places, and economies are wealthy and successful. *page 64* [**próspero**]

protest /PROH-test/ (*verb*) If people protest, they say or show publicly that they strongly disagree with something. *page 136, 140* [**protestar**]

Protestant /PROT-es-tant/ (*noun*) A Protestant is a Christian who belongs to the branch of the Christian church that separated from the Catholic church in the sixteenth century. *page 86* [**protestante**]

Prussia /PRUSH-a/ (*noun*) Prussia was the largest state that made up the German Empire founded in the nineteenth century. *page 102* [**Prusia**]

public /PUHB-lik/ (*noun*) The word public refers to people in general, or to people who belong to a particular country or community. *page 180* [**público**]

Puerto Rico /PORT-oh REE-koh/ (*noun*) Puerto Rico is an island in the Caribbean that was once controlled by Spain and whose people are now United States citizens. *page 174* [**Puerto Rico**]

pyramid /PIR-a-mid/ (*noun*) A pyramid is a three-dimensional shape with a flat base and flat triangular sides that slope upwards to a point. Ancient Egyptians buried their rulers in large structures in the shape of a pyramid. *page 58* [**pirámide**]

R

radio /RAYD-ee-oh/ (*noun*) 1. Radio is a system for broadcasting of programs for the public to listen to, by sending out signals from a transmitter. 2. A radio is a piece of equipment used for listening to these broadcasts. *page 186* [**radio**]

raid /RAYD/ (*noun*) A raid is a sudden attack on a place or enemy. *page 160* [**incursión**]

railroad /RAYL-rohd/ (*noun*) A railroad is a route between two places along which trains travel on steel rails. *page 100* [**ferrocarril**]

rainforest /RAYN-for-est/ (*noun*) A rainforest is a thick forest of tall trees found mainly in tropical areas where there is a lot of rain. *page 22* [**bosque tropical**]

ranch /RANCH/ (*noun*) A ranch is a large farm used for raising animals. *page 150* [**rancho**]

ration /RAY-shuhn/ (*noun*) Your ration is the limited amount of something, especially food, that you are allowed to have when there is not enough of it. *page 196* [**ración**]

reason /REE-zuhn/ (*noun*) Reason is the ability that people have to think and to make sensible judgments. *page 90* [**razón**]

rebel /re-BEL/ (*verb*) When someone rebels, they reject the rules, values, or laws of their society. *page 92* [**rebelarse**]

Redcoat /RED-koht/ (*noun*) A Redcoat was a British soldier who fought in the American Revolution. *page 138* [**Redcoat**]

reduce /re-DOOS/ (*verb*) If you reduce something, you make it smaller. *page 113* [**reducir**]

Reformation /ref-er-MAY-shuhn/ (*noun*) The Reformation was the movement to reform the Catholic Church in the sixteenth century, which led to formation of the Protestant Church. *page 86* [**la Reforma**]

refugee /ref-yoo-JEE/ (*noun*) Refugees are people who have been forced to leave their homes or their country, either because there is a war there, or because of their political or religious beliefs. *pages 34, 209* [**refugiado(a)**]

region /REE-juhn/ (*noun*) A region is an area of a country or of the world. *pages 69, 128* [**región**]

reject /re-JEKT/ (*verb*) If you reject something such as a proposal or a request, you do not accept it or agree to it. *page 221* [**rechazar**]

religion /ree-LIJ-uhn/ (*noun*) A religion is a particular system of belief in a god or gods, and the activities that are connected with it. *page 14* [**religión**]

religious freedom /ree-LIJ-us FREE-duhm/ (*noun*) People who have religious freedom may choose to follow any religion that they wish. *page 130* [**libertad de religión**]

Renaissance /ren-e-SANS/ (noun) The Renaissance was the period in Europe, especially in Italy, in the fourteenth through sixteenth centuries, when there was a new interest in art, literature, science, and learning. *page 28* [**Renacimiento**]

renewable energy /ree-NOO-ah-bel en-er-JEE/ (noun) Renewable energy is any form of energy that is always available. It is taken from natural resources such as wind, water, or sunlight. *page 210* [**energía reanudable**]

republic /re-PUHB-lik/ (noun) A republic is a country that has a president, or a country whose system of government is based on the idea that every citizen has equal status. *page 214* [**república**]

Republican Party /re-PUHB-lik-an PAHRT-ee/ (noun) The Republican Party generally believes in lower taxes. This sometimes limits the party's support for social and economic programs. *pages 161, 234* [**Partido Republicano**]

representative /rep-re-ZENT-a-tiv/ (noun) In the United States, a representative is a member of the House of Representatives, one of the two parts of Congress. *page 218* [**representante**]

reservation /rez-er-VAY-shuhn/ (noun) A reservation is land in North America the United States government set aside for Native Americans to live on. *page 154* [**reserva**]

response /re-SPONS/ (noun) Your response to an event or to something that is said or done is your reply or reaction to it. *page 196* [**respuesta**]

reunite /ree-yu-NEYET/ (verb) If a divided organization or country is reunited, or if it reunites, it becomes one united organization or country again. *page 165* [**reunir**]

revolution /rev-a-LOO-shuhn/ (noun) A revolution is a successful attempt by a large group of people to change the political system of their country by force. *page 90* [**revolución**]

rice paddy /REYES pah-DEE/ (noun) A rice paddy is a field where rice is grown, commonly seen in eastern Asia. *page 46* [**arrozal**]

river /RIV-er/ (noun) A river is a large amount of fresh water flowing continuously in a long line across the land. *page 10* [**río**]

Rocky Mountains /ROK-ee MOWNT-enz/ (noun) The Rocky Mountains are the chief mountain range in North America stretching from New Mexico to Alaska. *page 154* [**Montañas Rocosas**]

Roman Empire /ROH-man EM-peye-yer/ (noun) The Roman Empire stretched around the Mediterranean Sea, including land in Europe, the Middle East, and North Africa. *page 62* [**Imperio Romano**]

Roman Peace /ROH-man pees/ (noun) The Roman Peace was the name for a long period of peace and well being during the Roman Empire. *page 64* [**Paz Romana**]

root /ROOT/ (noun) The roots of a plant are the parts of it that grow underground. *page 13* [**raíz**]

Rough Riders /RUF REYE-derz/ (noun) The Rough Riders were a group of American volunteer soldiers who fought in the Spanish-American War. *page 174* [**1er Regimiento de Caballería Voluntaria de Estados Unidos**]

rubber /RUHB-er/ (noun) Rubber is a strong, waterproof, elastic substance used for making tires, boots, and other products. *page 48* [**goma**]

rugged /RUG-ed/ (adjective) A rugged area of land is uneven, and is usually covered with rocks. *page 148* [**escabroso**]

rural /RUR-al/ (adjective) Rural places are far away from large towns or cities. *page 36* [**rural**]

S

Sahel /sa-HEL/ (noun) The Sahel is the wide stretch of land that runs between North Africa and Sub-Saharan Africa. *page 34* [**Sahel**]

salt /SALT/ (noun) Salt is a strong-tasting substance, in the form of white powder or crystals, which is used to improve the flavor of food or to preserve it. *page 74* [**sal**]

saltwater /SALT WAH-ter/ (noun) Saltwater is water, especially from the ocean, which has salt in it. *page 12* [**agua salada**]

satellite /SAT-el-eyet/ (noun) A satellite is an object that has been sent into space in order to collect information. *page 120* [**satélite**]

savanna /sah-VAN-a/ *(noun)* A savanna is a large area of flat, grassy land, usually in Africa. *page 34* [sabana]

scale /SKAYL/ *(noun)* The scale of a map is the relationship between the size of something on the map and its size in the real world. *page 4* [escala]

Scandinavia /skan-di-NAY-vee-a/ *(noun)* Scandinavia is part of Europe made up of the countries of Denmark, Norway, and Sweden. Many Vikings left Scandinavia because of its cold climate and poor farmland. *page 69* [Escandinavia]

science /SEYE-ens/ *(noun)* Science is the study of the nature and behavior of physical things and the knowledge that we obtain about them. *page 90* [ciencia]

scribe /SKREYEB/ *(noun)* In the past, a scribe was someone who wrote copies of things such as letters or documents. *pages 56, 60* [escribiente]

sculpture /SKUHLP-chur/ *(noun)* A sculpture is a work of art that is produced by carving or shaping stone, wood, clay, or other materials. *page 82* [escultura]

sea /SEE/ *(noun)* The sea is the salty water that covers about two-thirds of the earth's surface. *page 12* [mar]

sea level /SEE LEV-el/ *(noun)* A way to measure a place's elevation. Land near the coast is at sea level. Mountains can be miles above sea level. *page 12* [nivel del mar]

secede /se-SEED/ *(verb)* If a region or group secedes from the country or larger group to which it belongs, it formally becomes a separate country, or stops being a member of the larger group. *pages 161, 162* [separarse]

secondary sources /SEK-on-dair-ee SOR-ses/ *(noun)* Secondary sources are accounts of the past that were created by people writing about the events after they actually happened. *page 181* [fuentes secundarias]

secretary of state /SEK-re-tair-ee UHV STAYT/ *(noun)* In the United States, the secretary of state is the head of the government department that deals with foreign affairs. *page 222* [La secretaria de Estado]

segregate /seg-re-GAYT/ *(verb)* To segregate two groups of people or things means to keep them physically apart from each other. *page 196* [segregar]

segregation /seg-re-GAY-shuhn/ *(noun)* Segregation is the official practice of keeping people apart, usually when those people are of different sexes, races, or religions. *page 202* [segregación]

semi-arid /SEM-ee AIR-id/ *(adjective)* A place that is semi-arid receives very little rainfall, making it difficult to farm and raise crops. *page 32* [semiárido]

Senate /SEN-it/ *(noun)* The Senate is the smaller of the two houses of Congress. The Senate has 100 members, two members from each state. Senators are elected for six-year terms. There is no limit on the number of terms they can serve. *page 218* [el Senado]

separation of powers /sep-a-RAY-shuhn UHV POW-erz/ *(noun)* A separation of powers is when each part of government is separate from the other and has a special function. *page 214* [separación de poderes]

serf /SERF/ *(noun)* Serfs were a class of people who had to work on someone's land and could not leave without permission. *page 66* [siervo]

servant /SER-vant/ *(noun)* A servant is someone who is employed to work at another person's home. *page 101* [sirviente(a)]

service /SER-vis/ *(noun)* A service is something that an organization or group provides for public need. *page 16* [servicio]

settlement /SET-uhl-ment/ *(noun)* A settlement is a place where people have come to live and have built homes. *page 18* [asentamiento]

shelter /SHEL-ter/ *(noun)* A shelter is a small building or place that is made to protect people from bad weather or danger. *page 52* [refugio, albergue]

shopping mall /SHOP-ing MAWL/ *(noun)* A shopping mall is a specially built covered area containing shops and restaurants where cars are parked outside. *page 198* [parque commercial]

Sierra Nevada Mountains /see-air-ah ne-VAH-dah MOWNT-enz/ *(noun)* The Sierra Nevada Mountains are a mountain range that separates California from the rest of the United States to the east. *page 154* [Montañas de Sierra Nevada]

silk /SILK/ *(noun)* Silk is a smooth, shiny fabric that is made from the thread of silkworms. *page 70* [seda]

silt /SILT/ *(noun)* Silt is fine sand, soil, or mud that is carried along by a river. *page 48* [limo]

silver /SIL-ver/ *(noun)* Silver is a valuable pale gray metal that is used for making jewelry, coins, and ornaments. *page 94* [plata]

sin /SIN/ *(noun)* A sin is an action or type of behavior that is believed to break the laws of God. *page 88* [pecado]

sit-in /SIT-in/ *(noun)* A sit-in is an organized protest, where people occupy seats or spaces and refuse to leave until their demands are met. *page 202*

slave /SLAYV/ *(noun)* A slave is someone who is the property of another person and who has to work for that person. *page 136* [esclavo(a)]

slave state /SLAYV STAYT/ *(noun)* Until 1865, slave states were states where slavery was legally allowed. *page 158* [estado con esclavos]

slavery /SLAYV-er-ee/ *(noun)* Slavery is the system by which people are owned as slaves by other people. *page 134* [esclavitud]

slogan /SLOH-gan/ *(noun)* A slogan is a short phrase that is easy to remember. Slogans are used in advertisements and by political parties and other organizations who want people to remember what they are saying or selling. *page 184* [slogan]

smog /SMOG/ *(noun)* Smog is a mixture of fog and smoke that occurs in some busy industrial cities. *page 200* [niebla tóxica]

smoke /SMOHK/ *(noun)* Smoke is the gray or black cloud of gases and other materials that is produced by something that is burning. *page 100* [humo]

snow /SNOH/ *(noun)* Snow consists of a lot of soft white pieces of frozen water that fall from the sky in cold weather. *page 12* [nieve]

social class /SOH-shuhl KLAS/ *(noun)* A social class is a group in a society with common economic, cultural, or political status. *page 58* [clase social]

Social Security /SOH-shuhl she-KYOOR-i-tee/ *(noun)* Social Security is a system by which workers and employers in the United States have to pay money to the government. The government then gives money to people who are retired, who are disabled, or who cannot work. *page 190* [Seguridad Social]

socialist /SOH-shuhl-ist/ *(noun)* A socialist is a person who believes that the state should own and run factories, hospitals, schools, and so on, and that people in the society should have equal opportunities. *page 106* [socialista]

society /suh-SEYE-it-ee/ *(noun)* Society consists of all the people in an organized community, particularly considered in terms of their behavior, traditions, and law. *page 16, 126* [sociedad]

sod house /SOD HOWS/ *(noun)* A sod house is a house made of grass and soil. *page 148* [casa de tierra enzacatada]

soil /SOYL/ *(noun)* Soil is the top layer on the surface of the earth in which plants grow. *page 54* [tierra]

soldier /SOHL-jer/ *(noun)* A soldier is a member of an army. *page 140* [soldado]

south /SOWTH/ *(noun)* The south is the direction that is on your right when you are looking toward the direction where the sun rises. *page 4* [sur]

South America /SOWTH a-MER-i-ka/ *(noun)* South America is the continent between the South Atlantic and South Pacific Oceans. *page 22* [América del Sur, Sudamérica]

South Asia /SOWTH AY-zhah/ *(noun)* South Asia is comprised of the countries in the southern, central part of Asia. South Asia is separated from the rest of Asia by the Himalaya Mountains. *page 38* [Asia del Sur]

South Pole /SOWTH POHL/ (*noun*) The South Pole is the tip of land that is farthest toward the south on Earth. *page 2* **[Polo Sur]**

South Vietnam /SOWTH vee-et-NAHM/ (*noun*) South Vietnam was the part of Vietnam that opposed communism. *page 206* **[Vietnam del Sur]**

southeast /sow-THEEST/ (*noun*) The southeast is the direction that is between south and east. *page 129* **[sureste, sudeste]**

Southeast Asia / sow-THEEST AY-zhah/ (*noun*) Southeast Asia includes the land between China and India. *page 46* **[Sudeste de Asia]**

Southern Colonies (32) /SUHTH-ern KOL-uh-neez/ (*noun*) The southern colonies were Maryland, Virginia, North Carolina, South Carolina, and Georgia. *page 134* **[Colonias Sur]**

Southern Hemisphere /SUHTH-ern HEM-i-sfeer/ (*noun*) The Southern Hemisphere is the half of the earth that lies south of the equator line. *page 2* **[Hemisferio Sur]**

southwest (30) /SOWTH-west/ (*noun*) The southwest is the direction that is between south and west. *page 128* **[Sudoeste]**

Soviet Union /SOHV-ee-et YOON-yuhn/ (*noun*) The Soviet Union was a group of countries, including Russia, united under one government from 1922 to 1991. *page 114* **[Unión Soviética]**

Spanish /SPAN-ish/ (*noun*) Spanish is the official language of Spain, and of many countries in the Americas. *page 22* **[español]**

spice /SPEYES/ (*noun*) A spice is a part of a plant, or a powder made from that part, that you put in food to give it flavor. Cinnamon, ginger, and paprika are spices. *pages 70, 132* **[especia]**

spinning wheel /SPIN-ing WEEL/ (*noun*) A spinning wheel is a wooden machine that people used in their homes to make thread from wool in former times. *page 98* **[rueca]**

standard of living /STAN-derd UHV LIV-ing/ (*noun*) Your standard of living is the level of comfort and wealth that you have. *page 28* **[estándar de vida]**

steam engine /STEEEM en-JIN/ (*noun*) A steam engine provided power to machines and generated energy which helped people make products faster. *page 98* **[máquina de vapor]**

steamboat /STEEM BOHT/ (*noun*) A steamboat is a boat or ship that has an engine powered by steam. *page 100* **[barco de vapor]**

steppe /STEP/ (*noun*) Steppes are large areas of flat grassy land where there are no trees, especially in the area that stretches from Eastern Europe across the south of the former Soviet Union to Siberia. *page 42* **[estepa]**

stock market /STOK MAR-ket/ (*noun*) The stock market consists of the general activity of buying stocks and shares, and the people and institutions that organize it. *page 186* **[bolsa de valores]**

strait /STRAYT/ (*noun*) A strait is a narrow strip of ocean that joins two large areas of ocean. *page 18* **[estrecho]**

stream /STREEM/ (*noun*) A stream is a small narrow river. *page 10* **[arroyo]**

strike /STREYEK/ (*verb*) When workers strike, they stop doing their work for a period of time, usually in order to try to get better pay or working conditions from their employer. *page 170* **[declararse en huelga]**

structure /STRUK-chur/ (*noun*) A structure is something that is built from or consists of parts connected together in an ordered way. *page 16* **[estructura]**

submarine /sub-ma-REEN/ (*noun*) A submarine is a type of ship that can travel both above and below the surface of the ocean. *page 110* **[submarino]**

Sub-Saharan Africa /sub-sah-HAR-an AF-ri-ka/ (*noun*) Sub-Saharan Africa is the area of the African continent south of the Sahara Desert. *page 34* **[África Sub-sahariana]**

subsistence farming /sub-SIS-tents FARM-ing/ (*noun*) In subsistence farming or subsistence agriculture, farmers produce food to eat themselves rather than to sell. *page 36* **[agricultura de subsistencia]**

suburb /SUB-erb/ (*noun*) A suburb of a city or large town is a town or an area that is part of the city or large town but that is far from its center. *page 198* [suburbia]

succession /suk-SESH-uhn/ (*noun*) Succession is the act or right of being the next person to have an important job or position. *page 224* [sucesión, secuencia]

sue /SOO/ (*verb*) If you sue someone, you start a legal case against them, usually in order to claim money from them because they have harmed you in some way. *page 160* [demander]

Suez Canal /SOO-ez kuh-NAL/ (*noun*) The Suez Canal is one of the worlds' most important human-made waterways. It connects the Mediterranean Sea and the Red Sea. *page 30* [Canal de Suez]

suffrage /SUF-rij/ (*noun*) Suffrage is the right of people to vote for a government or national leader. *page 150* [sufragio]

suffragist /SUF-ra-jist/ (*noun*) A suffragist is a person who is in favor of women having the right to vote, especially in societies where women are not allowed to vote. *page 106* [sufragista]

sugar /SHUG-ar/ (*noun*) Sugar is a substance that is used to make food and drinks sweet. It is usually in the form of small white or brown crystals. *page 94* [azúcar]

superpower /SOO-per POW-er/ (*noun*) A superpower is a very powerful and influential country, usually one that is rich and has nuclear weapons. *page 118* [superpotencia]

surface /SUR-fas/ (*noun*) The surface of something is the flat top part of it or the outside of it. *page 12* [superficie]

Supreme Court /soo-PREEM CORT/ (*noun*) The highest court in the nation is the Supreme Court. It is made up of nine judges called justices. *pages 225, 226* [la Corte Suprema]

surrender /suh-REN-der/ (*verb*) If you surrender, you stop fighting or resisting someone and accept that you have been beaten. *pages 116, 141* [entregar]

swampy /SWAM-pee/ (*adjective*) A swampy area of land is always very wet. *page 129* [pantanoso]

sweatshop /SWET-shop/ (*noun*) If you describe a small factory as a sweatshop, you mean that many people work there in poor conditions for low pay. *page 178* [fábrica de explotación]

symbol /SIM-buhl/ (*noun*) A symbol of something such as an idea is a shape or design that is used to represent it. *page 56* [símbolo]

system /SIS-tem/ (*noun*) A system is a way of working, organizing, or doing something that follows a fixed plan or set of rules. *page 77* [sistema]

T

Taj Mahal /TAZH ma-HAHL/ (*noun*) The Taj Mahal is one of the most famous buildings of the world and is located in South Asia. A ruler built it in the 1600s to honor his wife. *page 38* [Taj Mahal]

tank /TANK/ (*noun*) A tank is a large military vehicle that is equipped with weapons and moves along on metal tracks that are fitted over the wheels. *page 110* [carro de combate]

tax /TAKS/ (*verb*) **1.** When a person or company is taxed they have to pay a part of their income or profits to the government. When goods are taxed, a percentage of their price has to be paid to the government. *page 136* [gravar]

(*noun*) **2.** Tax is an amount of money that you have to pay to the government so that it can pay for public services such as roads and schools. *pages 138, 230* [impuesto]

tea /TEE/ (*noun*) Tea is a drink made by pouring boiling water on the chopped dried leaves of a plant called the tea bush. *page 138* [té]

technology /tek-NOL-e-jee/ (*noun*) Technology refers to methods, systems, and devices that are the result of scientific knowledge being used for practical purposes. *page 122* [tecnología]

teepee /TEE-PEE/ (*noun*) A teepee is a round tent. Teepees were first made from animal skins by Native American people. *page 128* [tipi]

telephone /TEL-e-fohn/ (noun) The telephone is the electrical system of communication that you use to talk directly to someone else in a different place. You use the telephone by dialing a number on a piece of equipment and speaking into it. *page 178* [teléfono]

telescope /TEL-e-scohp/ (noun) A telescope is a long instrument shaped like a tube. It has lenses inside it that make distant things seem larger and nearer when you look through it. *page 82* [telescopio]

temperate climate /TEM-per-et KLEYE-mit/ (noun) A temperate climate changes through the year. Summers are warm or hot and winters are cool or cold. *page 20* [clima templado(a)]

tension /TEN-shuhn/ (noun) Tension is a feeling of anxiety produced by a difficult or dangerous situation, especially one in which there is a possibility of conflict or violence. *page 140* [tensión]

term /TERM/ (noun) A term is a period of time during which an elected official is in office. *pages 184, 224* [duración del mandato]

terrace farming /TER-as FARM-ing/ (noun) Terrace farming is the activity of growing crops on a flat area carved from a steep area of land such as a mountain side. *page 77* [cultivo en terrazas]

territory /TER-i-tor-ee/ (noun) A territory is an area that is controlled by a particular country or ruler. *page 152* [territorio]

terrorism /TER-er-iz-im/ (noun) Terrorism is the use of violence, especially murder and bombing, in order to achieve political aims. *page 210* [terrorismo]

Thanksgiving /THANKS-giv-ing/ (noun) In the United States, Thanksgiving or Thanksgiving Day is a public holiday on the fourth Thursday in November, when people remember the occasion on which the first European settlers celebrated a successful harvest with the Native Americans. *page 130* [el día de Acción de Gracias]

theocracy /thee-AH-cra-see/ (noun) A theocracy is a society that is ruled by priests or other religious officials who represent a god. *page 238* [teocracia]

thread /THRED/ (noun) Thread or a thread is a long very thin piece of a material such as cotton, nylon, or silk, especially one that is used in sewing. *page 98* [hilo]

throne /THROHN/ (noun) A throne is a decorative chair used by a king, queen, or emperor on important official occasions. *page 106* [trono]

Timbuktu /tim-buk-TOO/ (noun) Timbuktu was an early center of trade and culture in Africa. *page 74* [Timbuktu]

tin /TIN/ (noun) Tin is a soft, silvery-white metal. *page 48* [estaño]

tobacco /toh-BAK-oh/ (noun) Tobacco is the dried leaves of a plant, which people smoke in pipes, cigars, and cigarettes. *page 134* [tabaco]

tomb /TOOM/ (noun) A tomb is a stone structure containing the body of a dead person. *page 60* [tumba]

tool /TOOL/ (noun) A tool is any instrument or simple piece of equipment, for example a hammer or a knife, that you hold in your hands and use to do a particular kind of work. *page 50* [instrumento]

torpedo /tor-PEE-doh/ (noun) A torpedo is a bomb that is shaped like a tube and that travels under water. *page 112* [torpedo]

torture /TOR-chur/ (noun) Torture is when one person deliberately causes another person great pain over a period of time in order to punish them or to make them reveal information. *page 116* [tortura]

totalitarian /toh-tal-i-TER-ee-an/ (adjective) A totalitarian political system is one in which there is only one political party that controls everything and does not allow any opposition parties. *page 118* [totalitario]

tourist /TOR-ist/ (noun) A tourist is a person who is visiting a place for pleasure, especially when they are on vacation. *page 49* [turista]

town meeting /TOWN MEET-ing/ (noun) A town meeting is a meeting held by the residents of a town, or by the people who are eligible to vote in a town. *page 134* [reunión municipal]

trade /TRAYD/ (noun) Trade is the activity of buying, selling, or exchanging goods or services between people, companies, or countries. pages 128, 144 [comercio]

trade route /TRAYD ROOT/ (noun) A trade route is a route, often covering a long distance, that is used by traders. page 154 [ruta comercial]

trail /TRAYL/ (noun) A trail is a rough path across open country or through forests. page 154 [camino]

Trail of Tears /TRAYL UHV TEERZ/ (noun) The Trail of Tears refers to the forced movement of Native Americans from their land east of the Mississippi River to the West. page 146 [Camino de Lágrimas]

transaction /tranz-AK-shuhn/ (noun) A transaction is an act of buying or selling something. page 56 [transacción]

transportation /tranz-por-TAY-shuhn/ (noun) Transportation refers to any kind of vehicle that you can travel in or carry goods in. page 170 [transportación]

treason /TREEZ-uhn/ (noun) Treason is the crime of betraying your country. page 93 [traición]

treasure /TREZH-ur/ (noun) Treasures are valuable objects, especially works of art and items of historical value. pages 60, 69 [tesoro]

treaty /TREE-tee/ (noun) A treaty is a written agreement between countries. pages 112, 225 [tratado]

trench /TRENCH/ (noun) A trench is a long narrow channel that has been dug in the ground. page 112 [trinchera]

trial /TREYE-al/ (noun) A trial is a formal meeting in a law court at which a judge and jury listen to evidence and decide whether a person is guilty of a crime. page 226 [juicio]

troops /TROOPZ/ (noun) Troops are soldiers. page 102 [tropas]

tropical climate /TROP-i-kal KLEYE-mit/ (noun) In a tropical climate the weather is always hot. There is no winter. page 20 [clima tropical]

tsunami /soo-NAHM-ee/ (noun) A tsunami is a very large wave, often caused by an earthquake, that flows onto the land and can cause widespread death and destruction. page 48 [tsunami]

Tutankhamen /too-tan-KAHM-en/ (noun) Tutankhamen was the Egyptian king from 1361 to 1352 B.C.E. page 58 [Tutankhamen]

U

unconstitutional /un-kon-sti-TOOSH-in-al/ (adjective) If something is unconstitutional, it breaks the rules of a constitution. page 204 [inconstitucional]

Underground Railroad /UN-der-grownd RAYL-rohd/ (noun) The Underground Railroad was a system of secret routes and safe places that helped African American slaves escape from the South. page 158 ["ferrocarril subterráneo"]

unemployment /un-em-PLOY-ment/ (noun) Unemployment is a situation in which people who want jobs cannot get them. page 190 [desempleo]

Union /YOON-yuhn/ (noun) When two or more things, for example countries or organizations, have been joined together to form one thing, you can refer to them as a union. Together, the states of the United States of America form a union. page 163 [unión]

union /YOON-yuhn/ (noun) A union is a workers' organization that represents its members and that tries to improve things such as their working conditions and pay. page 170 [unión]

unite /YOO-neyet/ (verb) If a group of people or things unite, or if something unites them, they join together and act as a group. page 102 [unir]

United Nations /yoo-NEYET-ed NAY-shuhnz / (noun) The United Nations is an organization that most countries belong to. Its role is to encourage international peace, cooperation, and friendship. page 118 [Naciones Unidas]

United States Constitution /yoo-NEYET-ed STAYTS kon-sti-TOO-shuhn/ (noun) The Constitution is the highest law in the nation.

It explains how the national government works. *page 214* [**Constitución de Estados Unidos**]

unsanitary /un-SAN-i-tair-ee/ *(adjective)* Something that is unsanitary is dirty and unhealthy, so that you may catch a disease from it. *page 180* [**antihigiénico**]

upper class /UP-er KLAS/ *(noun)* The upper class or the upper classes are the group of people in a society who own the most property and have the highest social status. *page 101* [**clase alta**]

urban /ER-ban/ *(adjective)* Urban means belonging to, related to, or located in a city. *page 170* [**urbano(a)**]

U.S.S. *Maine* /U S S MAYN/ *(noun)* The U.S.S. *Maine* was an American ship that exploded in a harbor in Cuba in 1898. It killed 266 people and the United States declared war on Spain because it believed Spain caused the explosion. *page 175* [**U.S.S. Maine**]

Union /YOON-yuhn/ *(noun)* When two or more things, for example countries or organizations, have been joined together to form one thing, you can refer to them as a union. Together, the states of the United States of America form a union. *page 163* [**unión**]

union /YOON-yuhn/ *(noun)* A union is a workers' organization that represents its members and that tries to improve things such as their working conditions and pay. *page 170* [**unión**]

V

valley /VAL-ee/ *(noun)* A valley is a low stretch of land between hills, especially one that has a river flowing through it. *page 10* [**valle**]

vegetation /vej-e-TAY-shuhn/ *(noun)* Plants, trees, and flowers can be referred to as vegetation. *pages 32, 34, 40* [**vegetación**]

Venice /VEN-is/ *(noun)* Venice is a port city in northern Italy that is famous for its canals. *page 70* [**Venicia**]

vertical timeline /VERT-i-kal TEYEM LEYEN/ *(noun)* A vertical timeline usually lists the earliest, or first, event at the bottom of the timeline and the most recent, or last,

event at the top of the timeline. *page 6* [**cronología vertical**]

veteran /VET-e-ran/ *(noun)* A veteran is someone who has served in the armed forces of their country, especially during a war. *page 200* [**veterano**]

veto /VEE-toh/ *(verb)* If someone in authority vetoes something, they forbid it or stop it from being put into action. The president can veto a bill to stop it from becoming a law. *pages 221, 222* [**vetar**]

vice president /VEYEZ PREZ-id-ent/ *(noun)* The vice president is part of the executive branch of government. If something happens to the president, the vice president is first in line of succession to take over the president's duties. The vice president also presides over the Senate. *page 222* [**vicepresidente**]

Viet Cong / VEE-et KONG/ *(noun)* The Viet Cong was a communist guerrilla army in South Vietnam. *page 208* [**Viet Cong**]

Viking /VEYE-king/ *(noun)* The Vikings were men who sailed from Scandinavia and attacked villages in most parts of northwestern Europe from the eighth to the eleventh centuries. It is also believed that they may have sailed to North America. *page 66* [**vikingo(a)**]

volcano /vol-KAY-noh/ *(noun)* A mountain from which hot melted rock, gas, steam, and ash from inside the earth sometimes burst. *page 22, 48* [**volcán**]

volunteer /vol-uhn-TEER/ *(verb)* To volunteer is to give or offer a service without being paid. *page 230* [**ofrecerse voluntariamente**]

vote /VOHT/ *(verb)* **1.** To vote is to indicate your choice of candidate, or to indicate your view regarding some other public decision, in an election. [**votar**]; *(noun)* **2.** If you have the vote, you have the legal right to indicate your choice in an election. *page 230* [**voto**]

voting rights /VOHT-ing reyets/ *(noun)* When a person has the legal right to vote in a political or corporate environment, he or she has voting rights. *page 106* [**derechos votos**]

voyage /VOI-ij/ *(noun)* A voyage is a long journey on a ship or in a spacecraft. *page 98* [**viaje**]

W

wagon train /WAG-en TRAYN/ (*noun*) A wagon train is a line of horses and wagons, especially one that formerly carried supplies or settlers. *page 154* [tren de carro]

walled city /WAWLD SIT-ee / (*noun*) In the past, a walled city was a large settlement that was surrounded by a strong defensive wall. *page 42* [ciudad amurallada]

war /WAWR/ (*noun*) A war is a period of fighting or conflict, especially between countries. *page 110* [guerra]

Washington, D.C. /WAHSH in ten dee-cee/ (*noun*) Washington, D.C., is the capital of the United States. It is where the president lives and works in the White House, and where Congress is located. D.C. stands for "District of Columbia." *page 222* [Washington, D.C.]

waste /WAYST/ (*noun*) Waste is material that has been used and that is no longer wanted, for example, because the valuable or useful part of it has been taken out. *page 85* [residuos]

water buffalo /wat-UR BUF-a-loh/ (*noun*) A water buffalo is an animal like a large cow with long horns that curve upwards. In some countries water buffalos are kept for their milk and are used to draw plows. *page 46* [búfalo del agua]

waterfall /wat-UR fahl/ (*noun*) A waterfall is a place where water flows over the edge of a steep high cliff in hills or mountains and falls into a pool below. *page 10* [cascada]

weapon /WEP-on/ (*noun*) A weapon is an object such as a gun, a knife, or a missile, which is used to kill or hurt people in a fight or a war. *page 100, 110* [arma]

weaving /WEE-ving/ (*noun*) A weaving is made by crossing long plant stems or fibers over and under each other. *page 126* [tejido]

west /WEST/ (*noun*) The west is the direction in which the sun sets in the evening. *page 4* [oeste]

wheel /WEEL/ (*noun*) The wheels of a vehicle are the round objects that are attached underneath it and that allow it to move along the ground. *page 54* [rueda]

White House /WEYET HOWS/ (*noun*) The president lives and works in the White House in Washington, D.C. *page 222* [la Casa Blanca]

wilderness /WIL-der-ness/ (*noun*) A wilderness is a desert or other area of natural land that is not used by people. *page 148* [tierra salvaje]

wind /WIND/ (*noun*) A wind is a current of air that moves across the earth's surface. *page 40* [viento]

woodland /WUD-land/ (*noun*) Woodland is land that is covered with a lot of trees. *page 146* [bosque]

wound /WOOMD/ (*noun*) A wound is a damaged area on someone's body, especially a cut or hole in the flesh, which is caused by a gun, knife, or other weapon. *page 164* [herida]

yellow fever /YEL-oh FEE-ver/ (*noun*) Yellow fever is a serious infectious disease that people can catch in tropical countries. *page 176* [fiebre amarilla]

yellow journalism /YEL-oh JURN-al-iz-im/ (*noun*) Yellow journalism is reporting that exaggerates or falsifies the facts of a story. *page 176* [periodismo amarillo]

Y

Yucatán Peninsula /yoo-ka-TAN pe-NIN-soo-la/ (*noun*) The Yucatán Peninsula is a peninsula between the Caribbean Sea and the Gulf of Mexico. *page 94* [La Península Yucatán]

Index

The index for *Gateway to Social Studies* will help you locate social studies terms and topics quickly and easily. Each entry in the index is followed by the numbers of the pages on which it appears. A page number in **bold italic type** indicates a page on which the entry is used in a graphic or photograph.

Southern Hemisphere, *2*, 3
Soviet Union, *See also Cold War.*
   1922–1991, 114, *114*, 115, 116, *116*
     breakup of, 124–125, *125*
     and Cuban Missile Crisis, 199, 200
     and Sputnik, 119, 121
Space race, 120. *See also Cold War.*
Spain, 72, 79, 80, 97
Spanish-American War the, 174, 175–177
Spanish language, *22*, 23
Special interest groups, 236, *236*
Spices, 71, *71*, 132
Spinning wheel, 98, *98*, 99
Stamp Act, 135, 136, *136. See also America, Colonial.*
Standard of living, 28
Standard Oil Company, *172*
Stanton, Elizabeth Cady. 151, *151*, 152, *153.*
     See also Amendment, 19th and Women's
     voting rights.
State of the Union address, 225, *225*
Statue of Liberty, 181, *181*
Steam engine, 99, *99*
Steppe, 43, *43*
Stock market, 187
   1929 crash of, 187, *187*, 188–189, *188*, 191
Strait, 19, *19*
Strike, 171, *171*
Sub-Saharan Africa, 34–37
Suburbanization, 198, 199, 200
Suez Canal, 31, *31*
Suffrage, 151, *151,* 152. *See also Women's voting rights.*
Suffragist, *106*, 107, *108*, 151, 152. *See also Women's*
     voting rights.
Sugar Act, 136
Sumerians, 55–56
   cuneiform, 56, *56*
Sundiata, *76*
Superpower, 118, *118,* 119
Supreme Court, 160, 168, 204, 225, *226*, 227, 228,
     228, 233
Sustainable growth, 124
Sweatshop, 178, *178*, 179. *See also Industrial Revolution.*
Swift, Jonathan, 92

T

Taj Mahal, 38, *38*, 39
Taxes,
   and citizens, *230*, 230, 231, 232
   Colonial America, 136, 139, 140
Teepees, 128, *128*
Tenements, 173, *173*

Tennessee Valley Authority, 193
Terrace farming, 77, *77*
Terrorism, 124, *210*, 210, 211, 213, *213*
Texas, 20, 152. See also *Mexican-American War.*
   and Alamo, *152*
   independence of, 152
   joins the Union, 152
Thanksgiving, 131, *131*, 133
Theocracy, 239, *239*
Tigris River, 56, *56*
Timbuktu, 74, *74*, 75
Timelines
   horizontal, *6*, 7
   vertical, 7, *7*
Tobacco
   in colonial America, *134*, 135
Tokyo, 45
Totalitarian, 119, *119*
Trade routes, *54*
   between early civilizations, 55
   and Imperialism, 95, 97
   Silk Road, 61
   Triangular Trade, 81, *81*
Trail of Tears, 147, *147. See also Native Americans.*
Transcontinental railroad, 154, *154*, 155,
     156, *156*
Triangle Shirtwaist Factory, 180, *180*
Triangular Trade, 81, *81*
Tribal masks, 37, *37*
Trujillo, Rafael, *240*
Truman, Harry. *See also World War II.*
   as president, 195, *195*, 197.
   soldier in World War I, 185, *185*
Tubman, Harriet, *158*, 159, 160
Tutankhamen, *58*, 59

U

Underground Railroad, 159, *159*, 160. *See also*
     Tubman, Harriet.
Union, the, 162, *162. See also Civil War, the.*
Union Pacific Railroad, 156, *156*
Unions, labor, 170, *170,* 171, 180
United Farm Workers, 205. *See also César Chávez.*
United Nations, 118, *118*, 119
   Model United Nations, 241, *241*
United States, 11, 20, 21
   challenges facing the, 211, 212–213
   life expectancy in, 212
United States Constitution, 215, *215*, 216,
     216, 217. *See also Preamble to the*
     Constitution.

Skills Index

Social Studies Skills

Analyzing

Archaeological Artifacts, 56
A Comparison Chart, 232
Historical Photographs, 177, 192, 204
Line Graphs, 212
Political Cartoons, 120, 137
Primary Sources, 196, 201

Comparing

Photographs, 12

Comparing and Contrasting

Historical Maps, 125
Visual Images, 156

Distinguishing

Fact from Opinion, 84

Interpreting

Bar Graphs, 173
Charts, 60
A Concept Map, 92
A Diagram, 224
Graphic Information, 80
Historical Photographs, 192
A Painting, 68
A Photograph, 108, 128, 169
A Pie Chart, 117
A Political Cartoon, 208
Primary Source Documents, 160
A Timeline, 184
A Visual Image, 100

Making

Observations, 48

Reading

A Cause and Effect Diagram, 140
A Chart, 104
A Climate Map, 32
A Diagram, 228

Double Bar Graphs, 164
A Flow Chart, 220
A Graph, 189
A Historical Map, 64, 96, 145
A Line Graph, 29
A Map, 73, 112
A Map Key, 132, 153
A Migration Map, 52
A Natural Vegetation Map, 40
A Physical Map, 20, 44
A Pie Chart, 16
A Political Map, 241
A Population Density Map, 36
A Population Pyramid, 24
A Route Map, 148
A Table, 217, 236
A Tree Diagram, 88
A Venn Diagram, 76

Studying

Primary and Secondary Sources, 181

Word Study

Antonyms
integration, segregation, 202
rise, decline, 94
temporary, permanent, 190
Commonly Confused Words
desert, dessert, 30
Compound Words
grasslands, 34
muckrakers, 178
rice paddy, 46
sweatshop, 178
water buffalo, 46
Homonyms
by, buy, 186
knight, night, 66
Irregular plurals
life, lives, 162
Loan Words
ranch, rancho, 150
Multiple-Meaning Words
cabinet, 222
china, China, 70
court, 226
party, 234

reservation, 154
right, 214
rule, 174
state, 158
Noncount Nouns
rice, tobacco, cotton, 134
Nouns Used as Verbs
bomb, 194
export, import, 210
vote, 230
Parts of Speech
settle (v.), settler (n.), 18
Prefixes
com-, 218
con-, 218
inter-, 14
mon-, 90
mono-, 90
multi-, 122
post-, 118
pre-, 50
re-, 86
trans-, 170
un-, 206
Suffixes
-er, 42
-ious, 38
-ize, 166
-less, 146
-ous, 38
Superlative Adjectives
-est, 22
Syllabification
constitution, 142
exploration, 78
propaganda, 182
Synonyms
voyage, journey, 130
Word Families
aggressive, aggression, 114
hostile, hostility, 102
prosperous, prosper, prosperity, 198
trade, 94
Word History
boycott, 138
Word Meanings
czar, 106
Word Origins
civilization, 54

Critical Thinking Skills

Academic Vocabulary

Credits

Illustrators

Peter Bull: pp. 66 (bottom), 92, 93, 116, 123, 130 (bottom), 136, 139 (center), 159, 202 (left), 206 (left), 211, 214, 226, 228, 234, 238, 239 (bottom).

Phil Foster: pp. 119.

Jeff Mangiat: pp. 14 (left, and center), 17 (top left), 50 (top), 64 (right) 72 (bottom), 79 (bottom), 86, 88 (bottom), 90 (bottom right), 92 (right), 106 (bottom) 113, 118 (center), 138 (center), 152, 157, 168, 185, 193, 208.

Maps.com: pp. 4, 5, 18–20, 22, 24, 26–28, 30–36, 38, 44, 46–47, 52, 54–56, 62, 64, 73–75, 80–81, 102, 110, 112, 118, 126, 128, 130, 132, 134, 136, 146–147, 150, 153, 156, 158, 162, 174, 195, 196, 206, 210, 222, 241.

Tom Newsom: pp. 18-19, 48–49, 50 (center), 58, 60 (top), 69, 76 (bottom), 82, 85, 87 (top), 91 (top), 126 (right, and center left), 127, 129, 132, 158, 167, 196, 230-231.

Frank Riccio: pp. 76, 78, 90 (top), 99 (bottom), 132 (right), 156.

Rob Schuster: pp. 10, 22, 57, 60 (center), 63, 66, 88 (center), 118 (bottom), 122, 130 (flag), 183, 186, 190, 202 (top), 207, 215, 217, 218, 223, 235, 139 (top).

Daniela Terrazzini: pp. 59.

Photos

Unit Icon Photos: Geography: ©Ladyann / Shutterstock; Resources: ©ImageZoo / Alamy; ©Vladimir Wrangler / Alamy; World History: ©Frank Whitney / The Image Bank / Getty Images; American History: ©Jean-Claude Marlaud / PhotoAlto / Corbis; ©Tom Grill / Corbis; Government: ©Joseph Sohm; Visions of America / Corbis; ©Pgiam / iStockphoto

2-3 (background): ©Petra Roeder / Alamy; 3 (top): ©M-Sat Ltd. / Photo Researchers, Inc.; 3 (bottom): ©Doug Taylor / Alamy; 4-5 (background): ©Stephen Sweet / Alamy; 6 (center left): ©INTERFOTO / Alamy; 6 (center): ©Hulton Collection / Getty Images; 6 (center right): ©GIPhotoStock / Photo Researchers; 6 (bottom left): ©ClassicStock / Alamy; 6 (bottom center): ©Museum of Flight / Corbis; 8-9 (background): ©Library of Congress; 8 (1): ©Library of Congress; 8 (2): ©Anne Frank Fonds / Getty Images; 8 (3): ©Bildarchiv Preussischer Kulturbesitz / Art Resource, NY; 8 (4): ©Bettmann / Corbis; 9 (5): ©Peter Newark American Pictures / Bridgeman Art Library International; 9 (6): ©North Wind / North Wind Picture Archives; 9 (7): ©Library of Congress; 12 (top): ©Morey Milbradt / Getty Images; 12 (center): ©Larry Prosor / Superstock / PhotoLibrary; 12 (bottom): ©Tetra Images / Corbis; 13 (top): ©Micha Pawlitzki / Corbis; 13 (bottom): ©Chris Ison / PA Wire / AP Images; 14 (top): ©John Lund / Getty Images; 14 (center): ©Donald Pye / Alamy; 14 (bottom): ©Tibor Bognár / Corbis; 15 (top): ©Brooks Kraft / Corbis; 15 (center): ©Raimund Koch / Corbis; 15 (bottom left): ©Alan Schein Photography / CORBIS; 15 (bottom right): ©Prisma Bildagentur AG / Alamy; 16 (top): ©Radius / Superstock; 16 (bottom left): ©Ben Molyneux / Alamy; 15 (bottom right): ©Ocean / Corbis; 17 (top): ©Construction Photography / Corbis; 17 (center): ©Massimo Borchi / Atlantide Phototravel / Corbis; 17 (bottom): ©James Houck / Alamy; 19 (center): ©Gary Hincks / Photo Researchers, Inc.; 19 (bottom): ©The New York Public Library; 20 (bottom left): ©Jack Fletcher / National Geographic Society / Corbis; 20 (bottom right): ©AGStockUSA / Alamy; 21: ©Louie Psihoyos / Corbis; 23 (top): ©Dennis Drenner / Getty Images; 23 (bottom): ©Martin Rietze / Westend61 / Corbis; 24 (bottom left): ©Stapleton Collection / Corbis; 24 (visual cue, clockwise from top): ©Mathew Imaging / WireImage / Getty Images; ©Jose Luis Pelaez Inc. / Getty Images; ©Keith Dannemiller / Alamy; ©Frans Lanting / Corbis; 25 (top): ©KARIM JAAFAR / AFP / Getty Images; 25 (bottom): ©Bartosz Hadyniak / iStockphoto; 26: ©Ayzek / iStockphoto; 27 (top): ©Creativ Studio Heinemann / Getty Images; 27 (top center): ©Steve Stock / Alamy; 28 (center left): ©Yuri Maselov / Alamy; 28 (center right): ©Cultura / Alamy; 28 (bottom right): ©PANORAMIC STOCK IMAGES / National Geographic Stock; 30 (center): ©MBI / Alamy; 30 (bottom): ©Michel Gounot / Godong / Corbis; 31 (5): ©Eugene Reshetov / Alamy; 31 (6): ©Image Source / Alamy; 31 (8): ©M-Sat Ltd. / Photo Researchers, Inc.; 31 (9): ©Seleznev Oleg / Shutterstock;

32 (top): ©Luis Orteo / Hemis / Corbis; 32 (bottom): ©Fine Art Photographic Library / Corbis; 33 (center): ©Thinkstock / Comstock Images / Getty Images; 33 (bottom): ©Israel images / Alamy; 34 (center): ©Radius / Superstock; 34 (bottom): ©Michel de Nijs / iStockphoto; 35 (top): ©Julian Nieman / Alamy; 35 (bottom): ©Mike Goldwater / Alamy; 36 (bottom left): ©Ariadne Van Zandbergen / Alamy; 36 (bottom right): ©Images of Africa Photobank / Alamy; 37 (center): ©Robert Harding Images / Masterfile; 37 (bottom): ©Danita Delimont / Getty Images; 38 (1): ©JOHN SCOFIELD / National Geographic Stock; 38 (3): ©Rafal Cichawa / Shutterstock; 38 (4): ©Frédéric Soltan / Sygma / Corbis; 38 (5): ©David Pearson / Alamy; 39 (6): ©michaeljung / Shutterstock; 39 (7): ©Jordan Rooney / Alamy; 39 (8): ©Dbimages / Alamy; 39 (9): ©Jon Arnold Images Ltd. / Alamy; 40: ©Robert Harding World Imagery / Corbis; 41 (top): ©Fuse / Getty Images; 41 (center): ©iStockphoto / Thinkstock; 41 (bottom): ©Associated Press; 42 (top): ©Stapleton Collection / Corbis; 42 (center): ©Stapleton Collection / Corbis; 42 (bottom): ©Keren Su / China Span / Alamy; 43 (5): ©Corbis; 43 (6): ©blackred / iStockphoto; 43 (7): ©Li Shao Bai / Redlink / Corbis; 43 (8): ©Image Source / Corbis; 44: ©Image Plan / Corbis; 45 (top): ©Keren Su / Corbis; 45 (bottom): ©Chris Willson / Alamy; 46 (top): ©Cyril Ruoso / JH Editorial / Minden Pictures / National Geographic Stock; 46 (bottom): ©Priit Vesilind / National Geographic Stock; 47 (top): ©Aaron Black / Corbis; 47 (center): ©Penny Tweedie / Corbis; 47 (bottom): ©Jason Edwards / National Geographic Stock; 48 (top center): ©Justin Guariglia / Corbis; 48 (bottom center): ©John Baker / Corbis; 4: ©Tororo Reaction / Shutterstock; 50 (center): ©The Natural History Museum / Alamy; 50 (bottom left): ©Gianni Dagli Orti / Corbis; 51 (bottom right): ©Ocean / Corbis; 51 (top left): ©DeadDuck / iStockphoto; 51 (top right): ©Science and Society / Superstock; 51 (bottom): ©Spencer Platt / Getty Images; 53 (top): ©Monkey Business Images /Shutterstock; 53 (bottom): ©Bettmann / Corbis; 54 (top): ©Images & Stories / Alamy; 54 (bottom left): ©Darren Kemper / Corbis; 54 (bottom right): ©Raymond Heinsius / iStockphoto; 55: ©Wolfgang Kaehler / Corbis; 55 (inset): ©studiomode / Alamy; 56 (center): ©Robert Harding Picture Library Ltd. / Alamy; 56 (bottom): ©Christian Larrieu-La Licorne / The Bridgeman Art Library International; 57 (top): ©Roger Wood / Corbis; 57 (bottom): ©Erich Lessing / Art Resource, NY; 58 (top): ©Destinations / Corbis; 58 (center): ©Baloncici / Shutterstock; 58 (bottom): ©Brand X Pictures / Getty Images; 59 (top): ©Tom Bean / Corbis; 59 (center): ©Alex Segre / Alamy; 6 (bottom left): ©Art Directors & TRIP /Alamy; 60 (bottom right): ©Ira Block / National Geographic / Getty Images; 61 (top): ©Gavin Hellier / Robert Harding World Imagery / Corbis; 61 (center): ©Archiv / Photo Researchers; 62 (center left): ©Finnbarr Webster / Alamy; 62 (center right): ©Jim Weber / ZUMA Press / Corbis; 62 (bottom): ©Paul Stokes / Alamy; 63 (top): ©DEA PICTURE LIBRARY / Getty Images; 63 (center): ©Wojciech Wójcik / Alamy; 64 (top): ©National Geographic Society / Corbis; 64 (center left): ©Ivy Close Images / Alamy;

64 (center right): ©NBAE / Getty Images; 65 (top): ©Bob Krist / Corbis; 65 (bottom): ©Hoberman Collection / Corbis; 66 (top): ©Mary Evans Picture Library / Alamy; 66 (center left): ©North Wind Picture Archives / North Wind Pictures; 66 (center): ©akg-images / British Library; 67 (top): ©Ivy Close Images / Alamy 66 (bottom): ©North Wind / North Wind Picture Archives; 68 (top): ©The Art Gallery Collection / Alamy; 68 (center): ©North Wind / North Wind Picture Archives; 70 (1): ©Mark L Stephenson / Corbis; 70 (2): ©Aliseenko / Shutterstock; 70 (3): ©Harry Taylor / Getty Images; 70 (4): ©Lisa Zador / Getty Images; 70 (5): ©North Wind Picture / North Wind Picture Archives; 71 (6): ©Rick Gayle / Corbis; 71 (7): ©Zlatko Kostic / iStockphoto; 71 (8): ©Peter Adams Photography Ltd. / Alamy; 71 (9): ©Panoramic Images / Getty Images; 71: fstockphoto / iStockphoto; 72 (top): ©Ocean / Corbis; 72 (center): ©Erich Lessing / Art Resource; 72 (bottom): ©Biblioteca Estense, Modena, Italy / Giraudon / Bridgeman Art Library; 74 (top): ©Thinkstock Images / Getty Images; 74 (center): ©HIP / Art Resource, NY; 74 (center right): ©artpartner-images / Getty Images; 74 (bottom): ©Hemis.fr / Superstock; 75 (top left): ©Erich Lessing / Art Resource, NY; 75 (top right): ©Lightworks Media / Alamy; 75 (center): ©Eduardo Rivero / Shutterstock; 76 (center): ©Joseph Sohm / Visions of America / Corbis; 77 (top): ©National Geographic Society / Corbis; 77 (bottom): ©Science and Society / Superstock; 78 (top): ©M.Brodie / Alamy; 78 (center): ©Réunion des Musées Nationaux / Art Resource, NY; 79 (top): ©Pictorial Press Ltd / Alamy; 79 (center): ©Mary Evans Picture Library / Alamy ; 80 (bottom): ©Schalkwijk / Art Resource, NY; 81 (top): ©INTERFOTO / Alamy; 82 (1): ©Rudy Sulgan / Corbis; 82 (3): ©Ken Welsh / Bridgeman Art Library; 82 (4): ©The Gallery Collection / Corbis; 82 (5): ©Alfredo Dagli Orti / Art Resource, NY; 82 (6): ©British Library Board / Bridgeman Art Library; 83 (7): ©Ken Welsh / Bridgeman Art Library; 83 (8): ©akg-images; 83 (9): ©North Wind Picture Archives / North Wind Pictures; 83 (10): ©Gjermund Alsos / Shutterstock; 83 (11): ©Gustavo Tomsich / Corbis; 83 (modern telescope): ©Marek Walisiewicz / Dorling Kindersley / Getty Images; 84 (top): ©Réunion des Musées Nationaux / Art Resource; 84 (center): ©Tetra Images / Corbis; 84 (bottom): ©imagebroker / Alamy; 85: ©Rick Maiman / Sygma / Corbis; 86 (top): ©Pier Paolo Cito / Associated Press; 86 (bottom): ©The Gallery Collection / Corbis; 87: ©North Wind / North Wind Picture Archives; 88 (top): ©akg-images / The Image Works; 88 (bottom): ©Scala / Ministero per i Beni e le Attività culturali / Art Resource, NY; 89: ©Classic Image / Alamy; 90 (center left): ©Janine Wiedel Photolibrary / Alamy; 90 (center right) ©Petworth House, West Sussex, UK / Bridgeman Art Library; 90 (bottom): ©Corbis; 91 (center): ©Chateau de Versailles, France / Bridgemant Art Library; 91 (bottom): ©Chateau de Versailles, France / Giraudon / Bridgemant Art Library; 92 (top): ©Alfredo Dagli Orti / The Art Archive / Corbis; 92 (center): ©PM Images / Getty Images; 94 (2): ©Rob Stark / Shutterstock; 94 (3): ©Archive Images / Alamy; 94 (4): ©GFC Collection / Alamy; 94 (5): ©Jabiru / Dreamstime; 95 (top): ©North Wind / North

154 (1 and 4): ©North Wind / North Wind Picture Archives; 154 (2): ©David R. Frazier Photolibrary, Inc. / Alamy; 154 (3): ©Art Resource; 155 (8): ©Dale Spartas / Corbis; 155 (9): ©Bettmann / Corbis; 156 (center): ©Bettmann / Corbis; 156 (bottom): ©North Wind / North Wind Picture Archives; 157 (top): ©Niday Picture Library / Alamy; 157 (bottom): ©Sal Maimone / Superstock; 158 (4, 5 and 6): ©North Wind / North Wind Picture Archives; 159 (7): ©North Wind / North Wind Picture Archives; 160 (top): ©North Wind / North Wind Picture Archives; 160 (center left): ©Photos 12 / Alamy; 160 (center right): ©Jupiterimages / Getty Images; 160 (bottom) ©Pictorial Press Ltd. / Alamy; 161: ©North Wind / North Wind Picture Archives; 162-163: ©North Wind / North Wind Picture Archives; 162: ©Archive Pics / Alamy; 163: ©Library of Congress; 164 (top): ©Peter Newark Military Pictures / Bridgeman Art Library; 164 (center): ©Shannon Fagan / Getty Images; 164 (bottom): ©Tom Lovell / National Geographic Stock; 165 (top): ©INTERFOTO / Alamy; 165 (bottom): ©Library of Congress; 166 (1): ©GL Archive / Alamy; 166 (2): ©Library of Congress; 166 (3): ©National Archives; 166 (4): ©Lass / Archive Photos / Getty Images; 167: ©The Granger Collection, NYC; 168 (top): ©Everett Collection Inc. / Alamy; 168 (center): ©Corbis; 168 (bottom): ©The Protected Art Archive / Alamy; 169: ©Bettmann / Corbis; 170 (1): ©Library of Congress - digital ve / Science Faction / Corbis; 170 (2): ©Minnesota Historical Society / Corbis; 170 (3 and 4): ©Mary Evans Picture Library / Alamy; 170 (5): ©The Granger Collection, NYC; 170 (6): ©White Packert / Iconica / Getty Images; 171 (7): ©Bettmann / Corbis; 171 (8): ©Edwin Levick / National Geographic Society / Corbis; 171 (9): ©Library of Congress; 172 (top): ©Bettmann / Corbis; 172 (center): ©Stephen Orsillo / Alamy; 173 (top left): ©YinYang / iStockphoto; 173 (top right and bottom): ©Bettmann / Corbis; 174 (top and bottom): ©The Granger Collection, NYC; 175 (top): ©Peter Newark American Pictures / Bridgeman Art Library; 175 (bottom): ©Richard Cummins / Getty Images; 176 (top): ©The Granger Collection, NYC; 176 (center): ©State Library and Archives of Florida / Memory Florida; 176 (bottom left): ©Bettmann / Corbis; 176 (bottom right): ©Corbis Bridge / Alamy; 177 (top): ©Library of Congress; 177 (bottom): ©David J. & Janice L. Frent Collection / Corbis; 178 (1): ©Kick Images / Photodisc / Getty Images; 178 (2 and 3): ©iStockphoto / Thinkstock; 178 (4): ©The Protected Art Archive / Alamy; 178 (5): ©North Wind / North Wind Picture Archives; 178 (6): ©Danny Lehman / Corbis; 179 (7): ©Time & Life Pictures / Getty Images; 179 (8): ©North Wind / North Wind Picture Archives; 179 (center): ©Underwood & Underwood / Corbis; 179 (bottom left): ©Bettmann / Corbis; 179 (bottom right): ©Thomas Del Brase / Getty Images; 180 (top): ©ClassicStock / Alamy; 180: ©Goodshoot / Thinkstock; 181 (1): ©Corbis; 181 (2): ©The Granger Collection, NYC; 181 (3): ©Valua Vitaly / Shutterstock; 181 (4): ©Lebrecht Photo Library; 182 (5): ©Skip Brown / National Geographic Stock; 182 (6): ©Barbara Singer / Hulton Archive / Getty Images; 184 (center and bottom): ©Corbis; 185: ©The Art Archive / National Archives Washington DC; 186 (1): ©RSB Photo / Alamy; 186 (2): ©Bettmann / Corbis; 186 (3): ©Motoring Picture Library / Alamy; 186 (4): ©The Granger Collection, NYC; 187 (5): ©Pictorial Press Ltd. / Alamy; 187 (6): ©New York Daily News Archive / Getty Images; 187 (7): ©National Portrait Gallery, Smithsonian Institution / Art Resource, NY; 188 (top): ©INTERFOTO / Alamy; 188 (center): ©Images.com / Alamy; 188 (bottom): ©Gamma-Keystone / Getty Images; 189: ©ClassicStock / Alamy; 190 (2): ©Fotosearch / Stringer / Getty Images; 190 (3): ©ClassicStock / Alamy; 190 (4): ©World History Archive / Alamy; 191 (5): ©National Portrait Gallery, Smithsonian Institution / Art Resource, NY; 191 (6 and 7): ©Bettmann / Corbis; 192 (top): ©World History Archive / Alamy; 192 (center): ©Library of Congress; 192 (bottom left and right): ©Bettmann / Corbis; 193 (top): ©Library of Congress; 193 (bottom): ©The Granger Collection, NYC; 194 (1, 3 and 4): ©Corbis; 194 (2): ©Hulton-Deutsch Collection / Corbis; 195 (5): ©APIC / Getty Images; 195 (6): ©Bettmann / Corbis; 196 (top): ©Cengage Learning; 196 (center): ©Library of Congress; 196 (bottom): ©Hulton Archive / Getty Images; 197 (top): ©Joe Rosenthal / Associated Press; 197 (bottom): ©Associated Press; 198 (1): ©H. Armstrong Roberts / Getty Images; 198 (2): ©Time & Life Pictures / Getty Images; 198 (3): ©Everett Collection / SuperStock; 198 (4 and 5): ©Bettmann / Corbis; 199 (6 and 7): ©Everett Collection Inc. / Alamy; 199 (9 and 10): ©Bettmann / Corbis; 200 (top, center right and bottom): ©Bettmann / Corbis; 200 (center left): ©John Dominis / Time & Life Pictures / Getty Images; 201 (top): ©Bettmann / Corbis; 201 (bottom): ©Everett Collection Inc. / Alamy; 202 (3): ©Elliott Erwitt / Magnum Photos; 202 (4): ©Don Cravens / Time Life Pictures / Getty Images; 202 (5): ©Bettmann / Corbis; 203 (6): ©Bettmann / Corbis; 203 (7): ©Buyenlarge / Getty Images; 203 (8): ©Cathy Murphy / Getty Images; 203 (9): ©JP Laffont / Sygma / Corbis; 204 (top): ©World History Archive / Alamy; 204 (center): ©The Granger Collection, NYC; 204 (bottom left and bottom right): ©Bettmann / Corbis; 205 (top): ©Cathy Murphy / Getty Images; 205 (bottom): ©Scott Goldsmith / Getty Images; 206 (top): ©INTERFOTO / Alamy; 206 (bottom): ©BananaStock / Thinkstock; 207: ©Bettmann / Corbis; 208 (top): ©Bettmann / Corbis; 208 (center): ©Everett Collection Inc. / Alamy; 208 (bottom): ©The Herb Block Foundation; 209 (top): ©Bettmann / Corbis; 209 (bottom): ©Gregg Newton / Corbis; 210 (top): ©Images.com / Corbis; 210 (bottom): ©Robert Giroux / Getty Images; 211 (6, left to right): ©Mark Schneider / Visuals Unlimited / Getty Images; ©Richard Levine / Alamy; ©Bettmann / Corbis; 211 (7, clockwise from top): ©Greg Smith / Corbis; ©Bettmann / Corbis; ©Svenja-Foto / Corbis; 212 (top): ©Ilene MacDonald / Alamy; 212 (center): ©Kablonk! / PhotoLibrary; 213 (top): ©Bob Krist / Corbis; 213 (center): ©Timothy A. Clary / AFP / Getty Images; 213 (bottom): ©Graham Barclay / BWP Media / Getty Images; 214 (2): ©Lucy Nicholson / Reuters / Corbis; 214 (3): ©The Print Collector / Alamy; 214 (4): ©Musee Antoine Lecuyer, Saint-Quentin, France / Bridgeman Art